"George Alpert is unique first of all amongst men. This in turn makes him unique amongst photographers. In *The Queens* George Alpert reveals his insights, his deep understanding of the human soul. To many others, unusual subjects are generally rendered as photographic curiosities. But not so to George Alpert. His camera tears away whatever protective mask his subject may wish to wear, and reveals tenderly the inner soul of the person or persons involved, in an honest and sympathetic as well as empa-thetic manner. By telling us that before his camera he has great people, he gives us in substance great pictures."

—Norman Rothschild

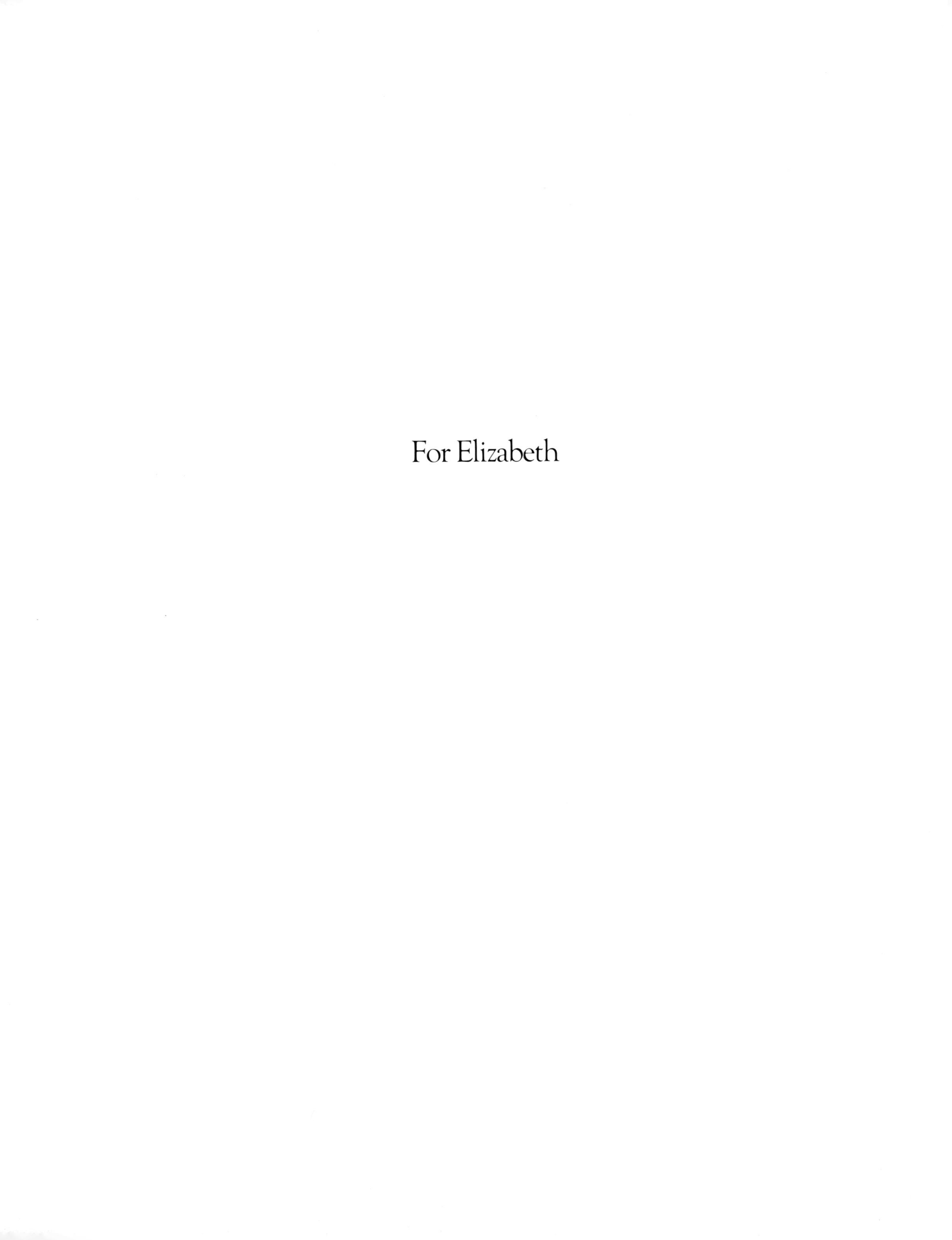

For Elizabeth

THE QUEENS

Photographs by GEORGE ALPERT

A DA CAPO PAPERBACK

Library of Congress Cataloging in Publication Data

Alpert, George, 1922-
  The queens.

  (A Da Capo paperback)
  1. Transvestism—Pictorial works. I. Title.
HQ77.A36   301.41'5   74-30498
ISBN 0-306-80012-8

First paperback printing 1975

ISBN: 0-306-80012-8

Published by Da Capo Press, Inc.
A subsidiary of Plenum Publishing Corporation
227 West 17th Street
New York, N.Y. 10011

Manufactured in the United States of America

Preface

To dress as a woman or to live as a woman part or all of the time is for some men an important part of their pursuit of happiness. For the men who appear in these pages, it is a vital way of life.

Some years ago, I met Mr. Kiki Hall, a producer of revues featuring female impressionists. Kiki is an impresario and is also an emcee and comedian. Through his occupation, he is in contact with scores of people in and out of show business who dress in drag. In our many conversations Kiki would relate marvelous anecdotes about queens and tell me their life stories. During one of these talks, Kiki suggested that it might be interesting to photograph some of the queens he knew. As we discussed this, I decided that the time had come to produce a photographic essay that would reveal something about the world of transvestism, and I encouraged Kiki to introduce me to some of his friends.

I started photographing Kiki's friends and then friends of their friends who were willing to be photographed and who understood that the photographs might eventually be published in a book. Not all of them accepted. Those who did told me that they were opening themselves up to me in the hope that as individuals and as a group they might be better understood by the straight world. The photographic results are here offered with that hope.

Although the photographs speak for themselves, I want to provide a few brief words about some of the people in the book. *Toni* has worked as a hairdresser (dressed as a man and as a woman) and as a cosmetician (dressed only as a woman). *Bobbie*, one of the twins, worked for a large company (as a woman) as the manager of inventory control. *Baby* is an exotic dancer and has appeared all over the world as a headliner with the Jewel Box Revue. *Bruno*, with an act of his own in which he is simultaneously half man and half woman, is also a superb designer of women's clothes. Many female impressionists rely upon Bruno for their wardrobes. Born in Italy, he was a featured dancer with La Scala, and when heard from most recently, was an owner-manager of a night club in Puerto Rico. *Jack* started out in show business as a chorus boy, was married for several years, and then became a comic working in drag. *Chrysis* appears as an actress and dancer and is usually featured in a show somewhere in the world. *Frankie* is a successful entertainer and producer of revues.

And so it goes. Although I had known some queens before I spent a year photographing for this book, it was during that period that I acquired my insight into the bitter-sweet life of transvestism. Despite our society's present mood of permissiveness, there is still prejudice and ridicule whenever a person who is "different" is concerned. Ultimately, the decision to become a woman is not an easy one for a man to make.

It is in this light that I was motivated to make these photographs. I hope they will help in making understood those people who may live in ways far different from the majority. I also hope that these photographs will inspire an appreciation of people who have the courage to be what they feel they are and who have a right, as we all do, to be what they are. That, finally, is what this book is all about.

To the people who were willing to share a portion of their lives by allowing me to photograph them, I want to dedicate this book. They did so in the interest of understanding, not sensationalism. In making these photographs, I have tried to be as honest with them as they have been with me and I sincerely hope that my insight in creating this photographic essay has not been less than their courage.

Finally, to my sister Ruth, I owe more for her interest and encouragement than I could possibly acknowledge. Her willingness to stay by my side for many hours in the darkroom and her helpful criticism of hundreds of prints were services well beyond the call of duty.

—George Alpert
New York, 1975

This is Baby

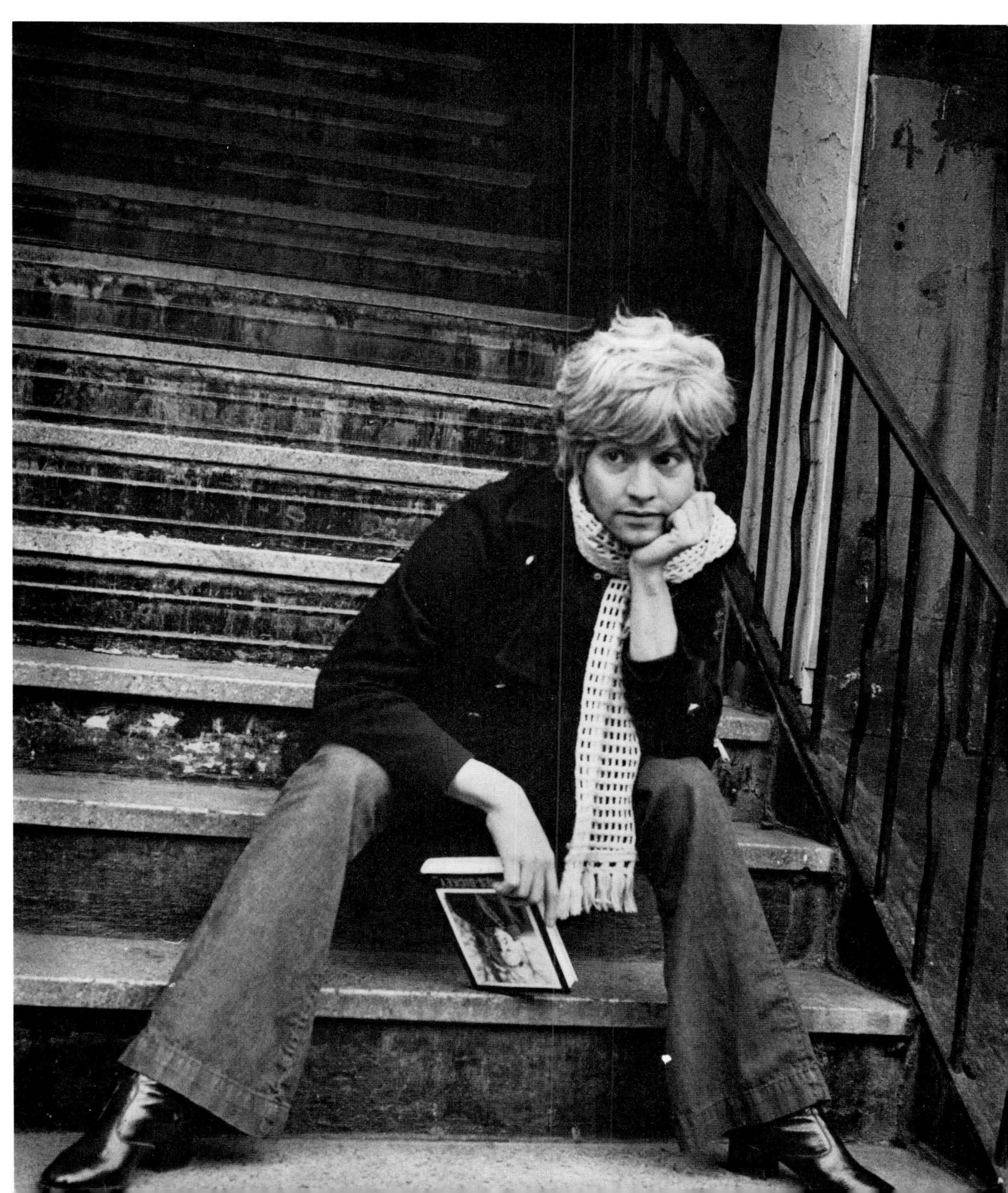

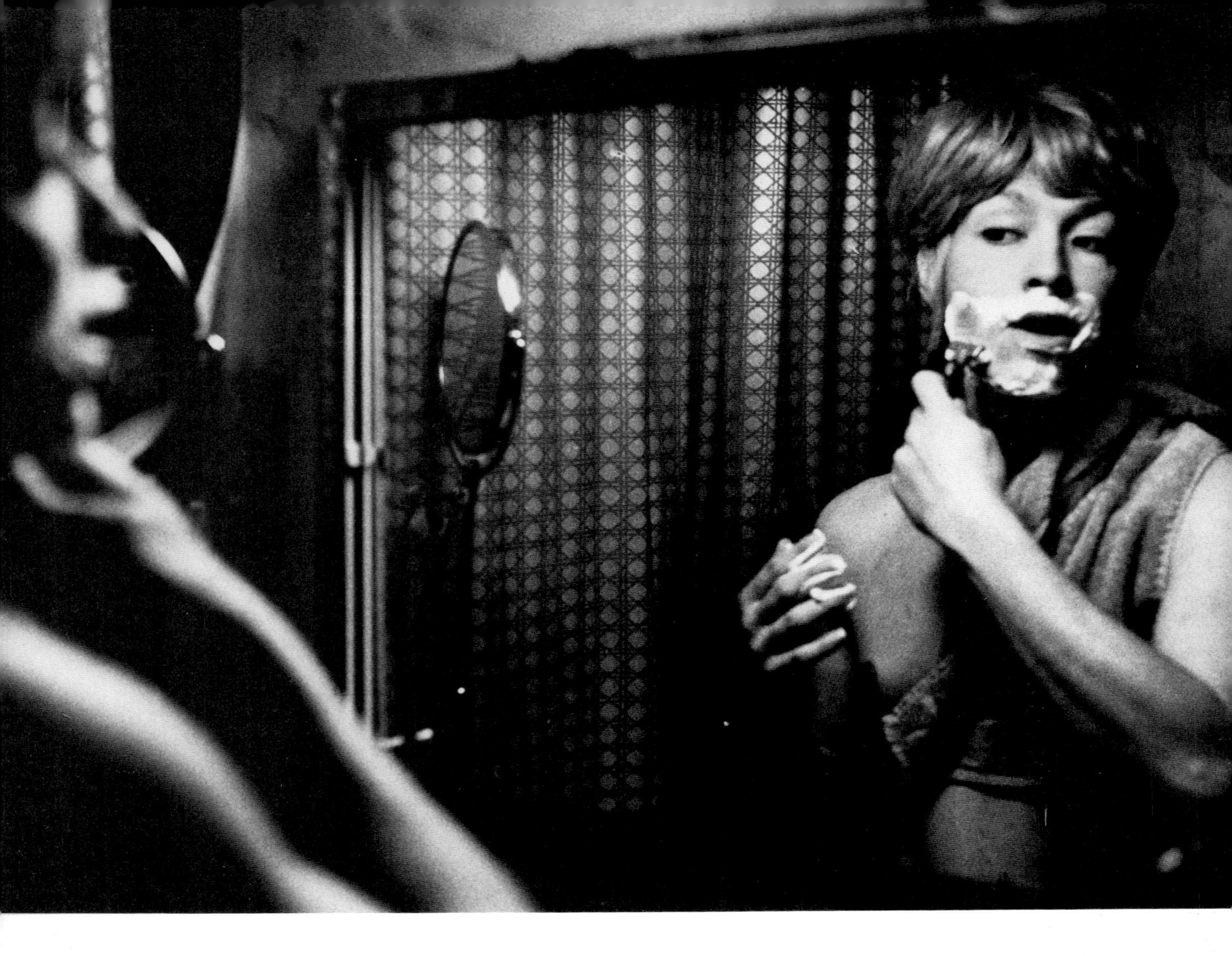

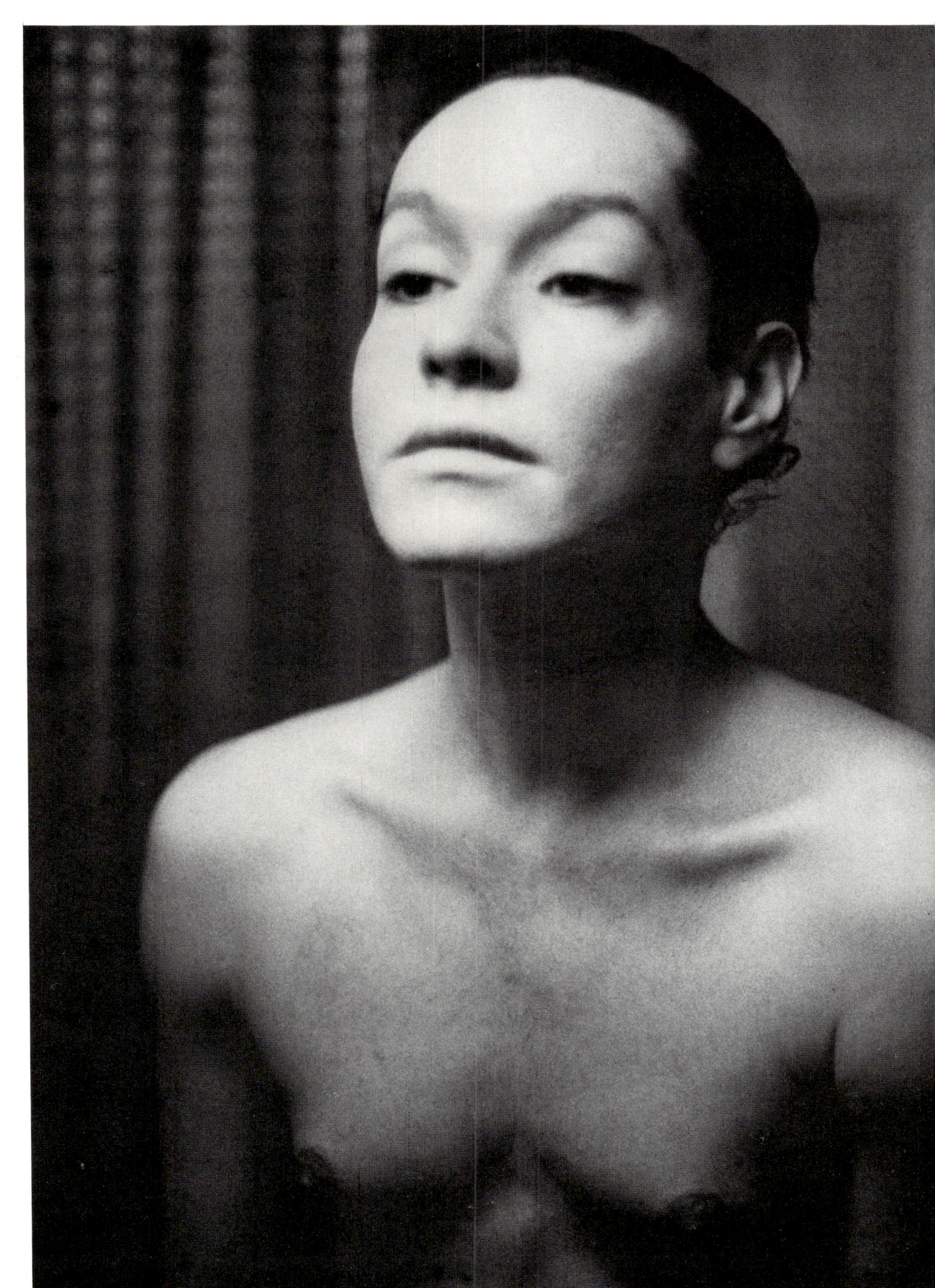

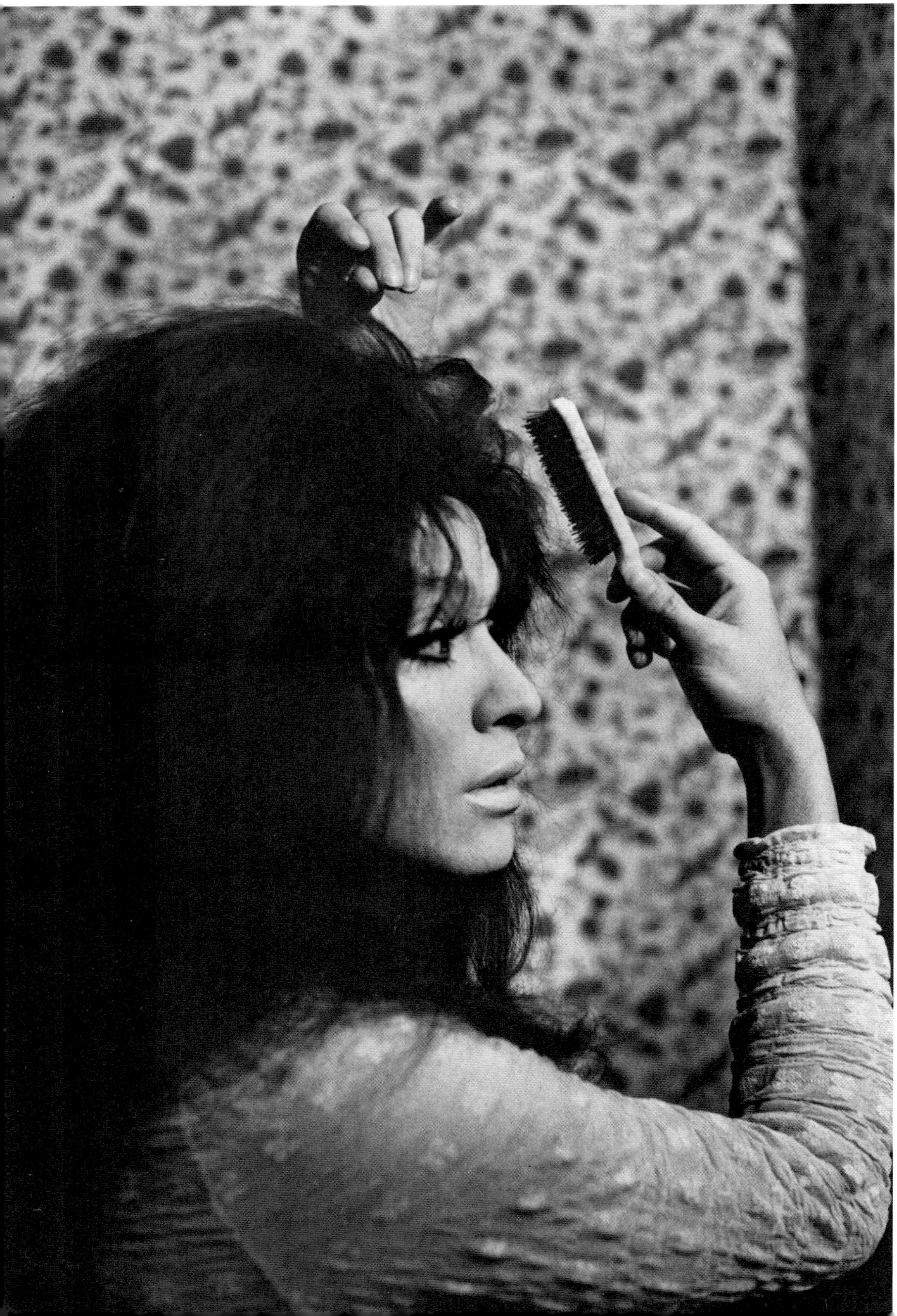

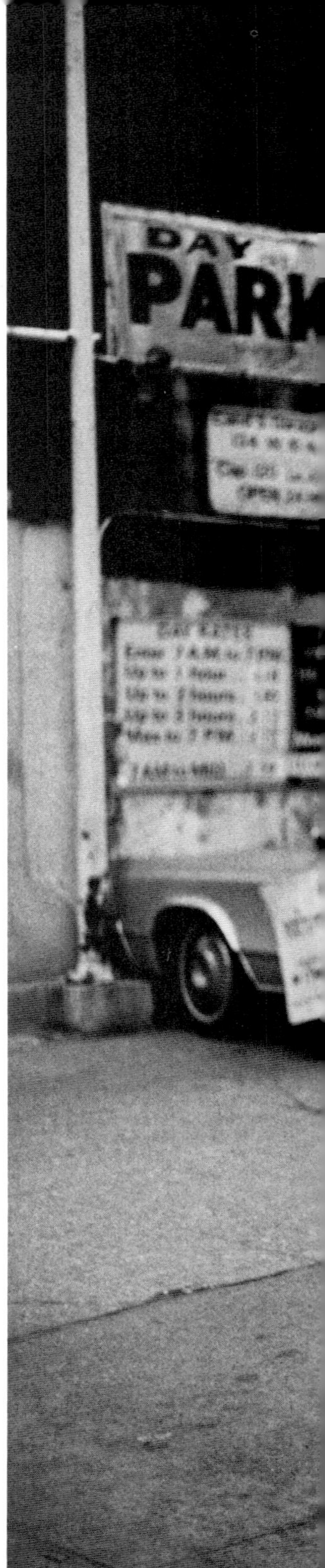
DAY
PARK

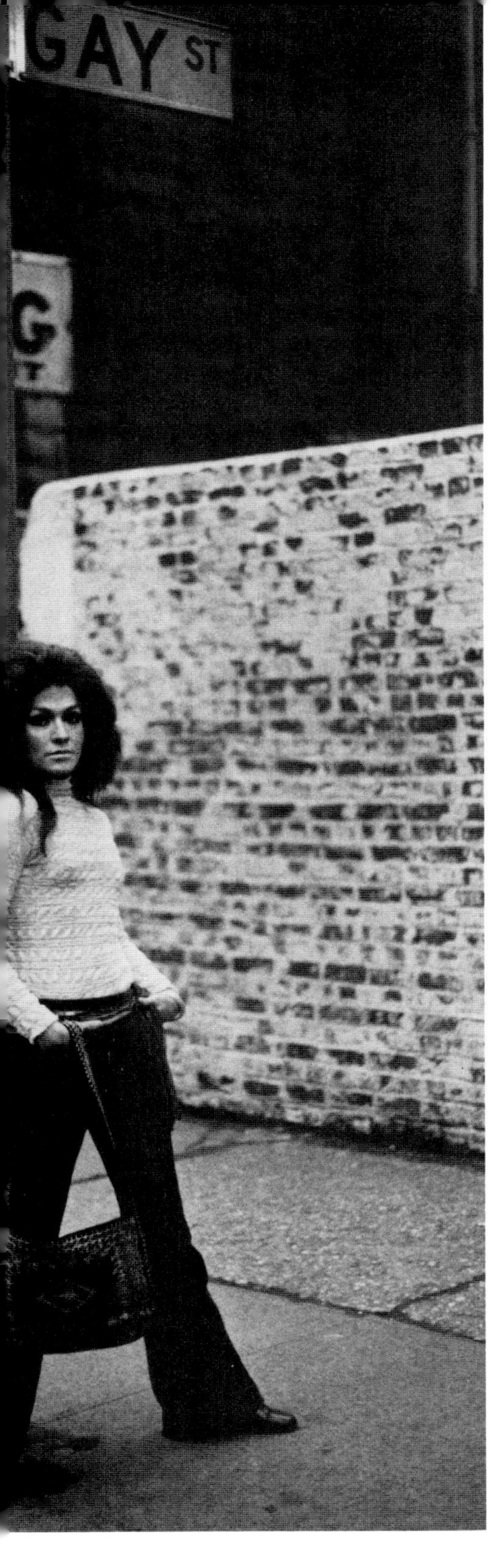

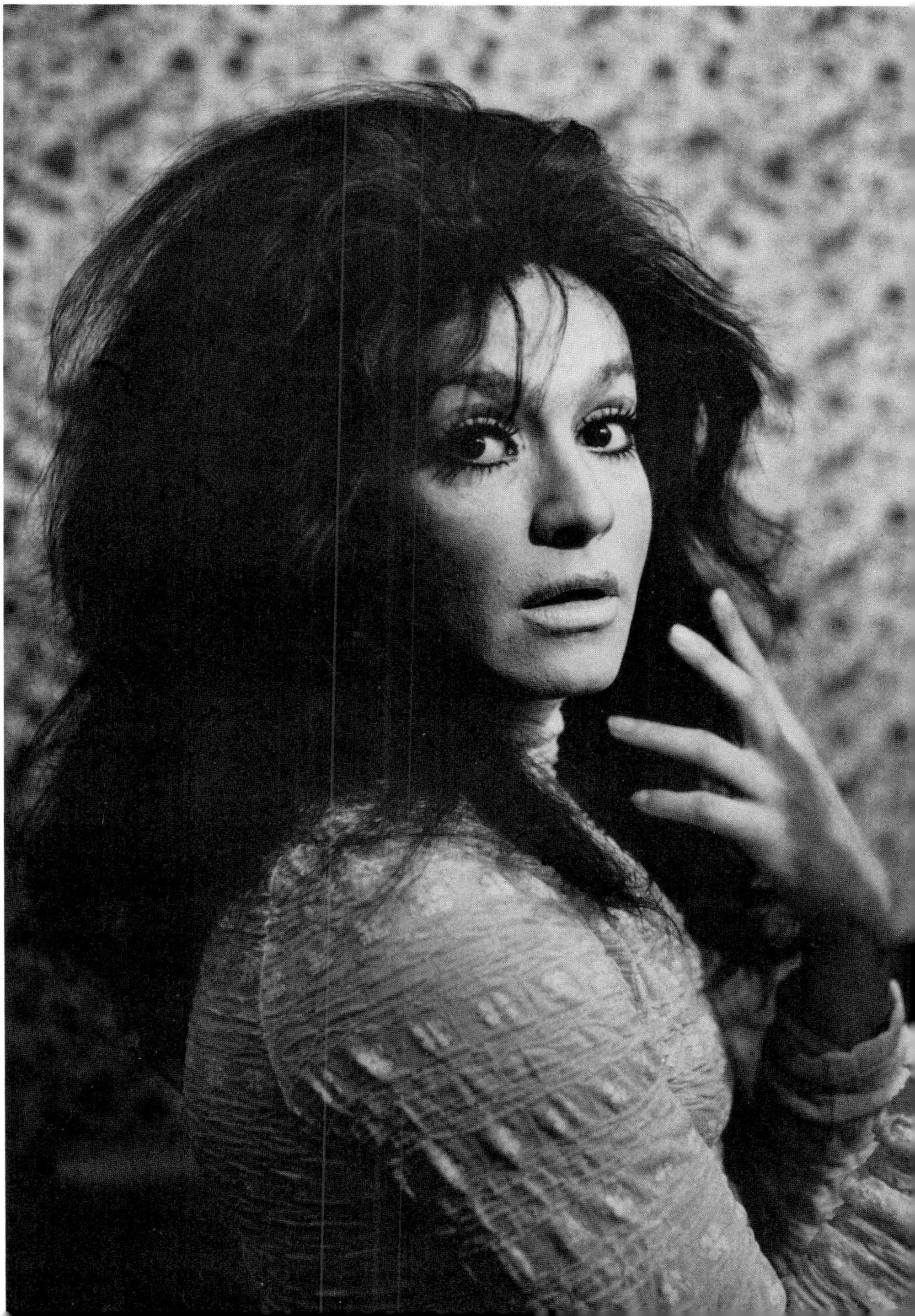

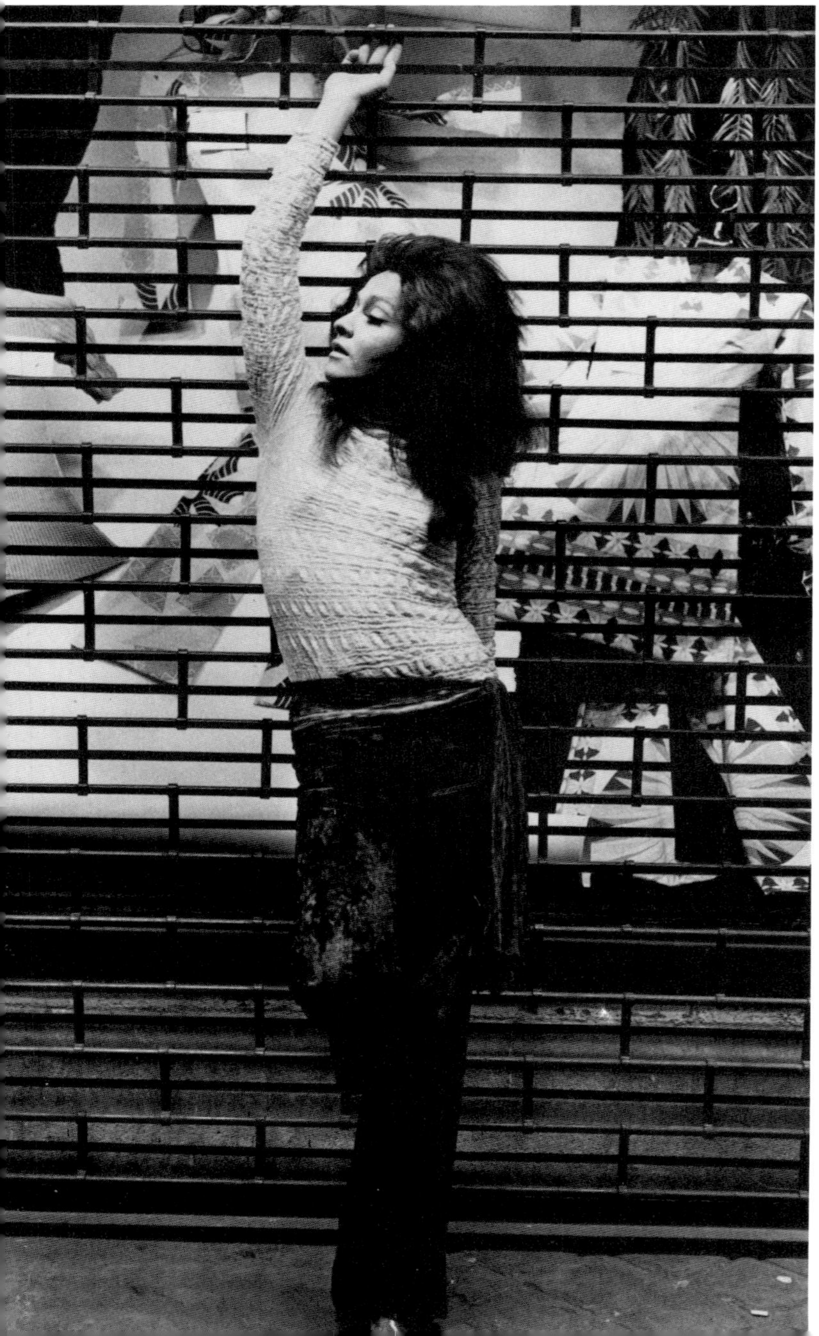

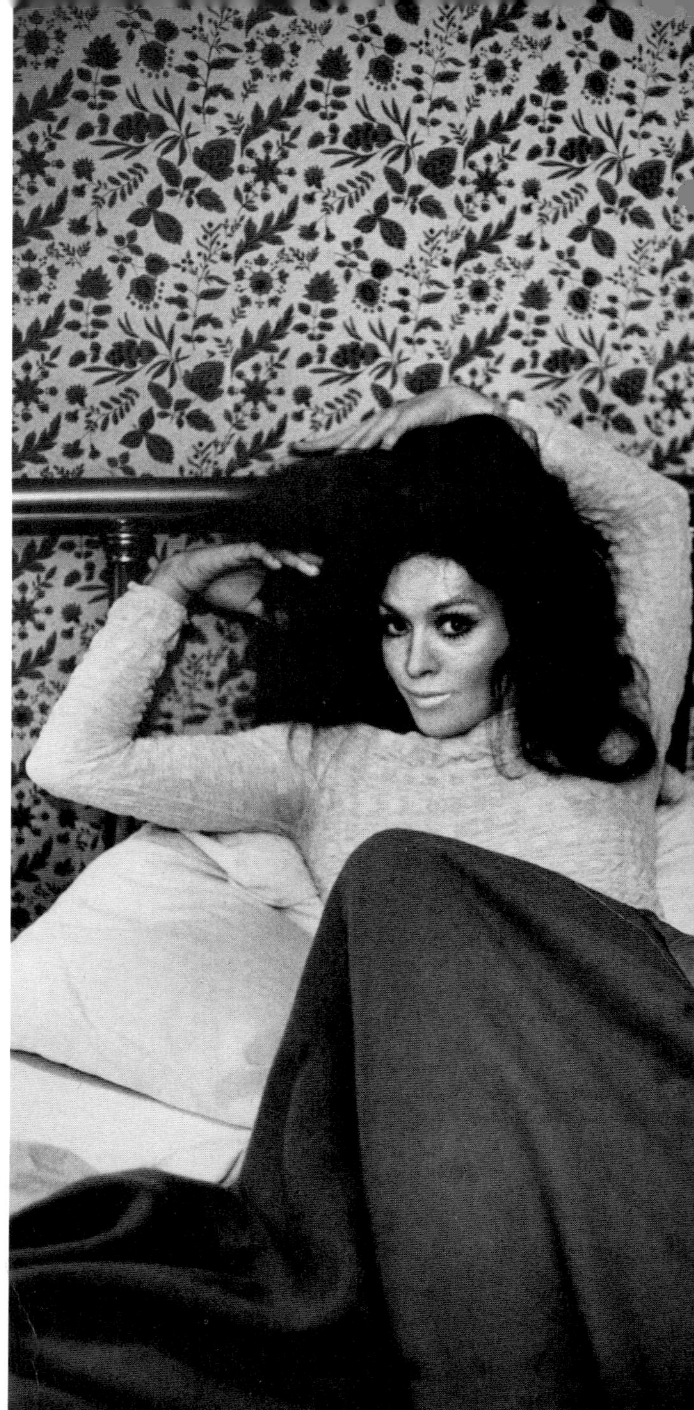

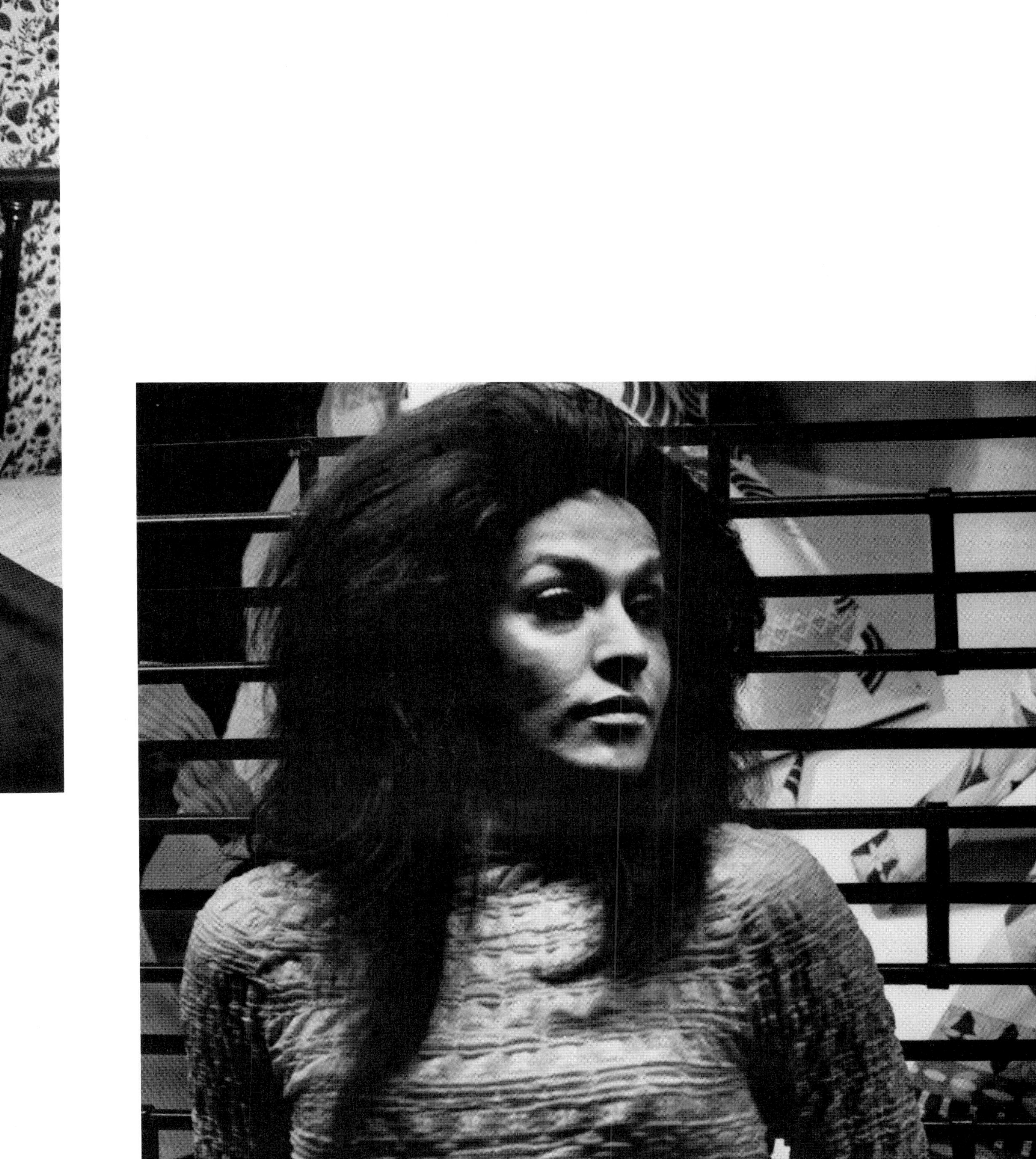

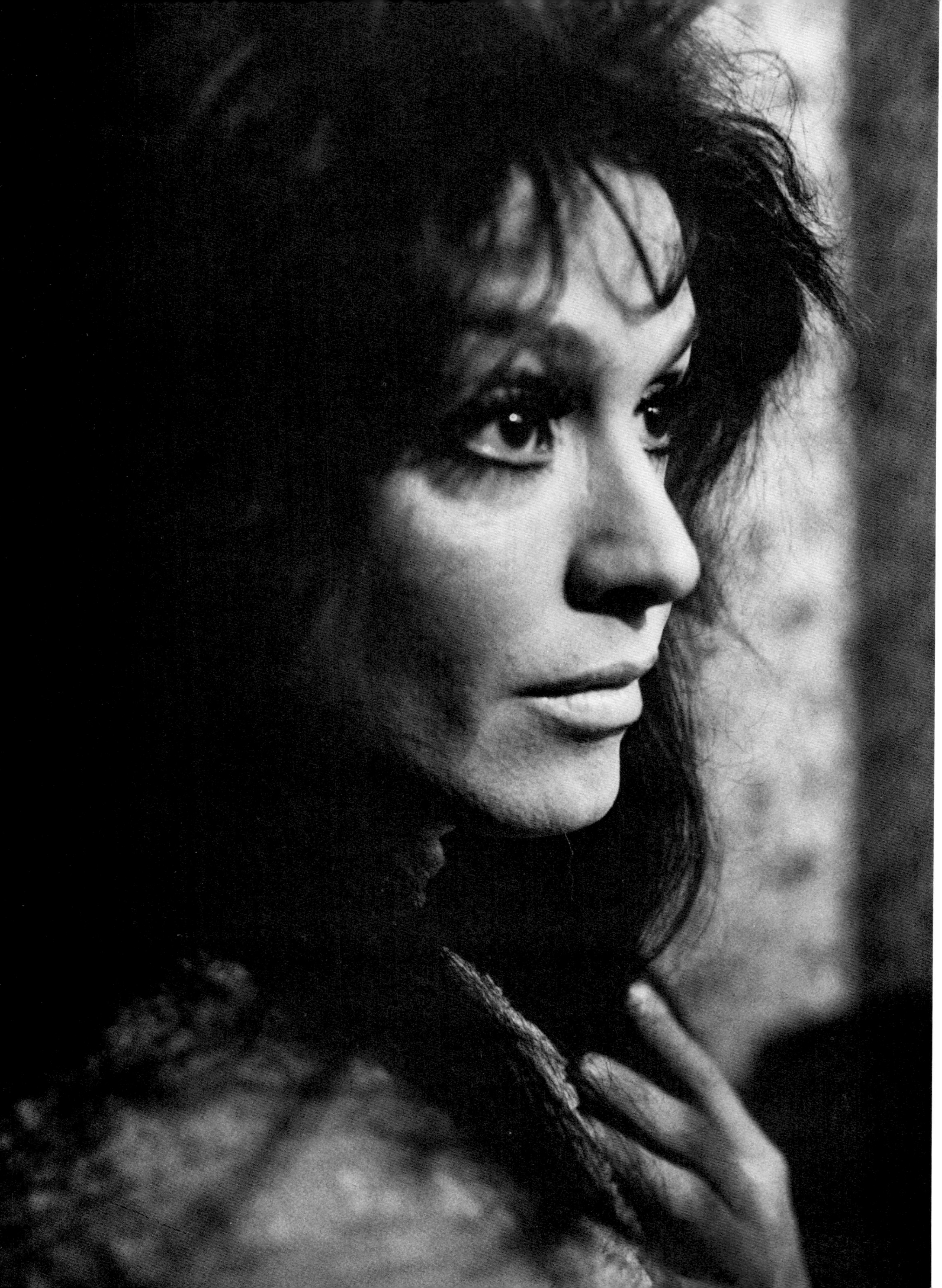

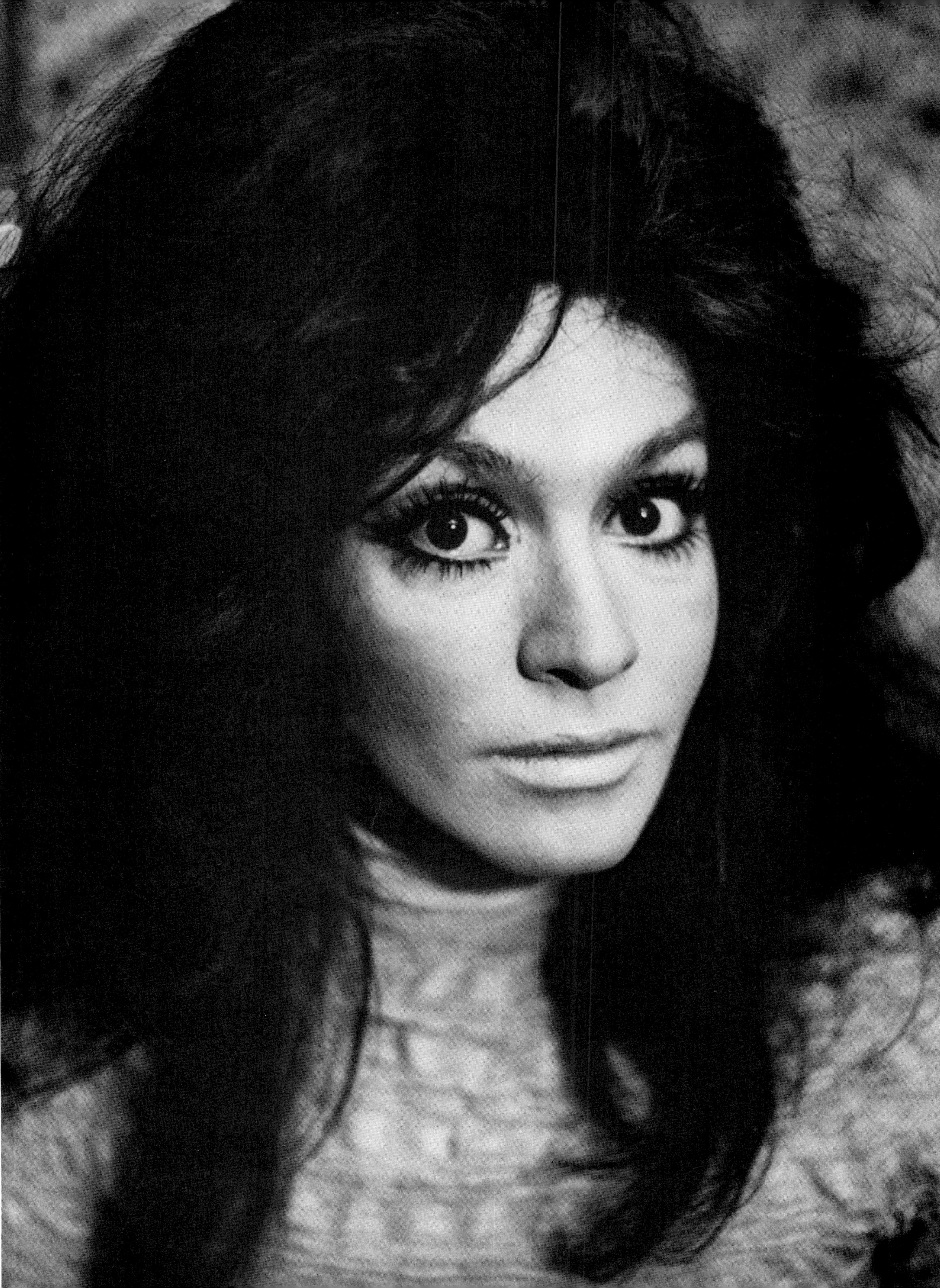

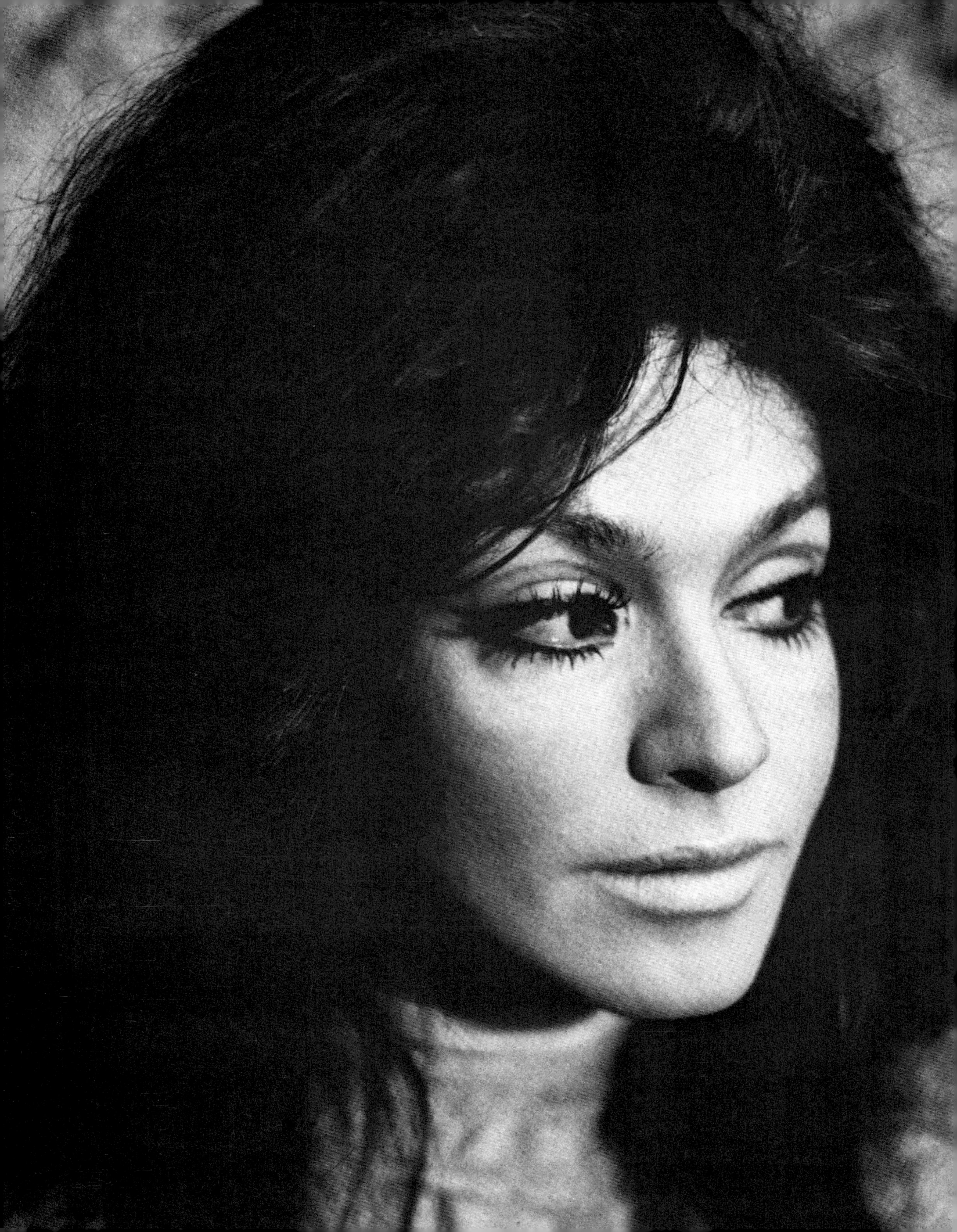

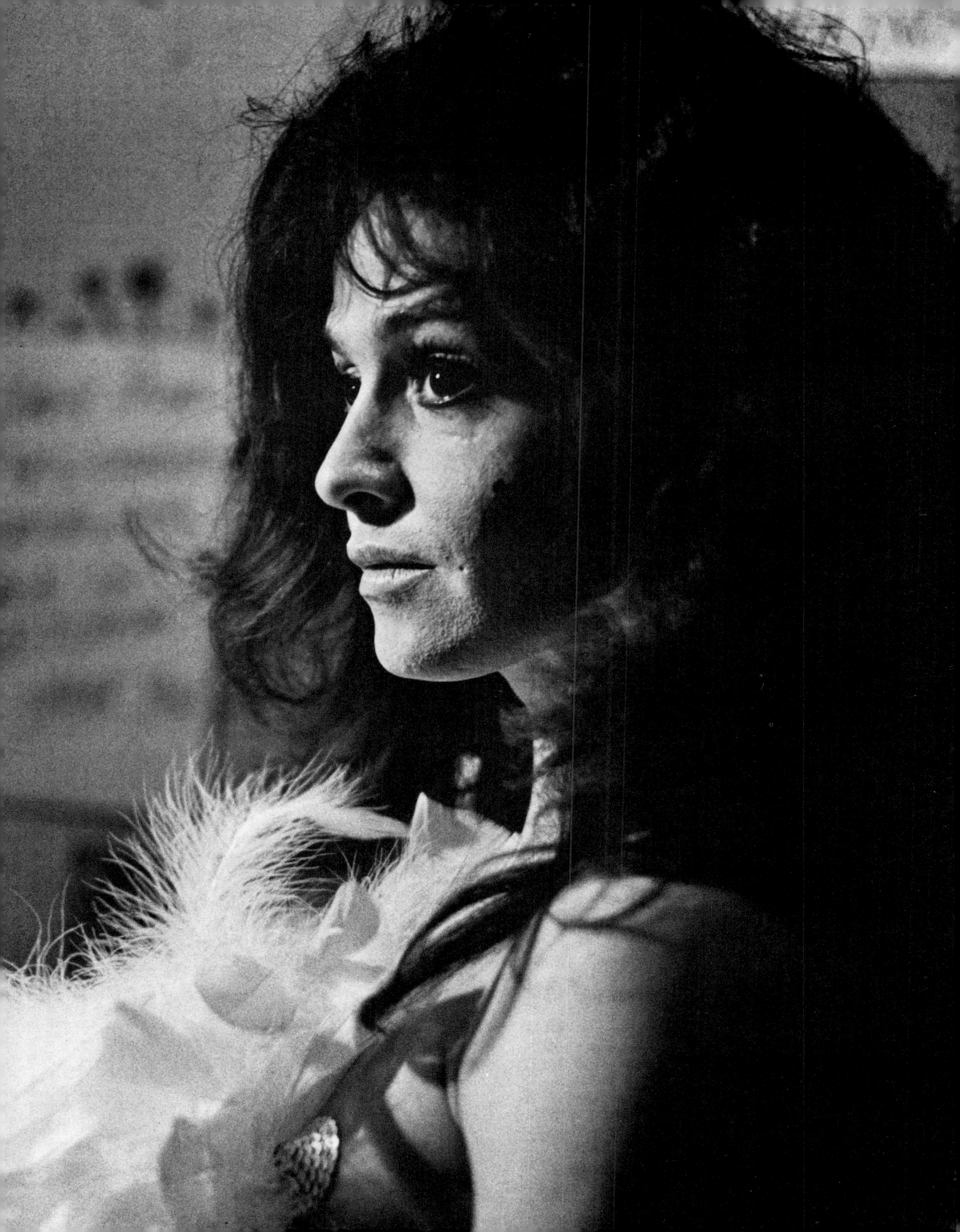

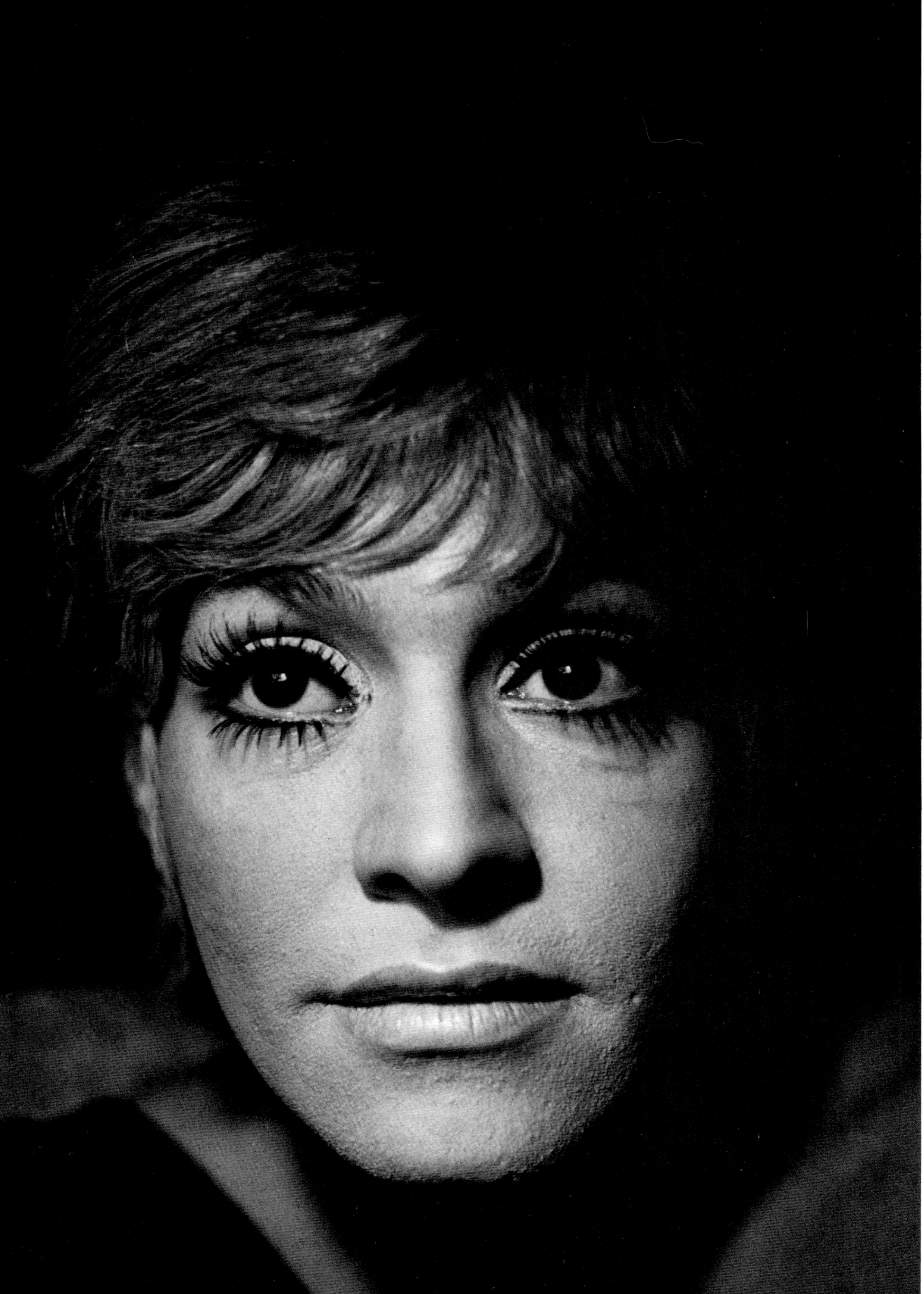

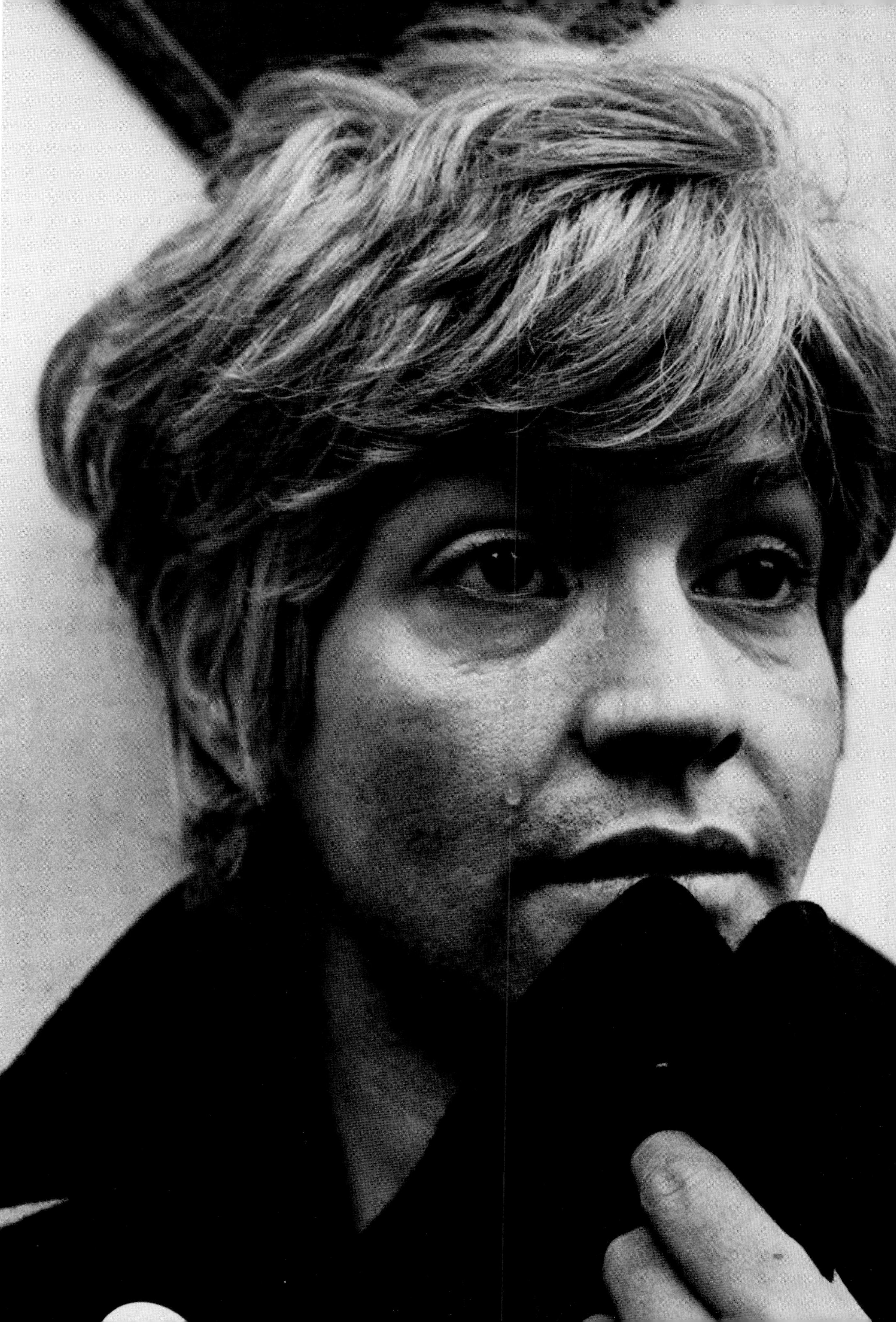

This is Bruno — La Fantastique!

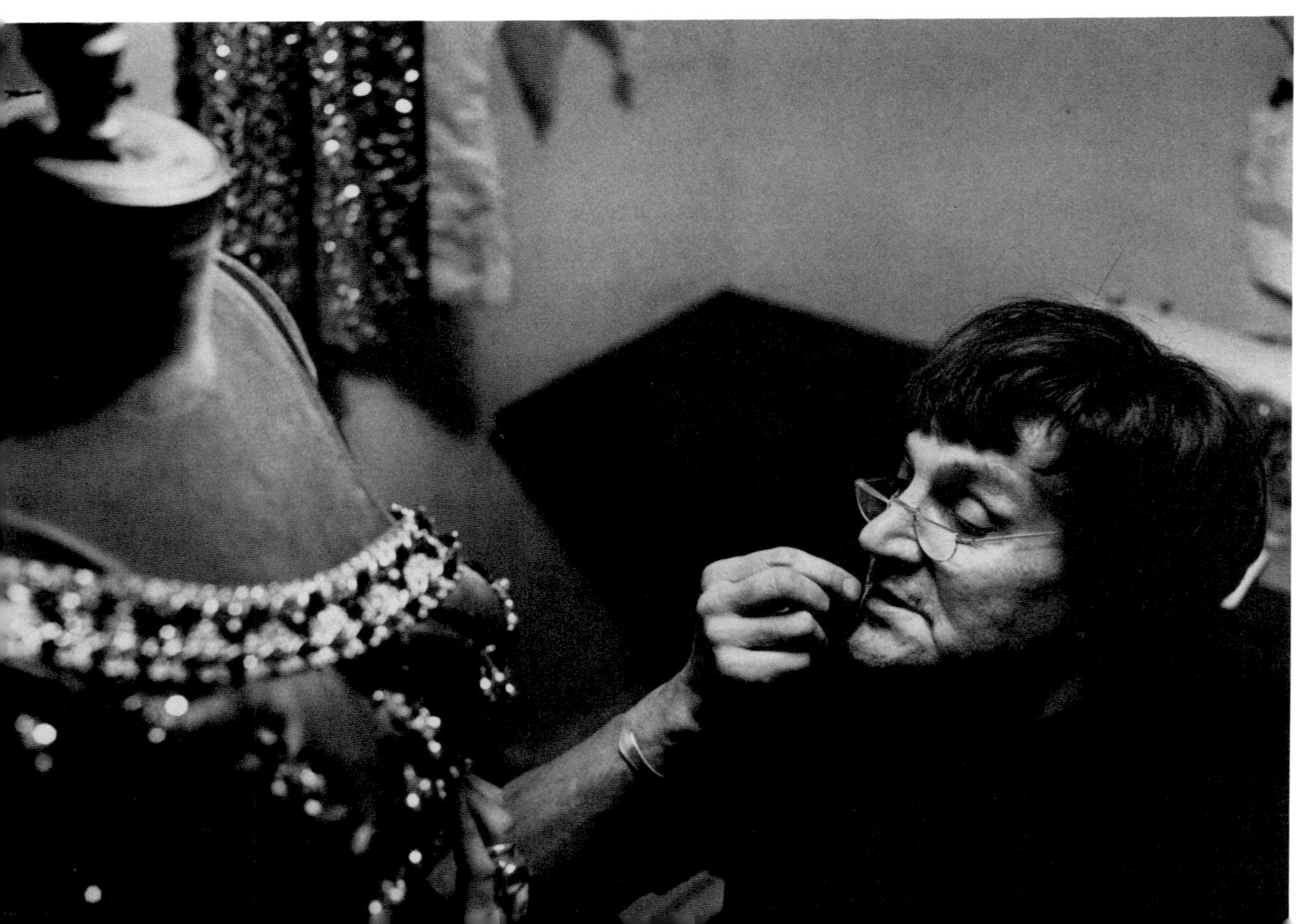

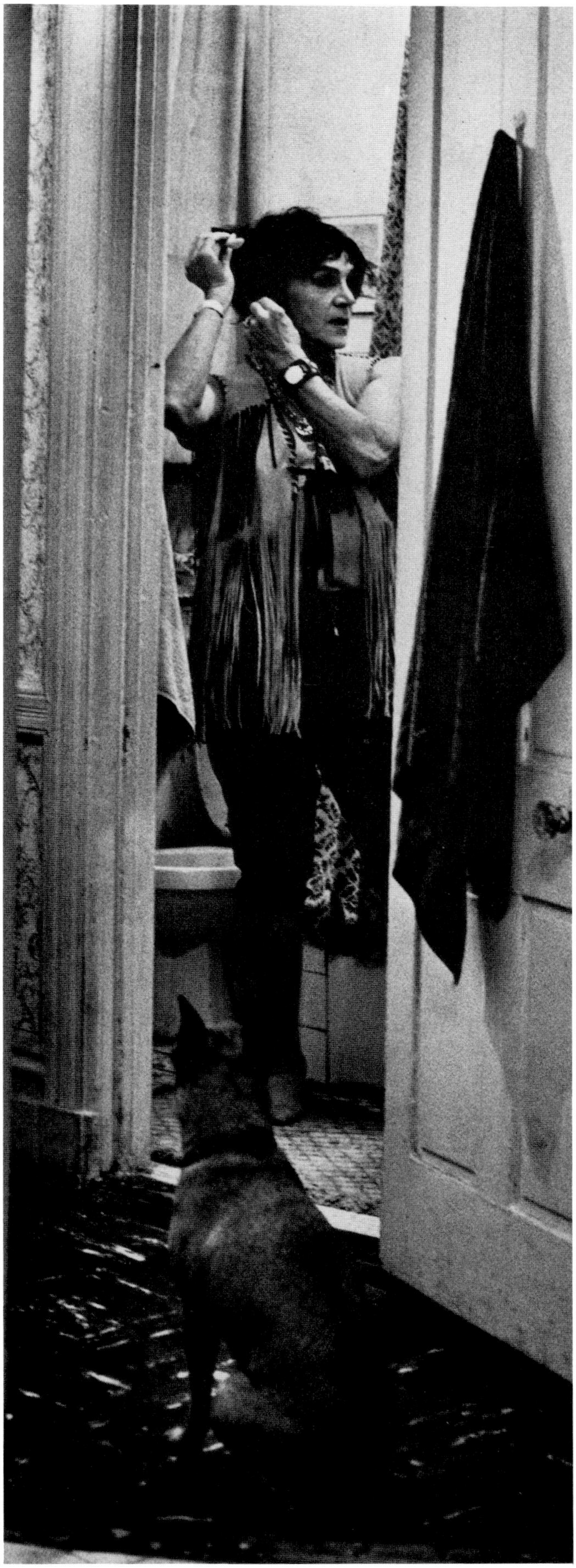

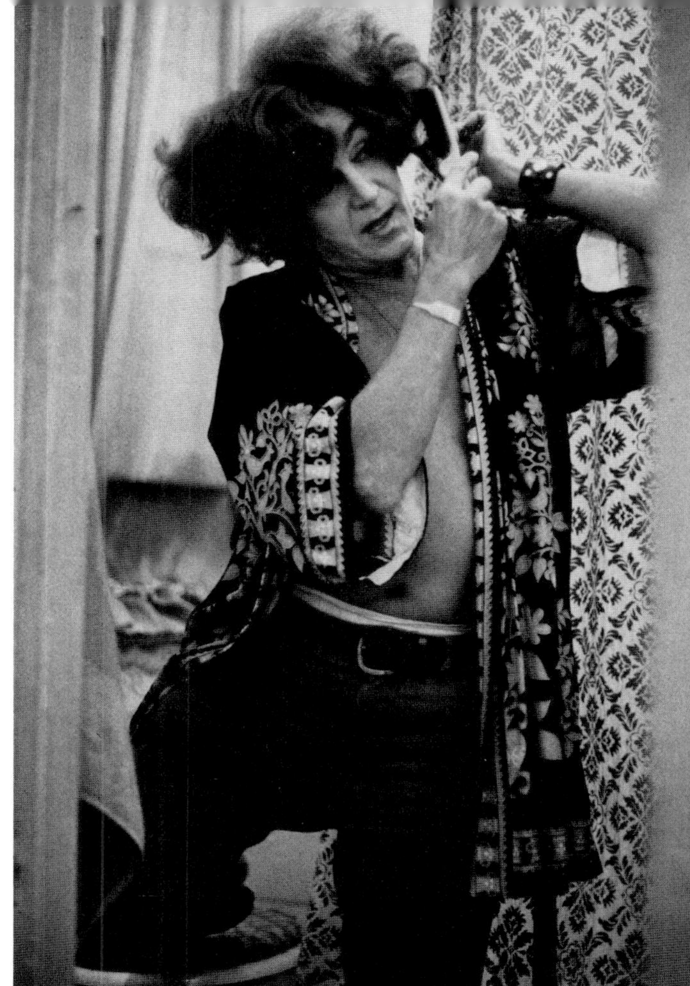
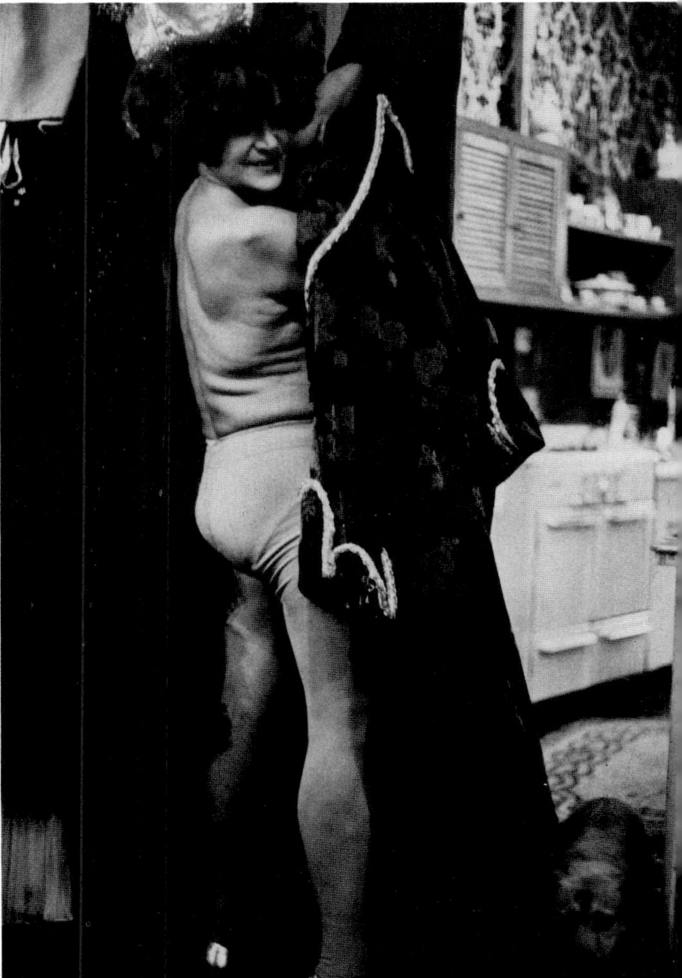

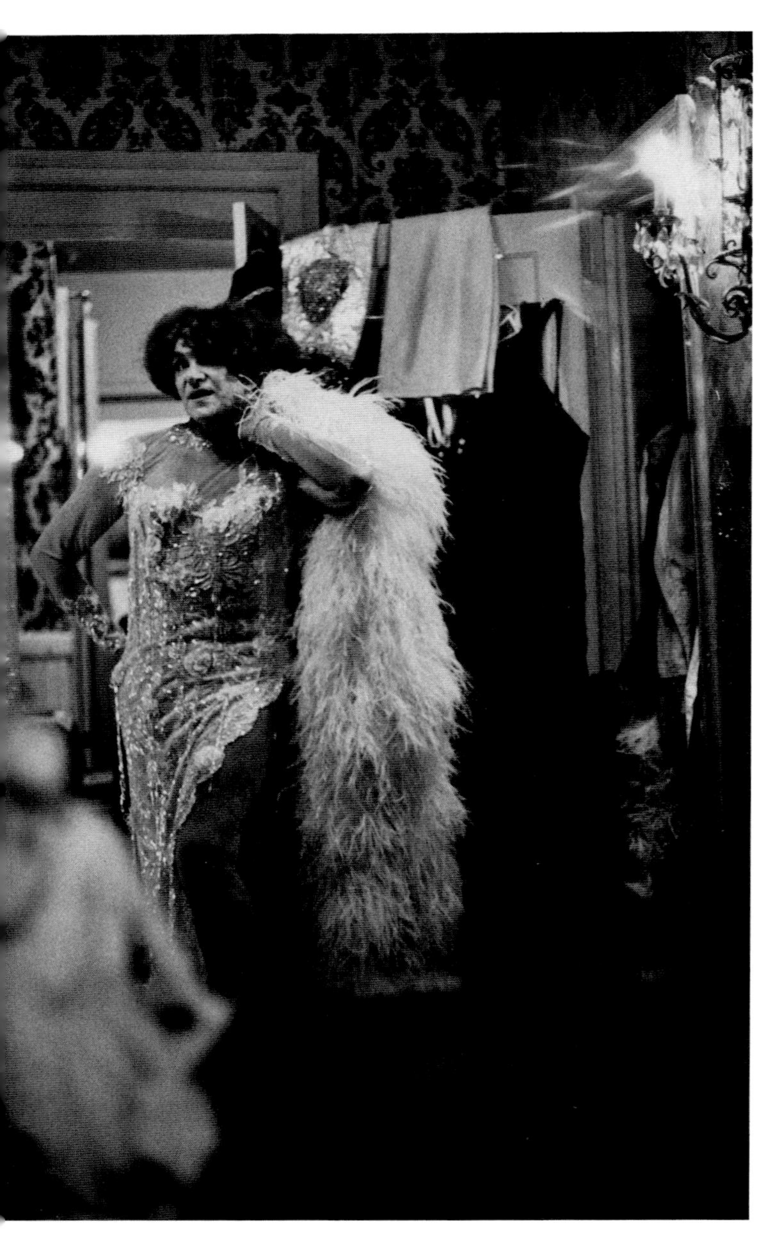
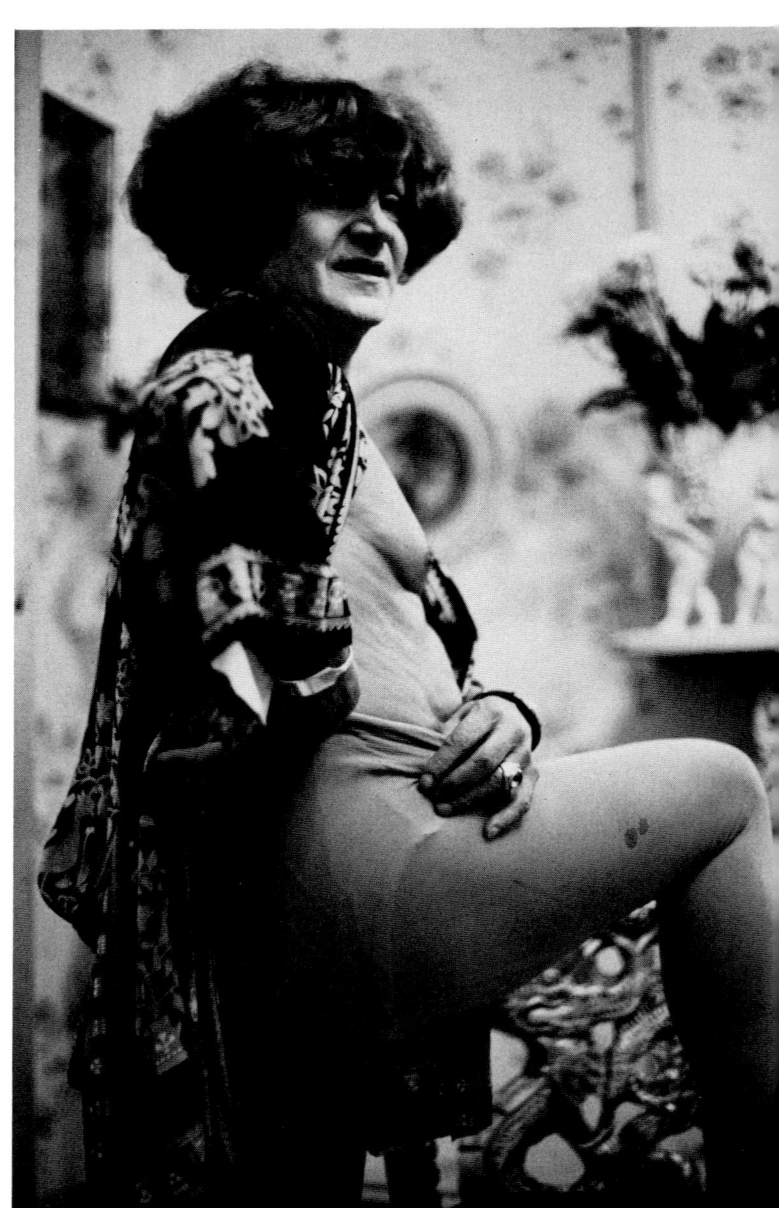

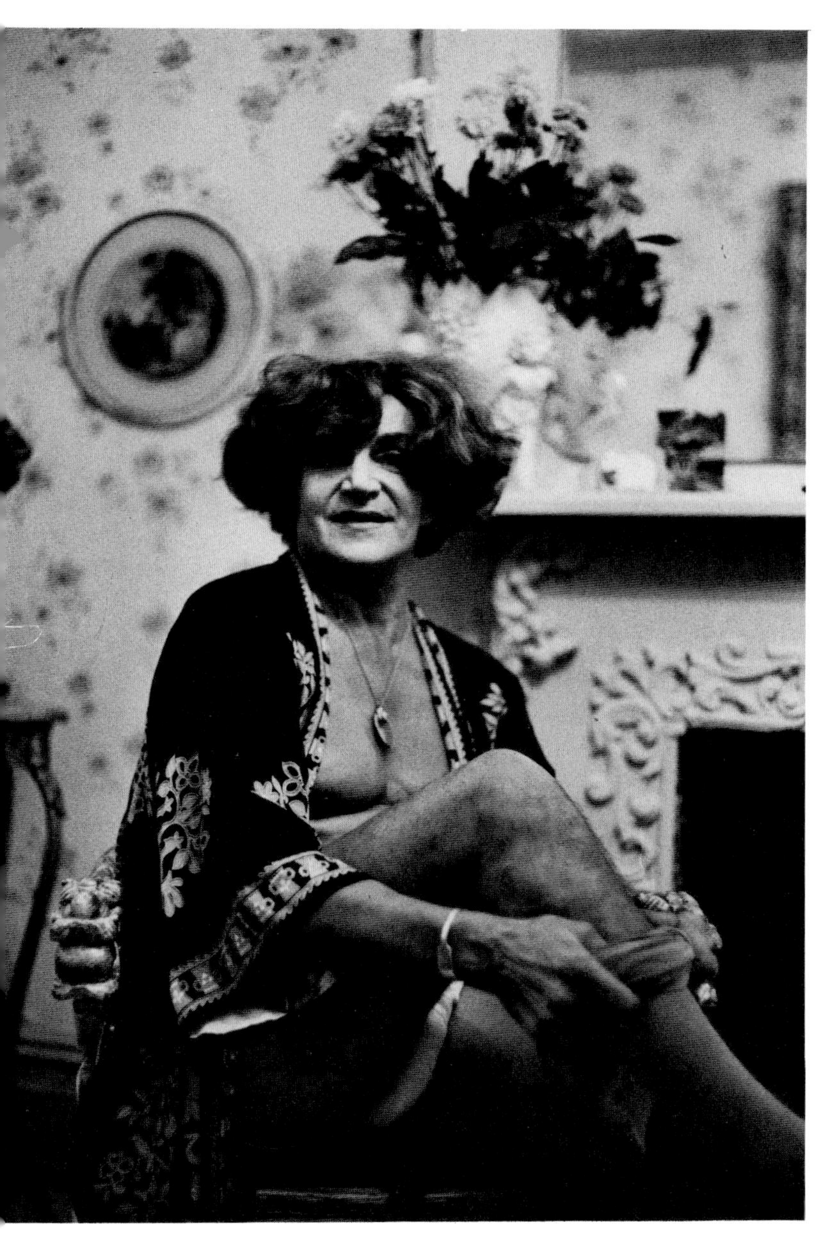
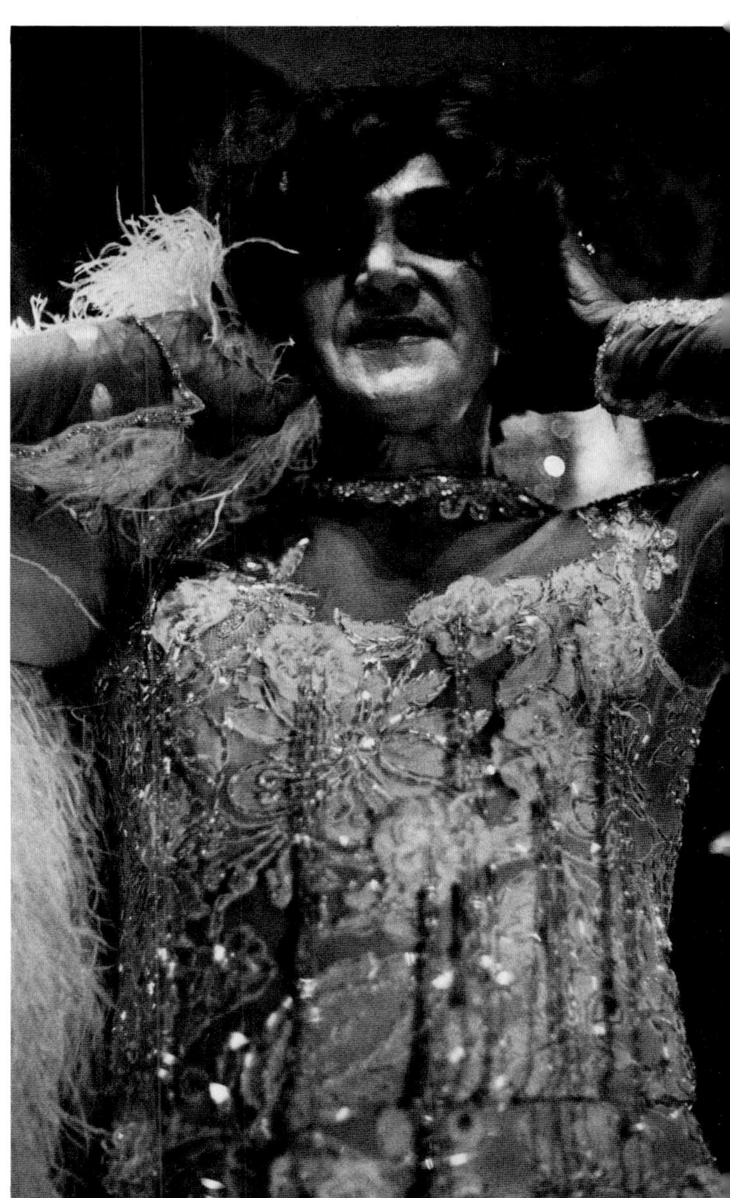

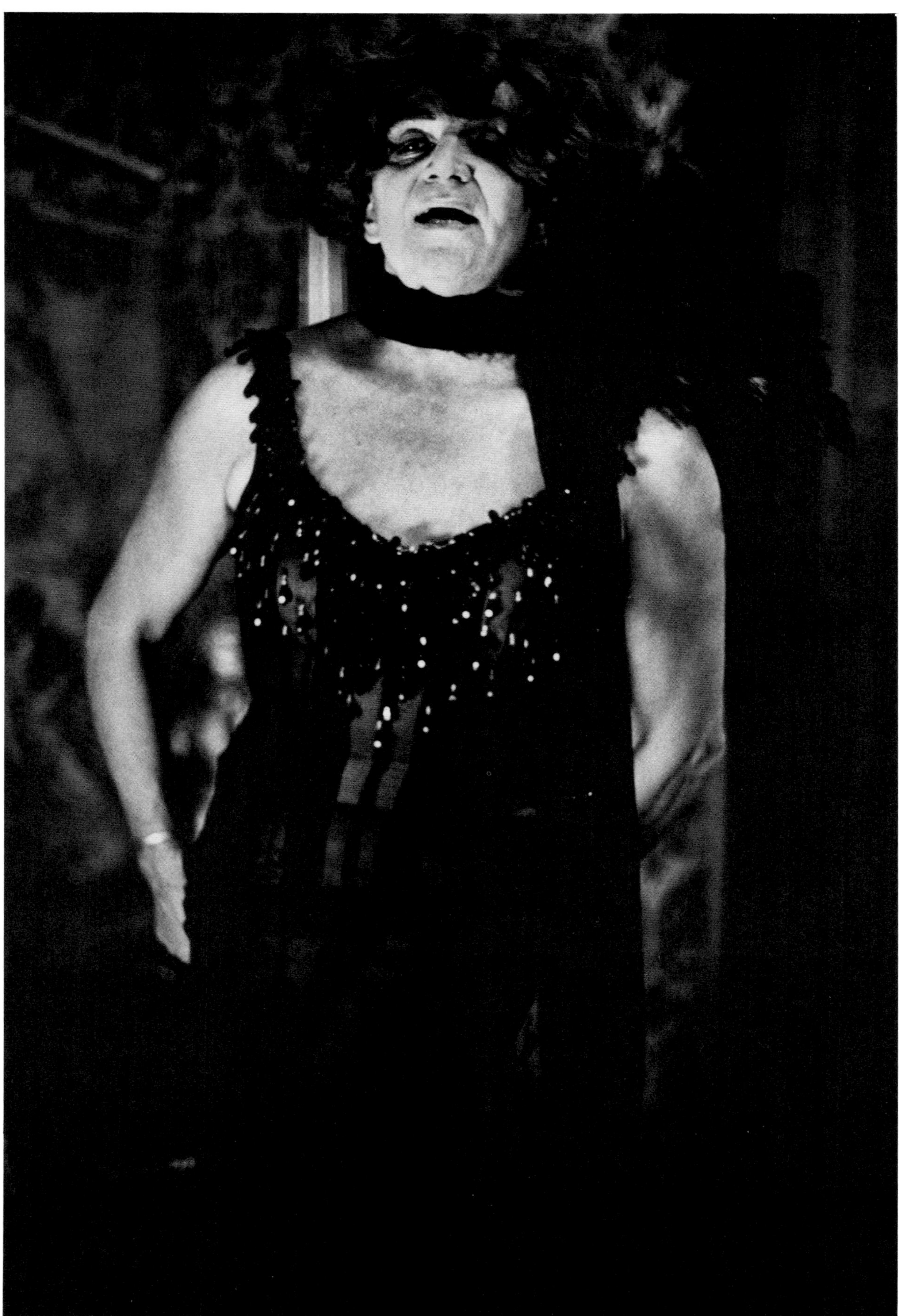

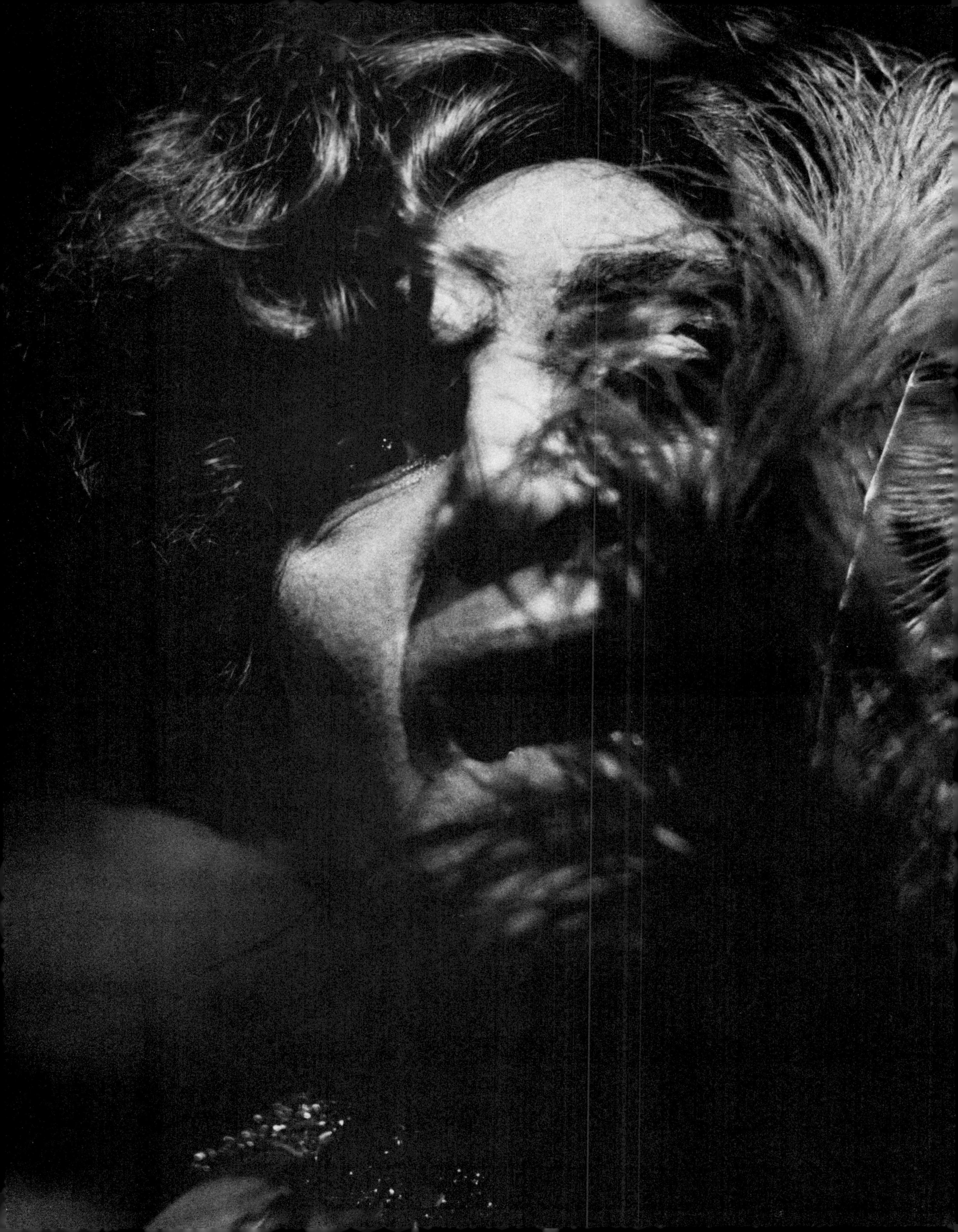

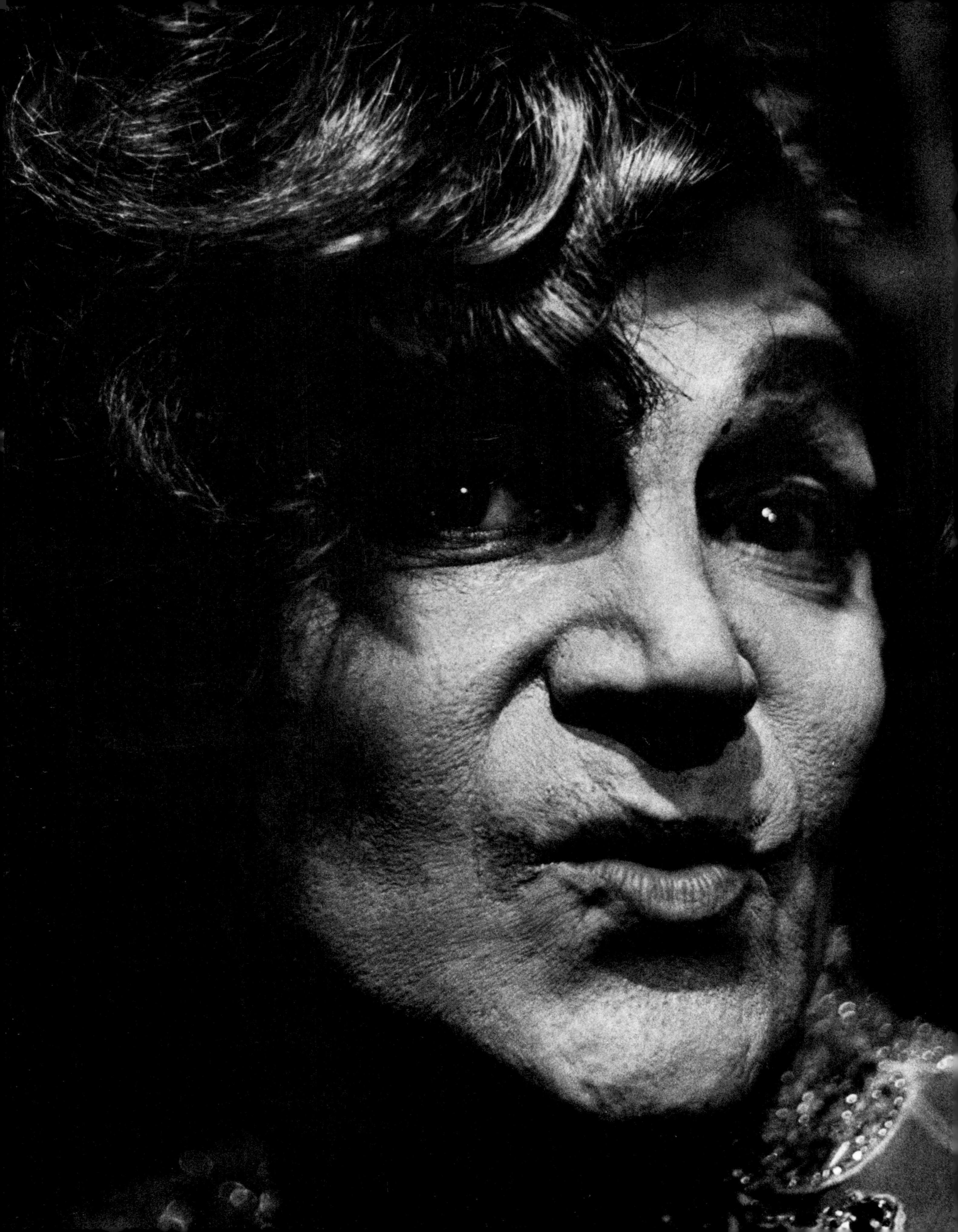

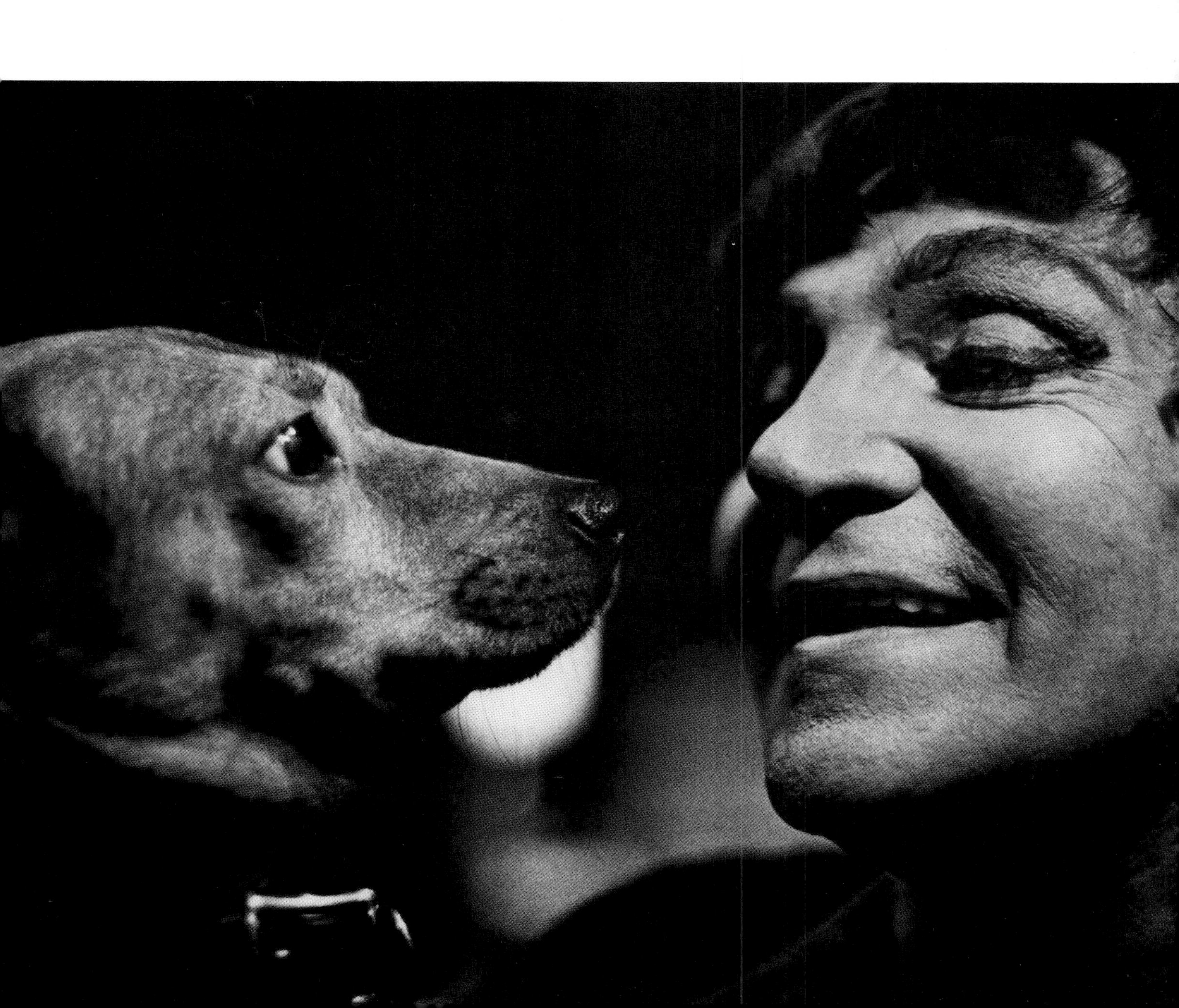

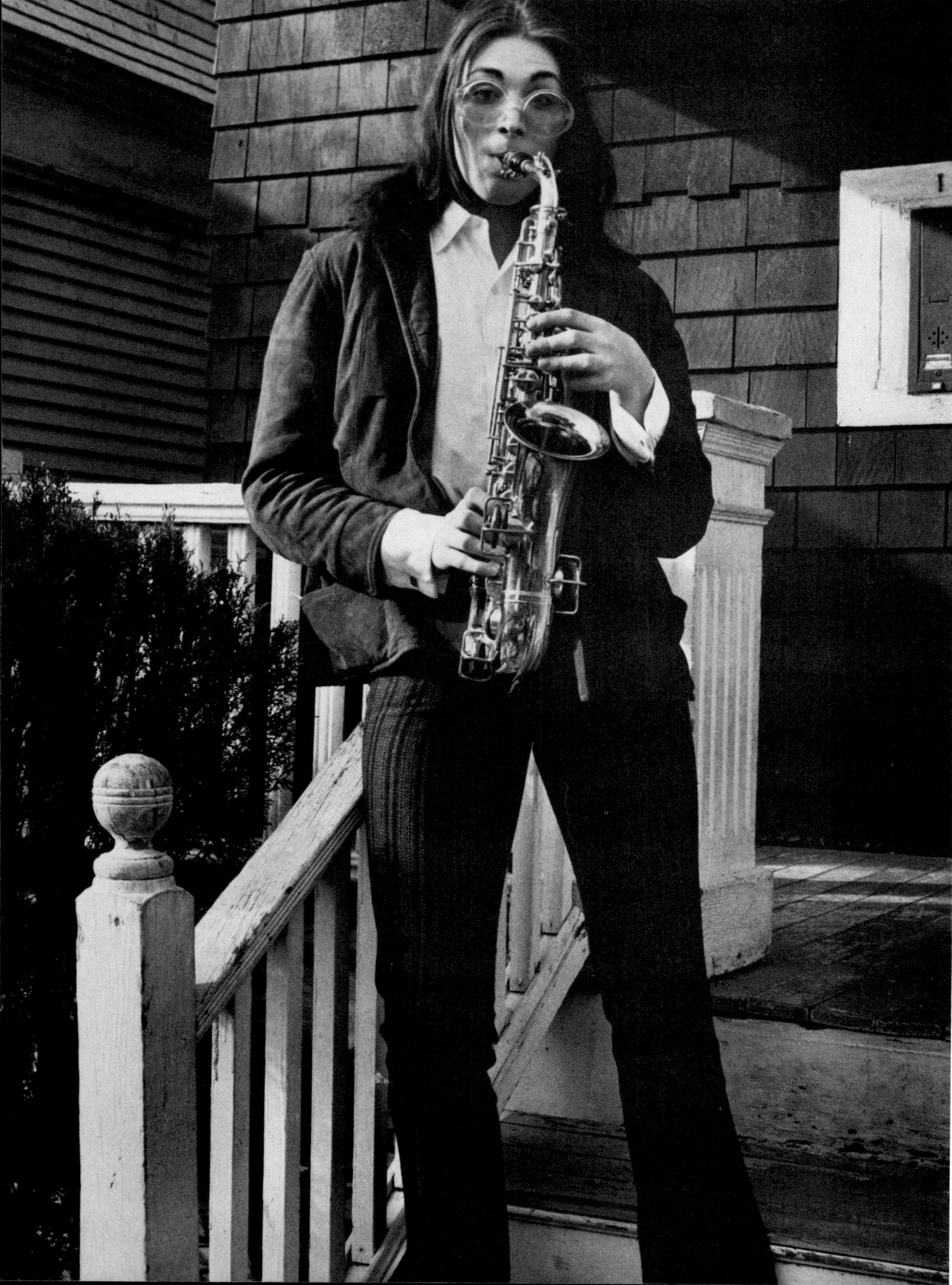

This is Caprice

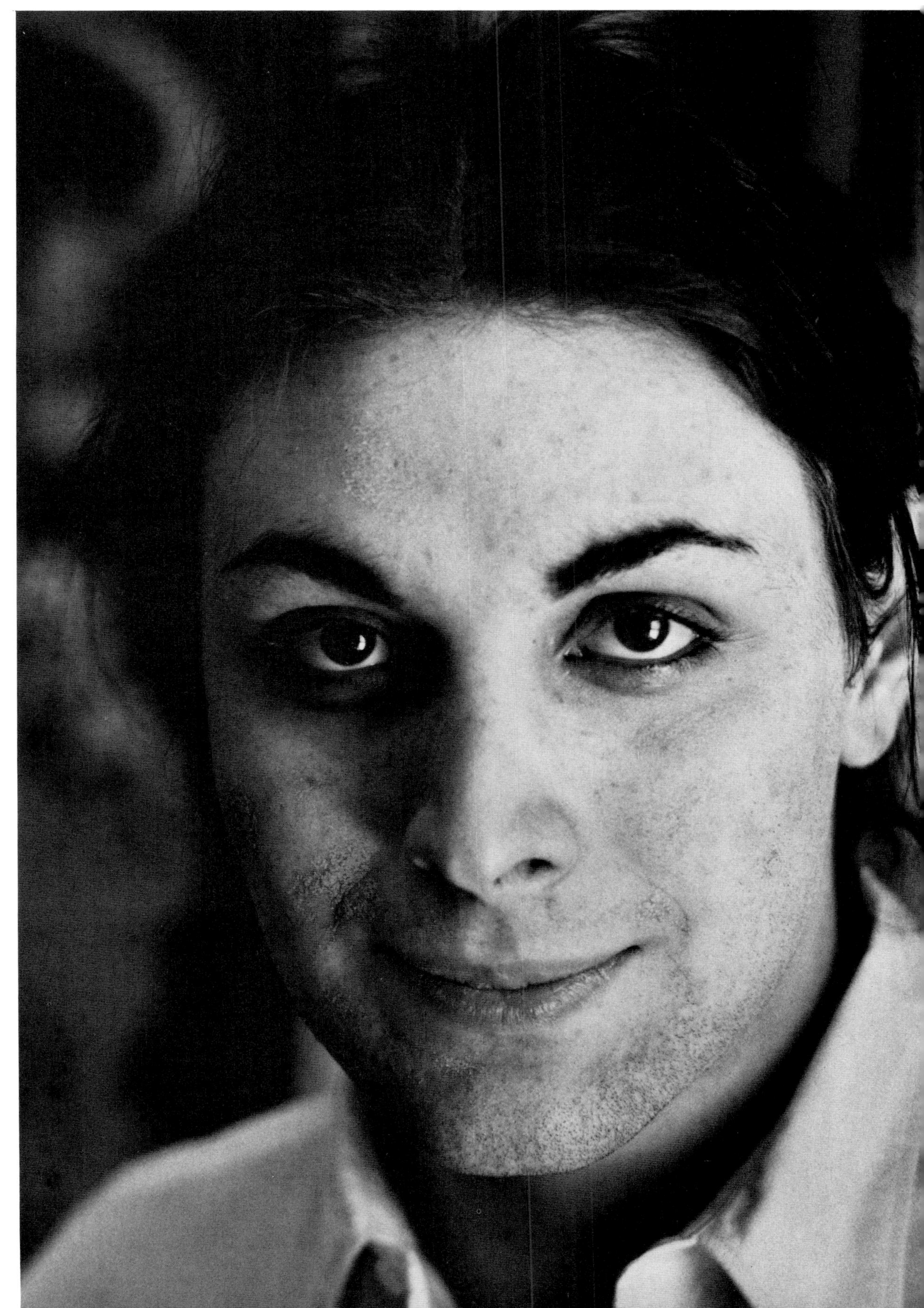

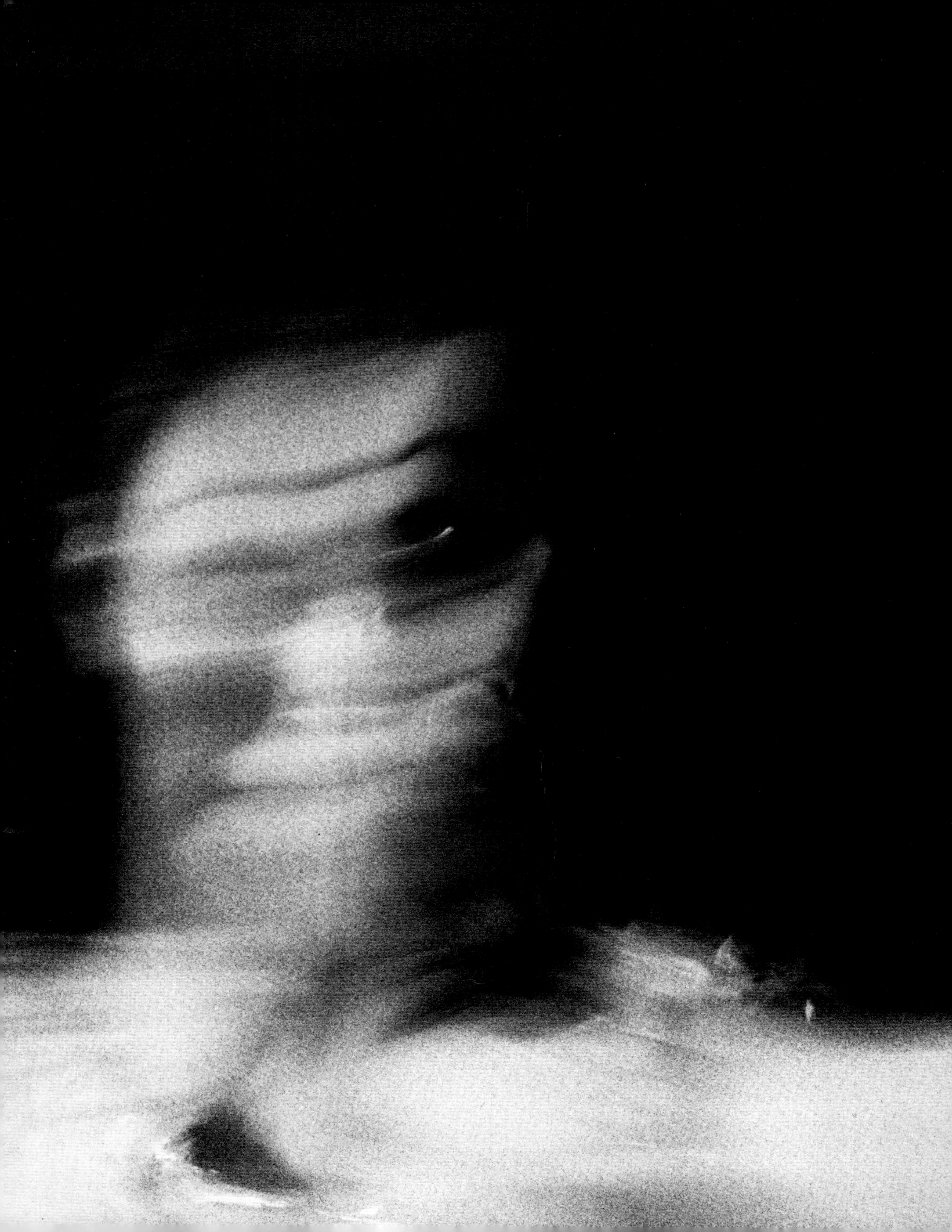

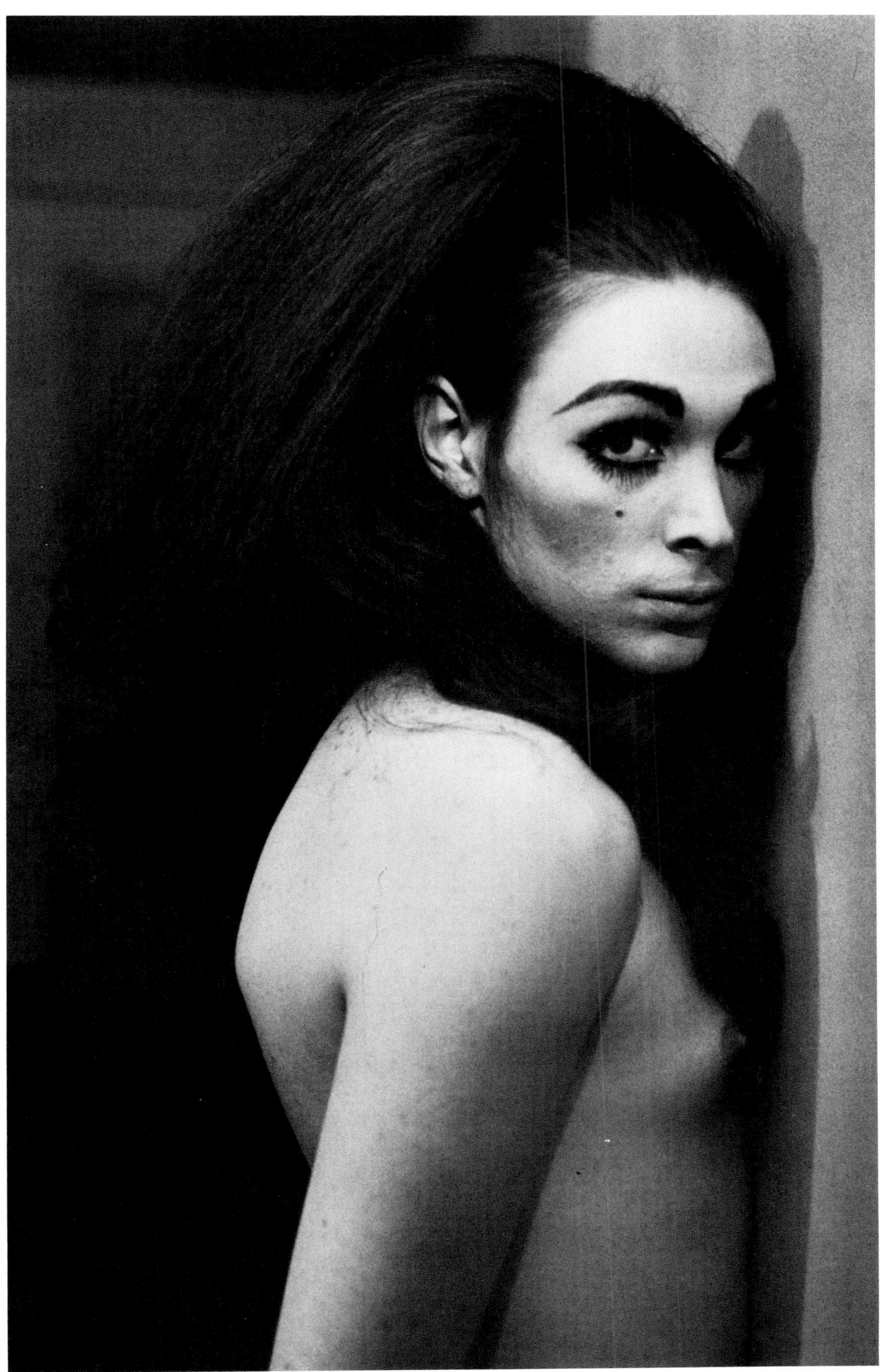

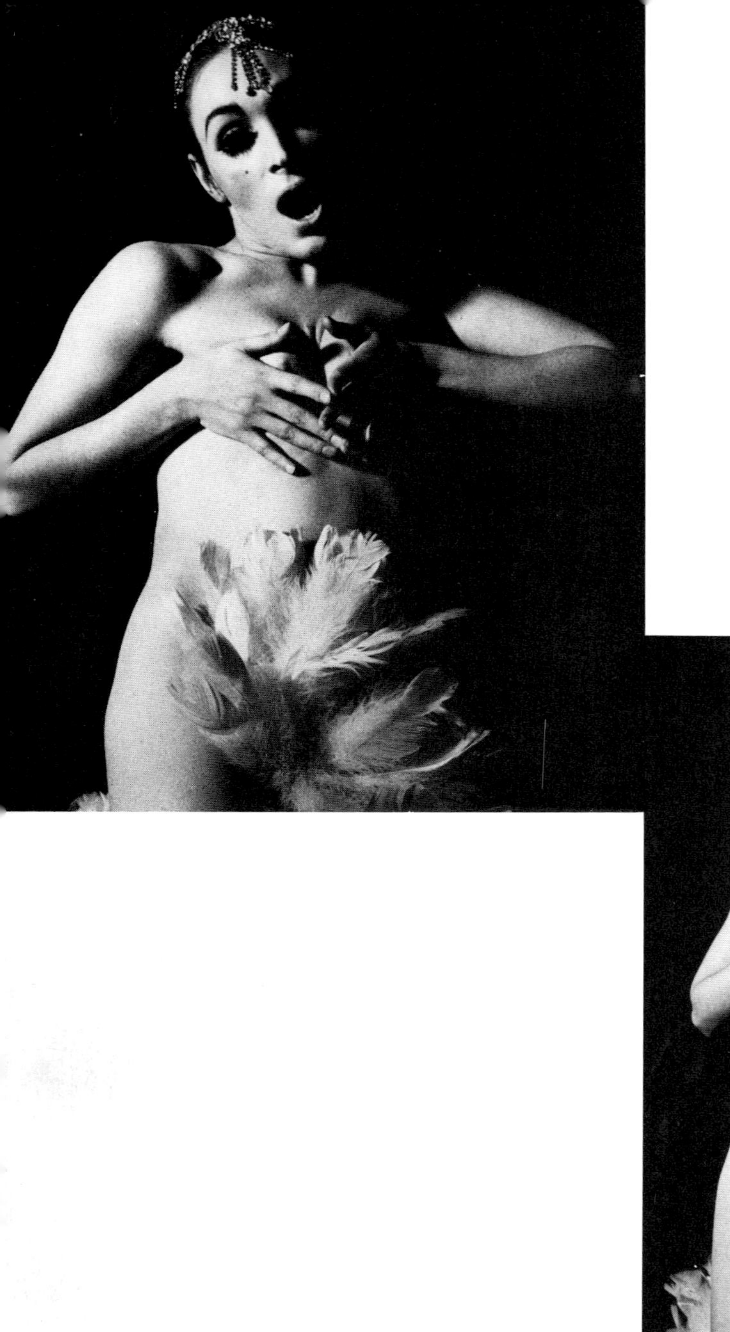
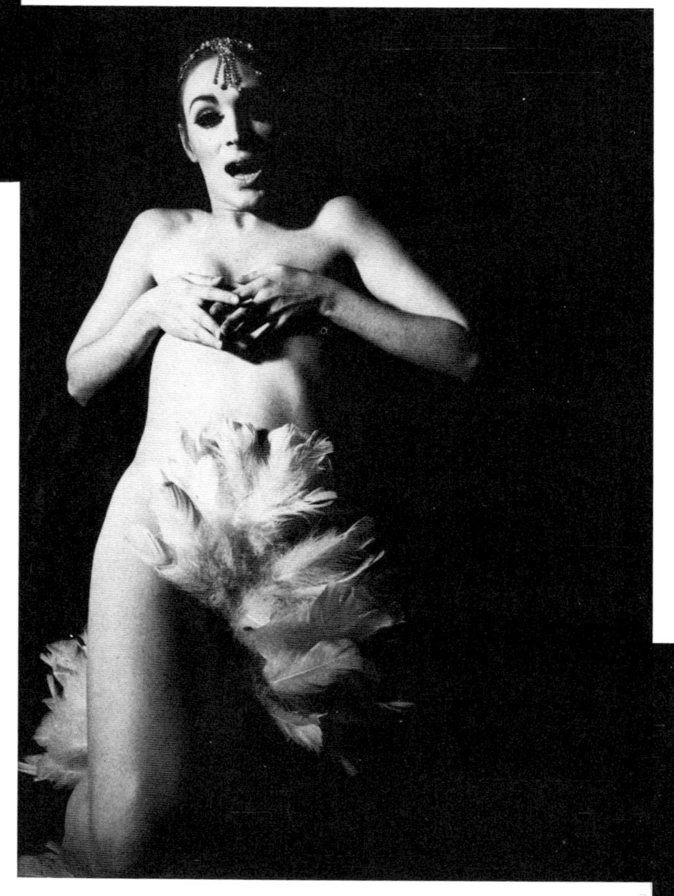

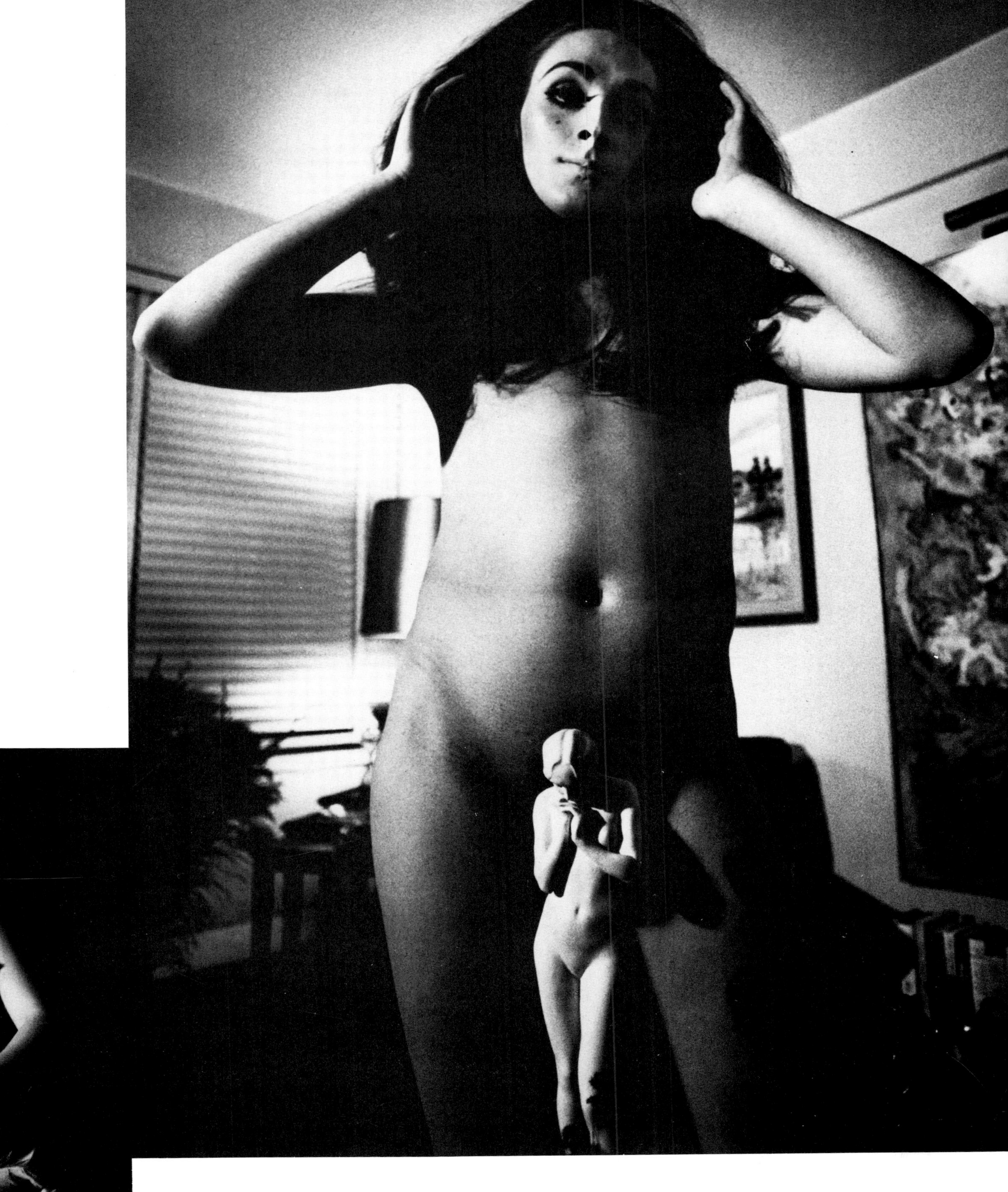

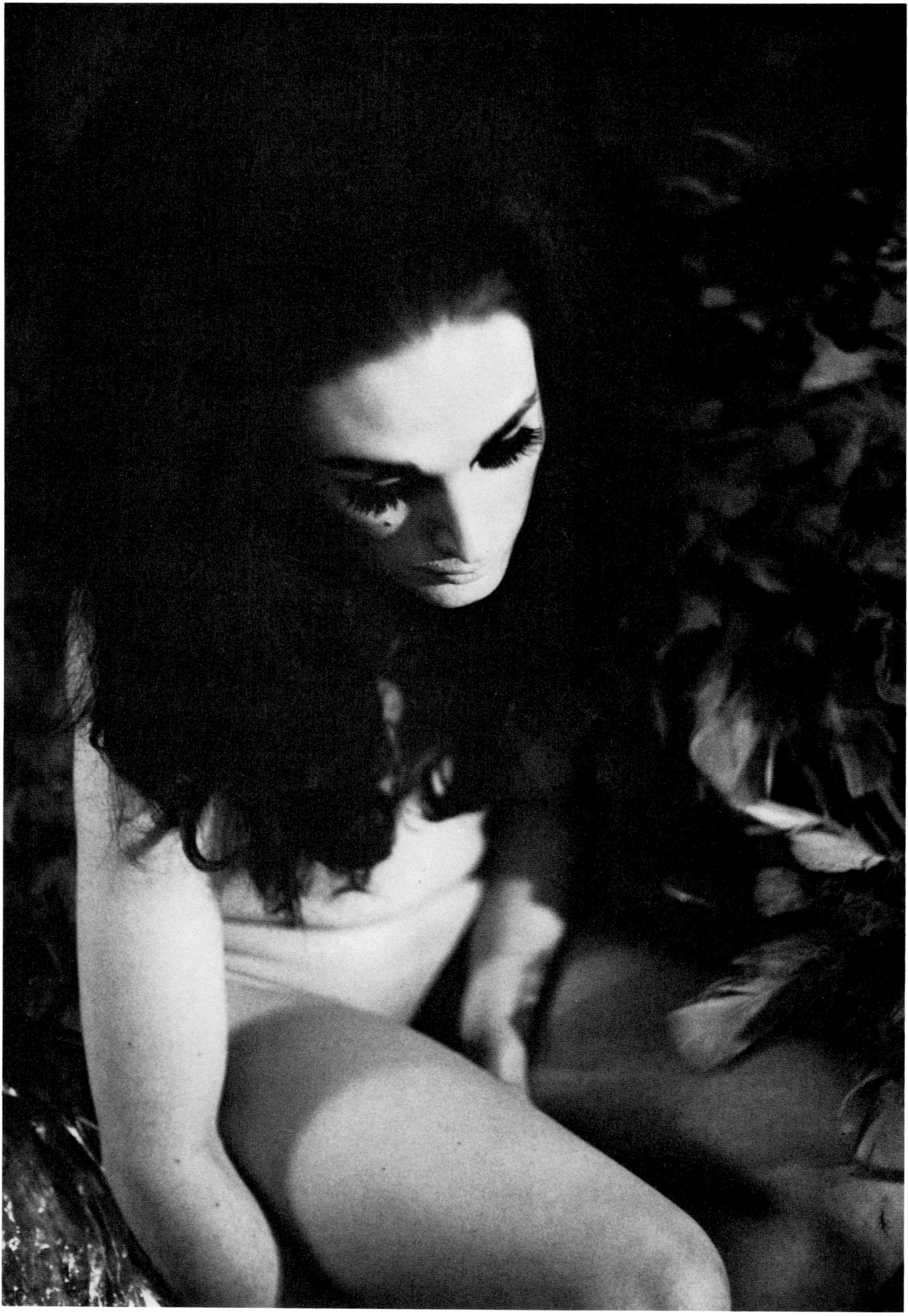

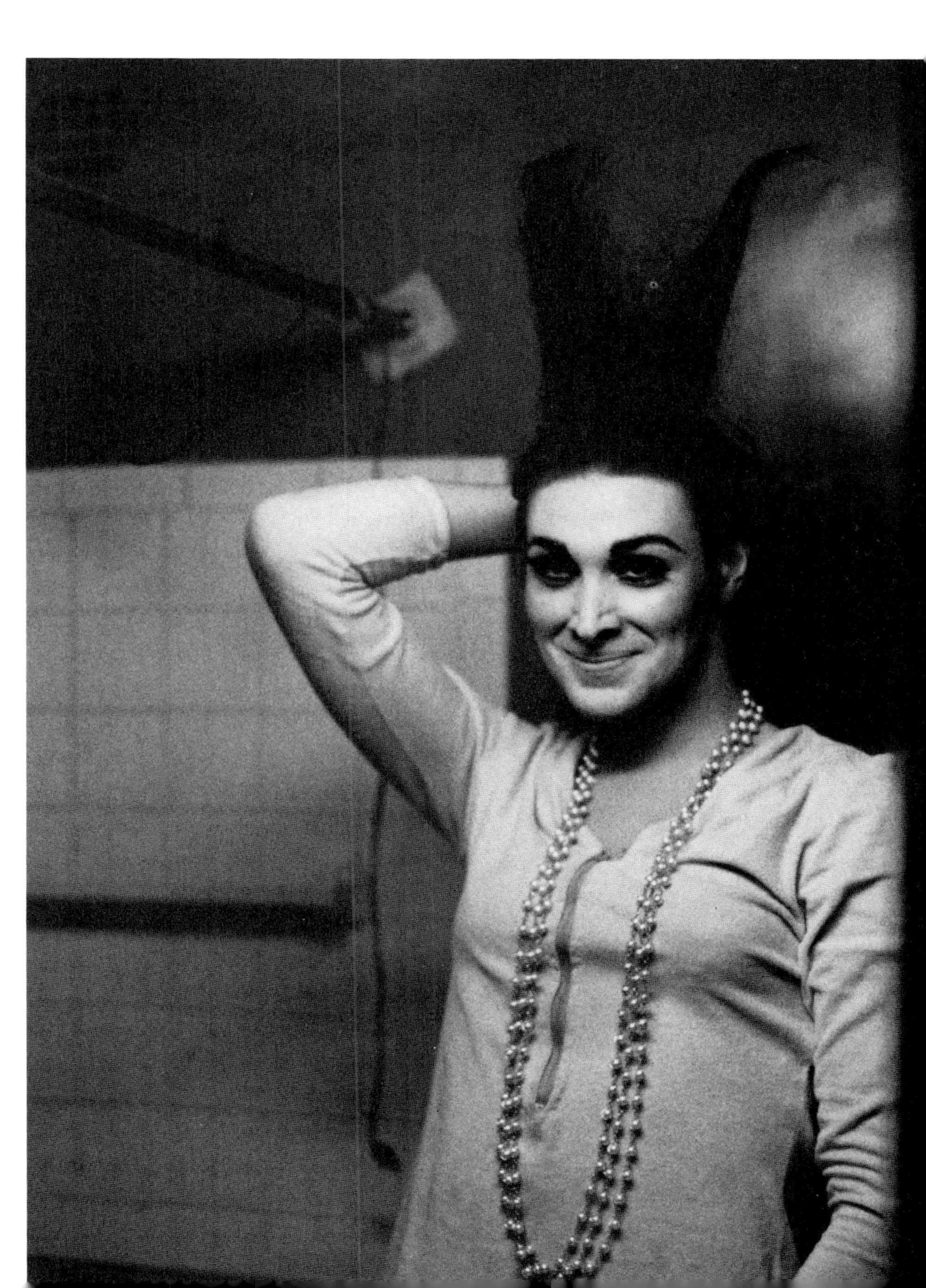

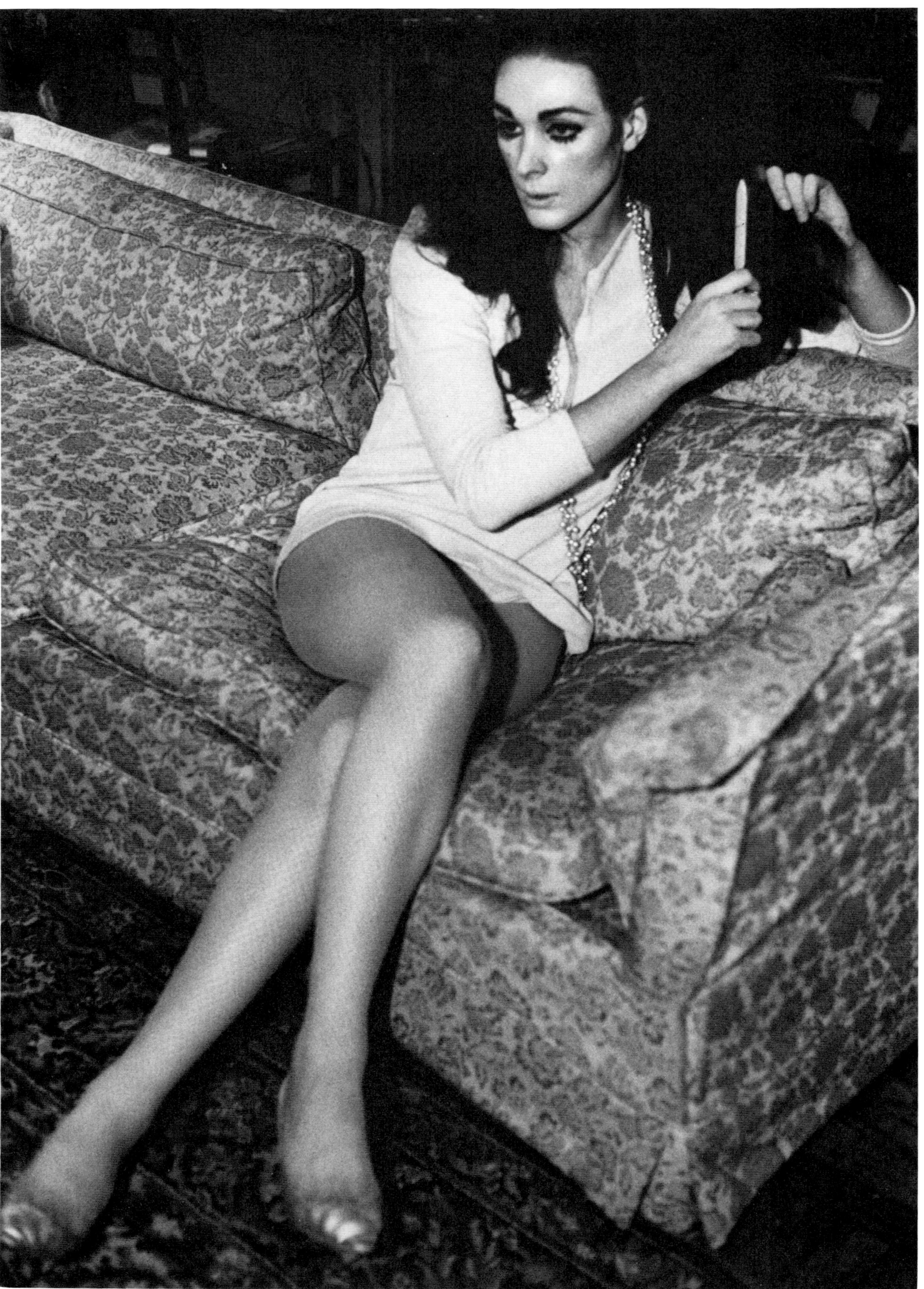

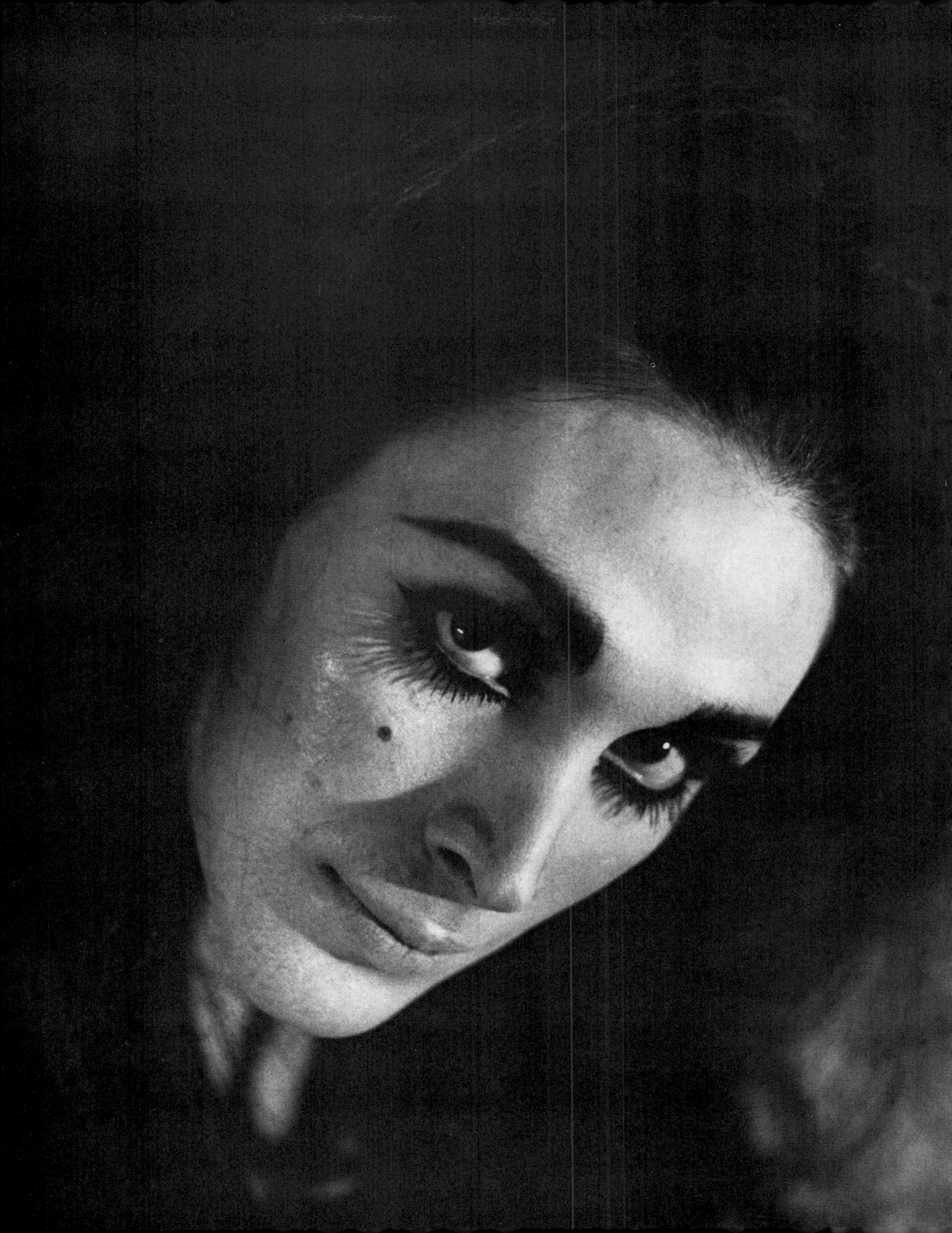

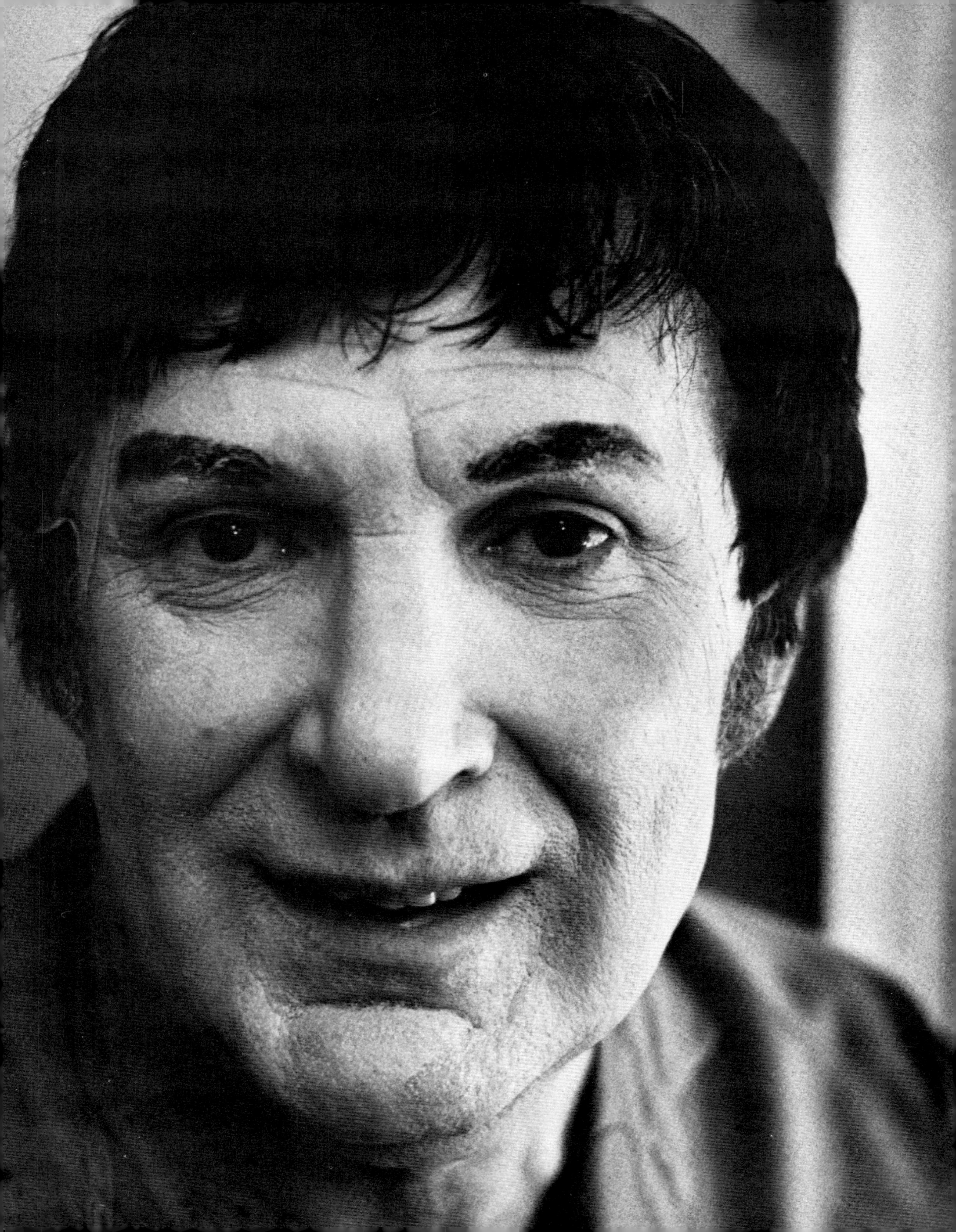

This is Frankie

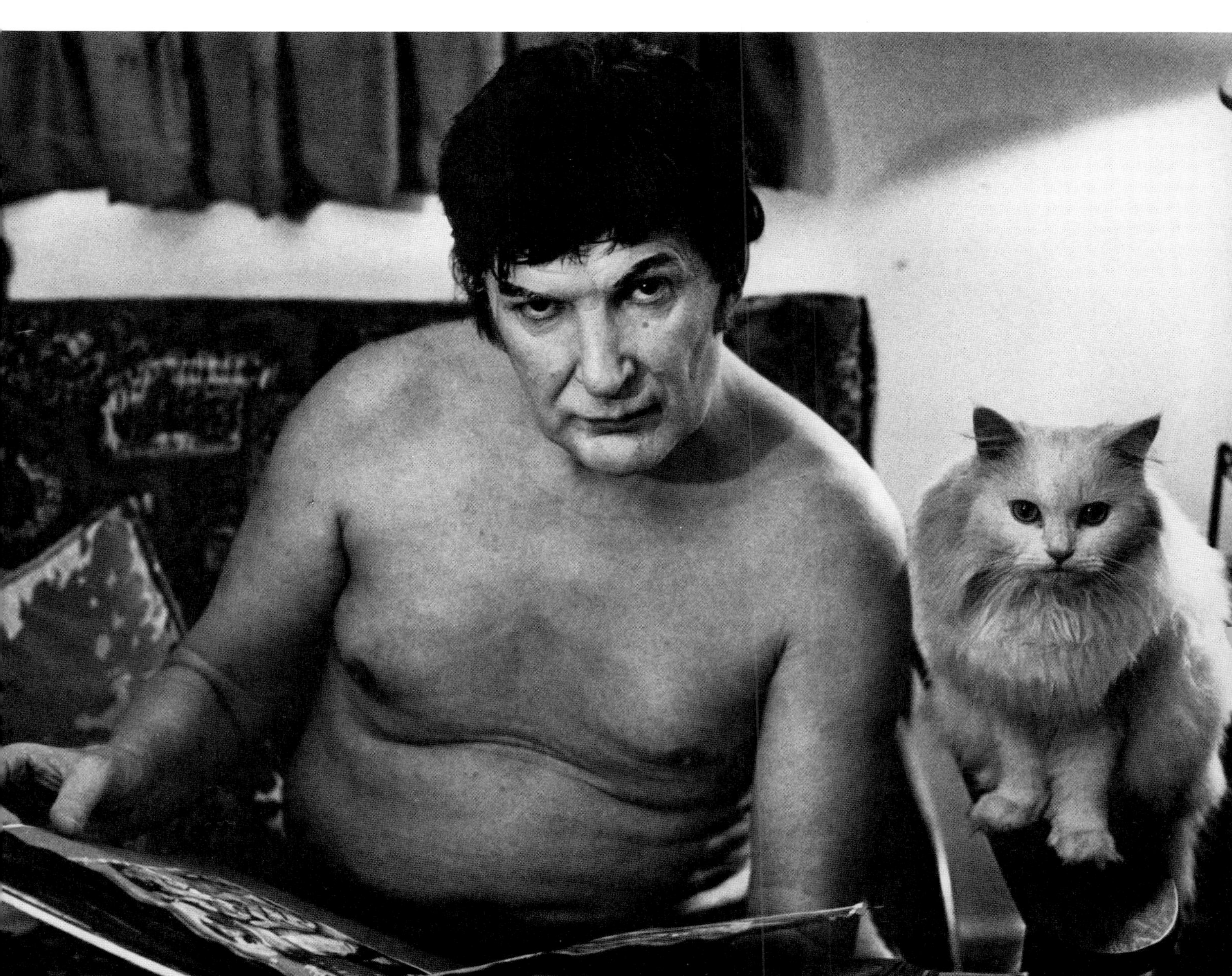

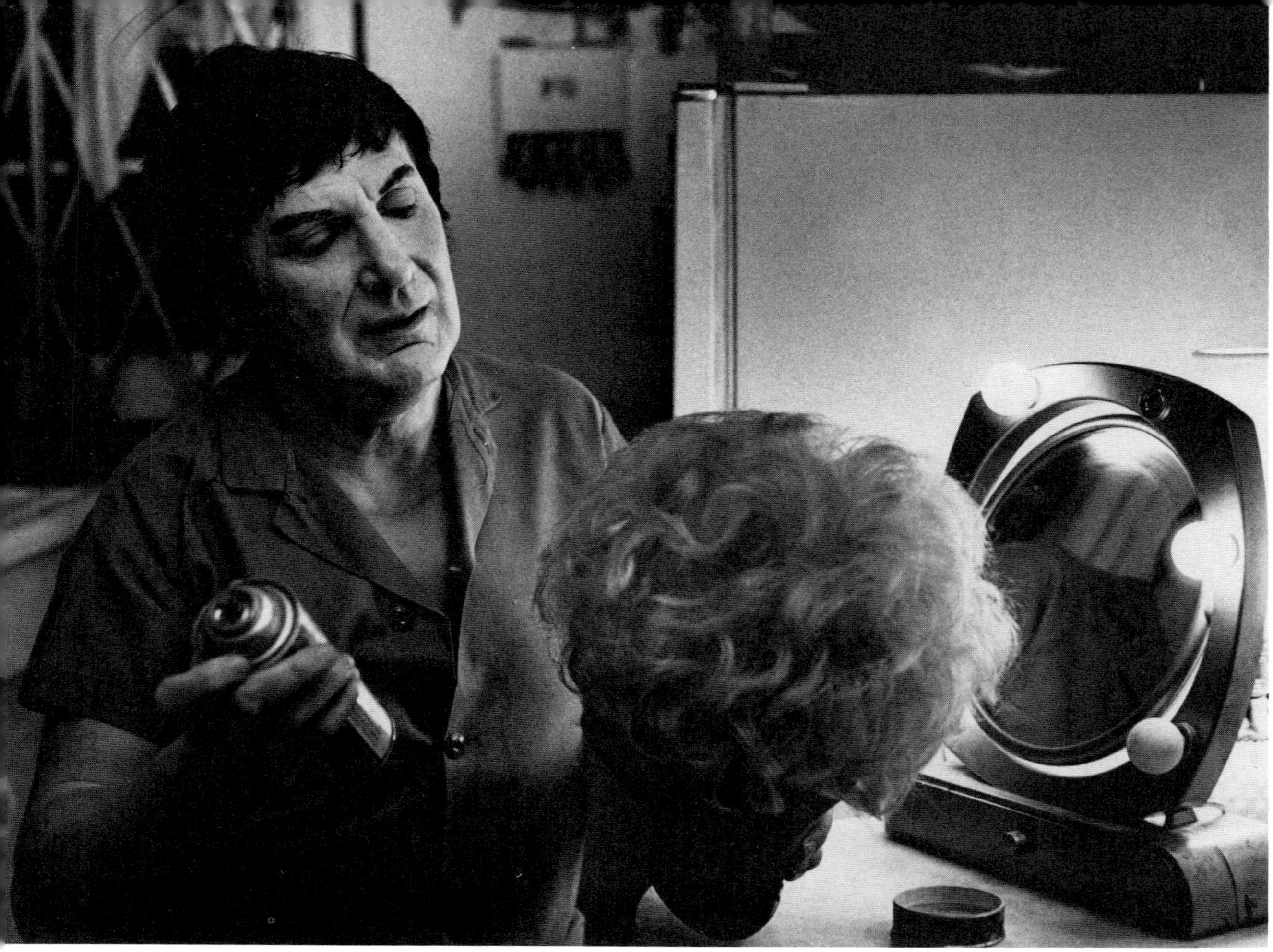

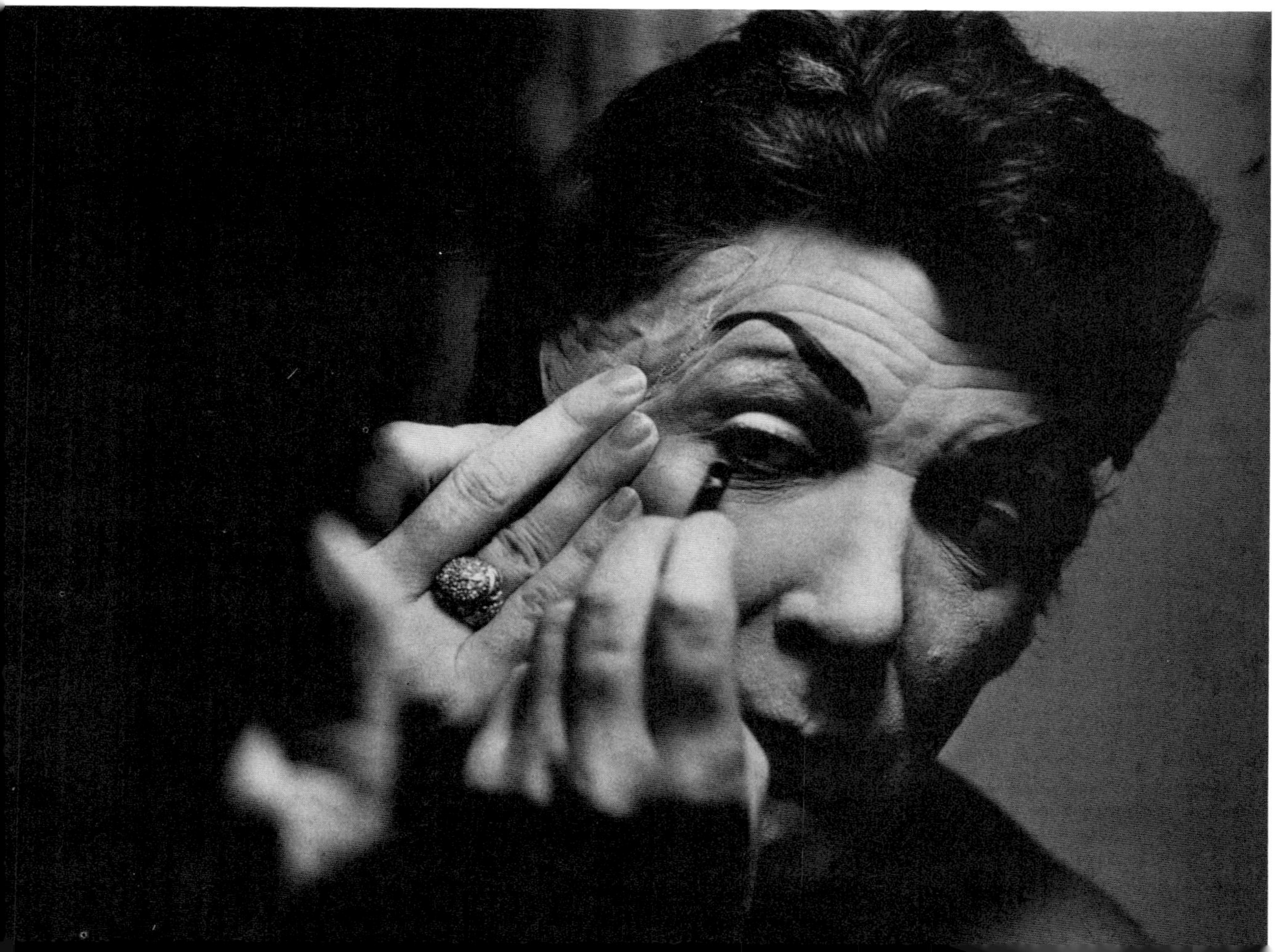

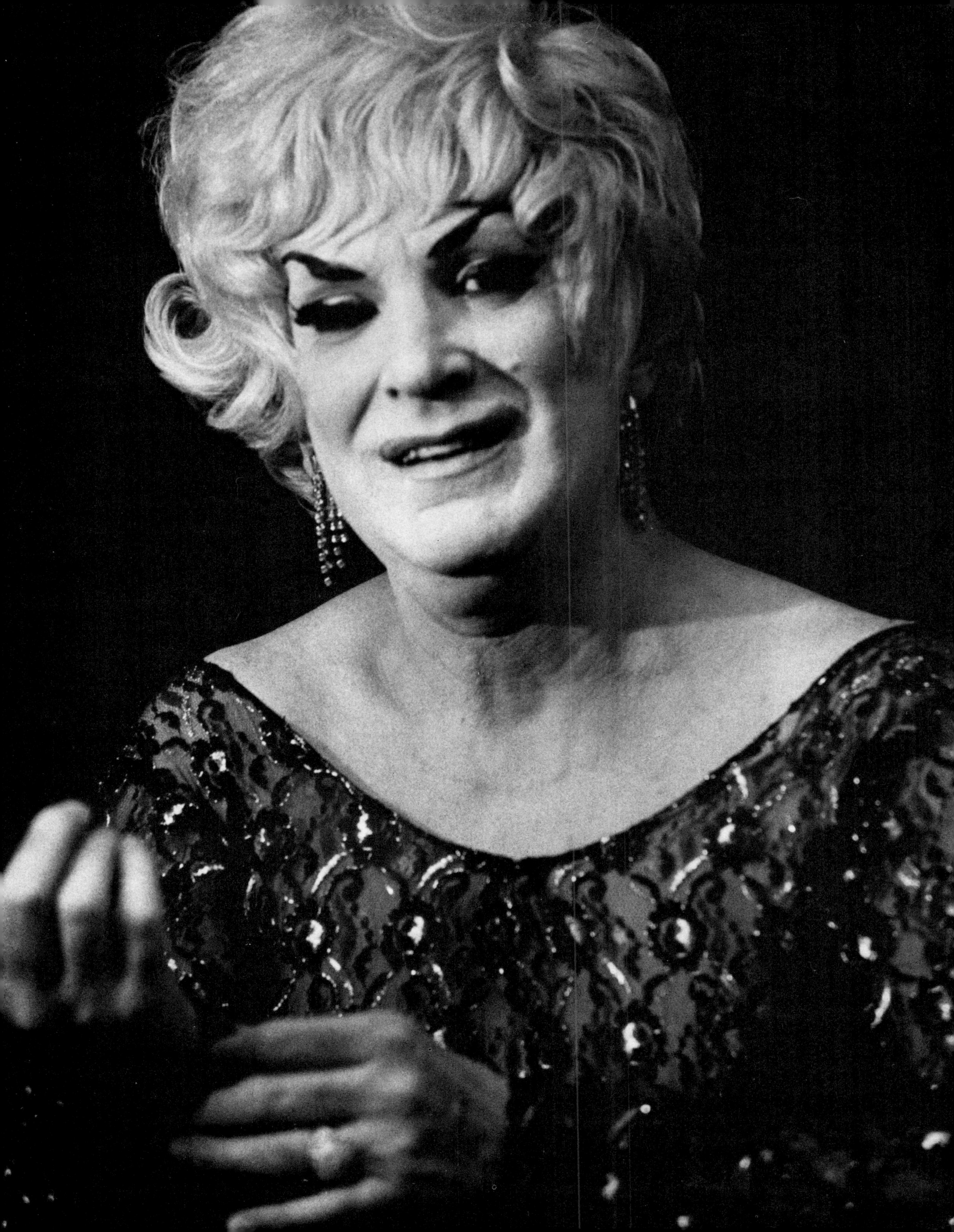

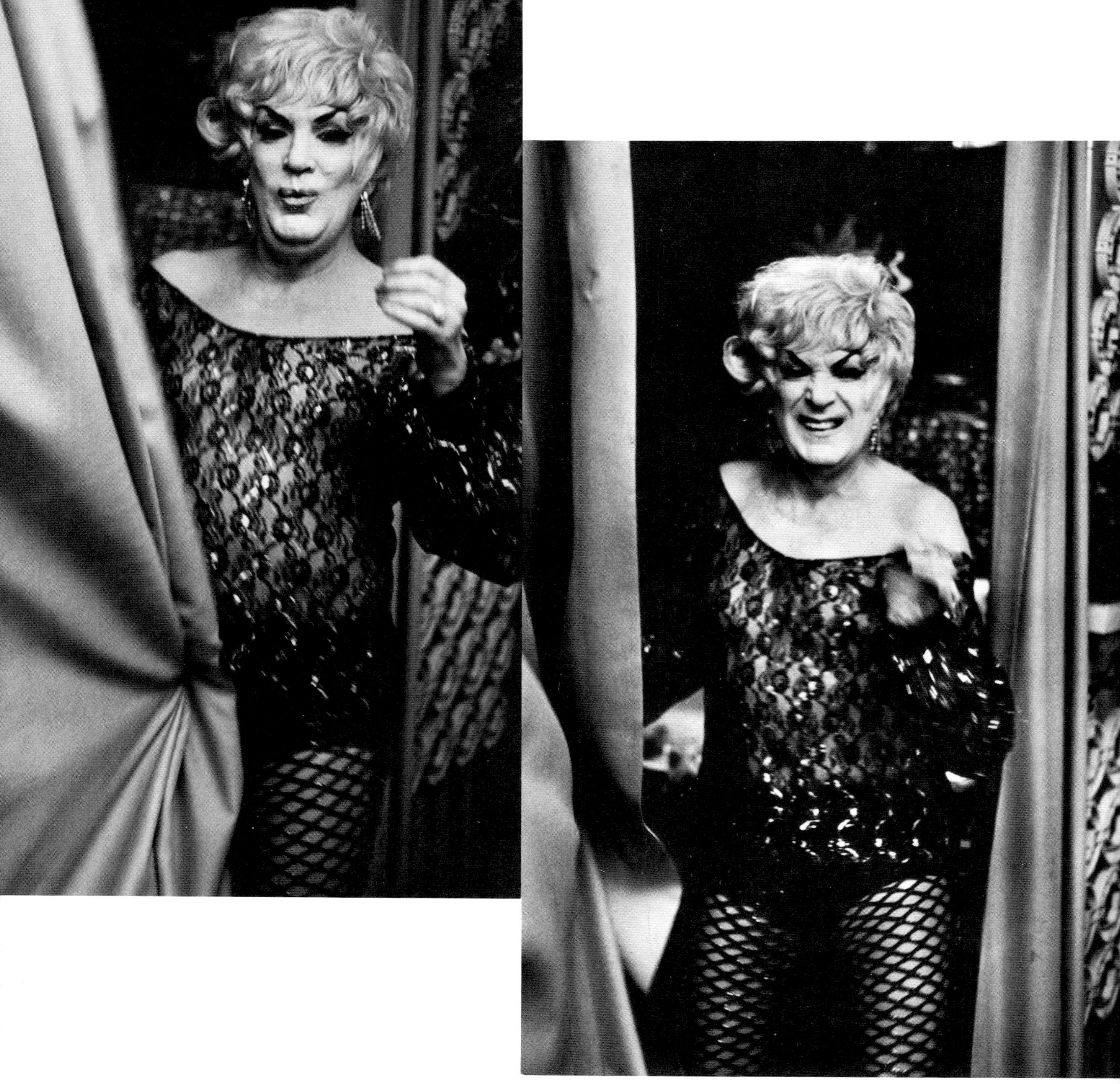

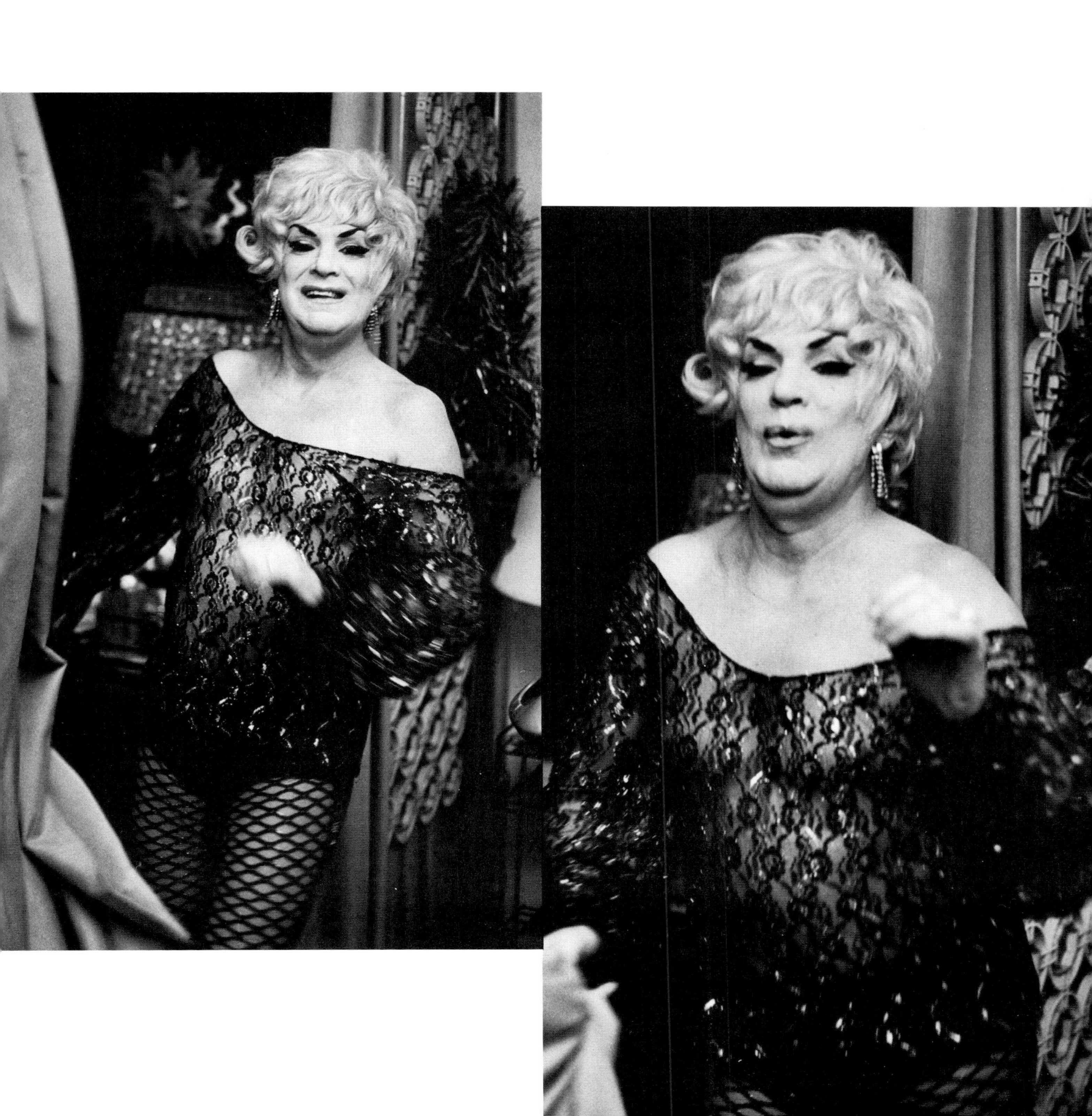

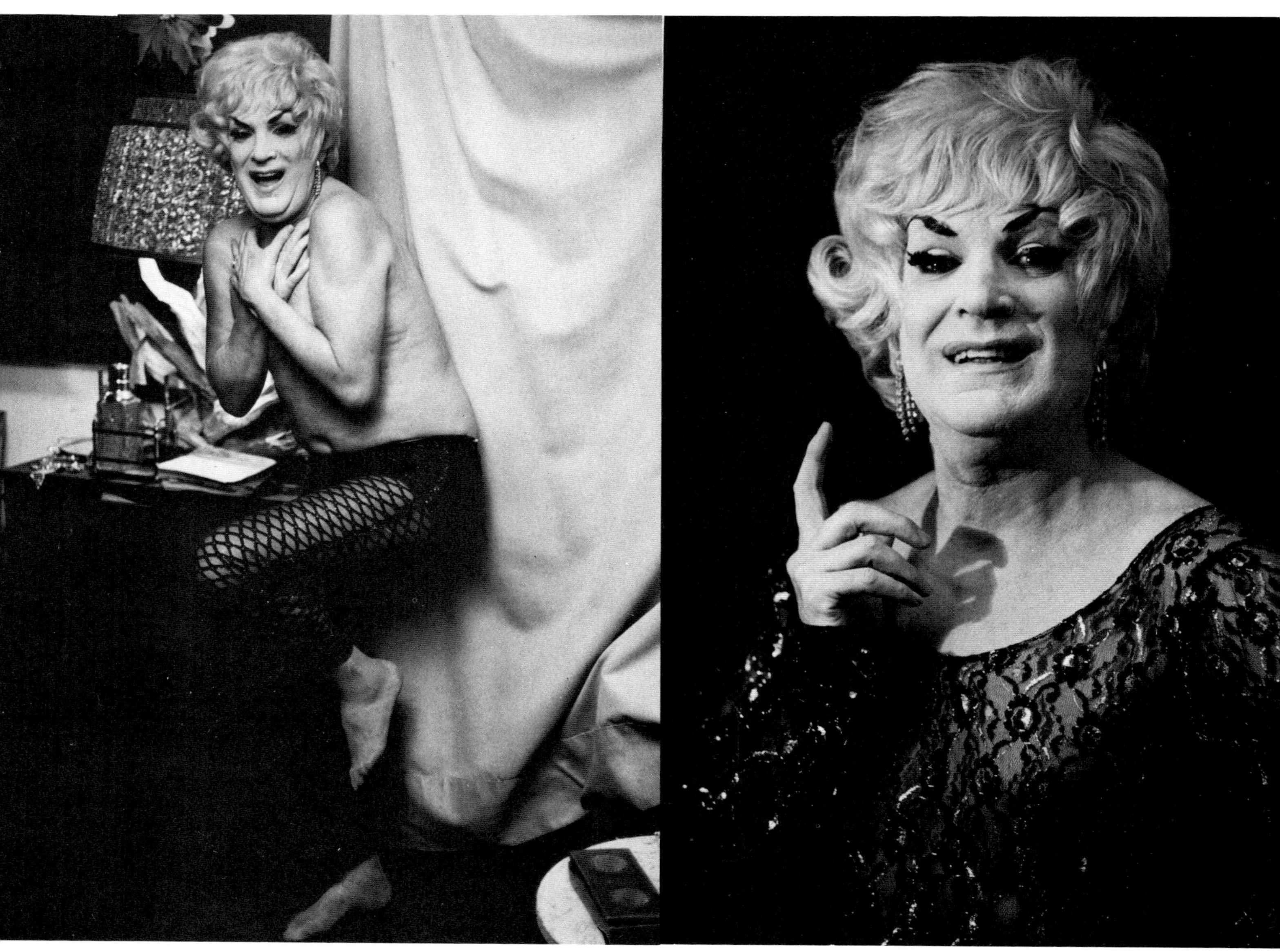

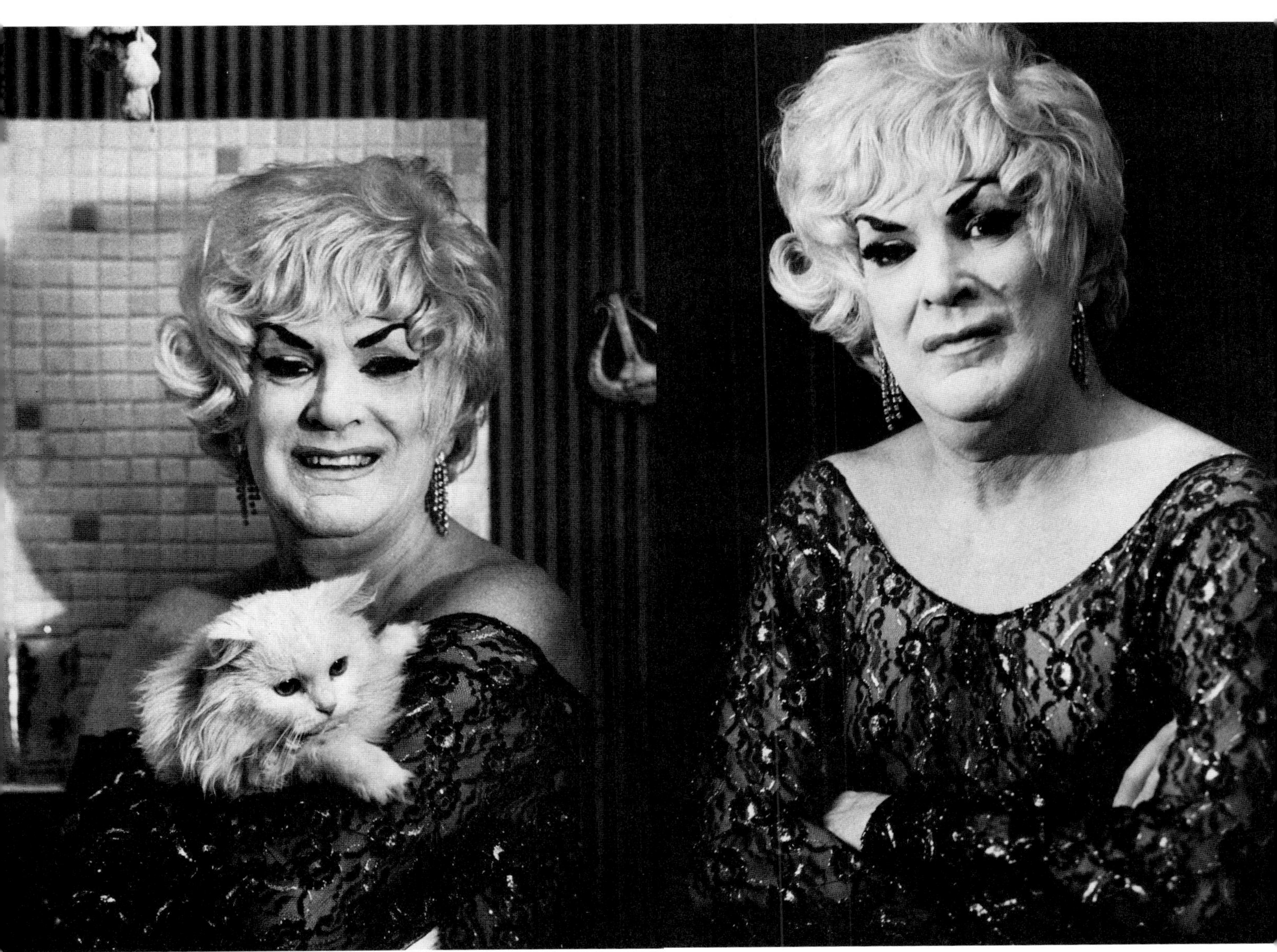

This is Chrysis

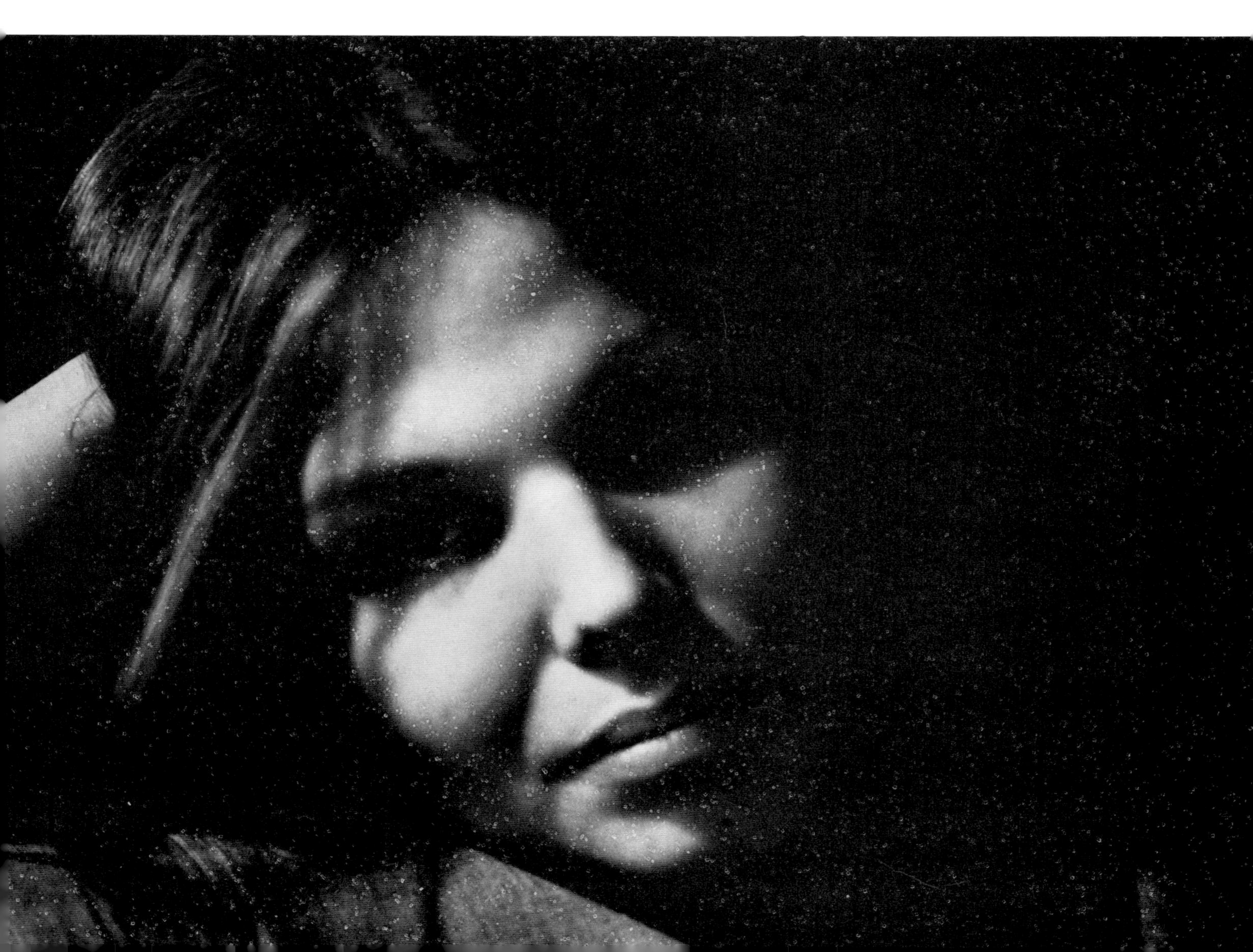

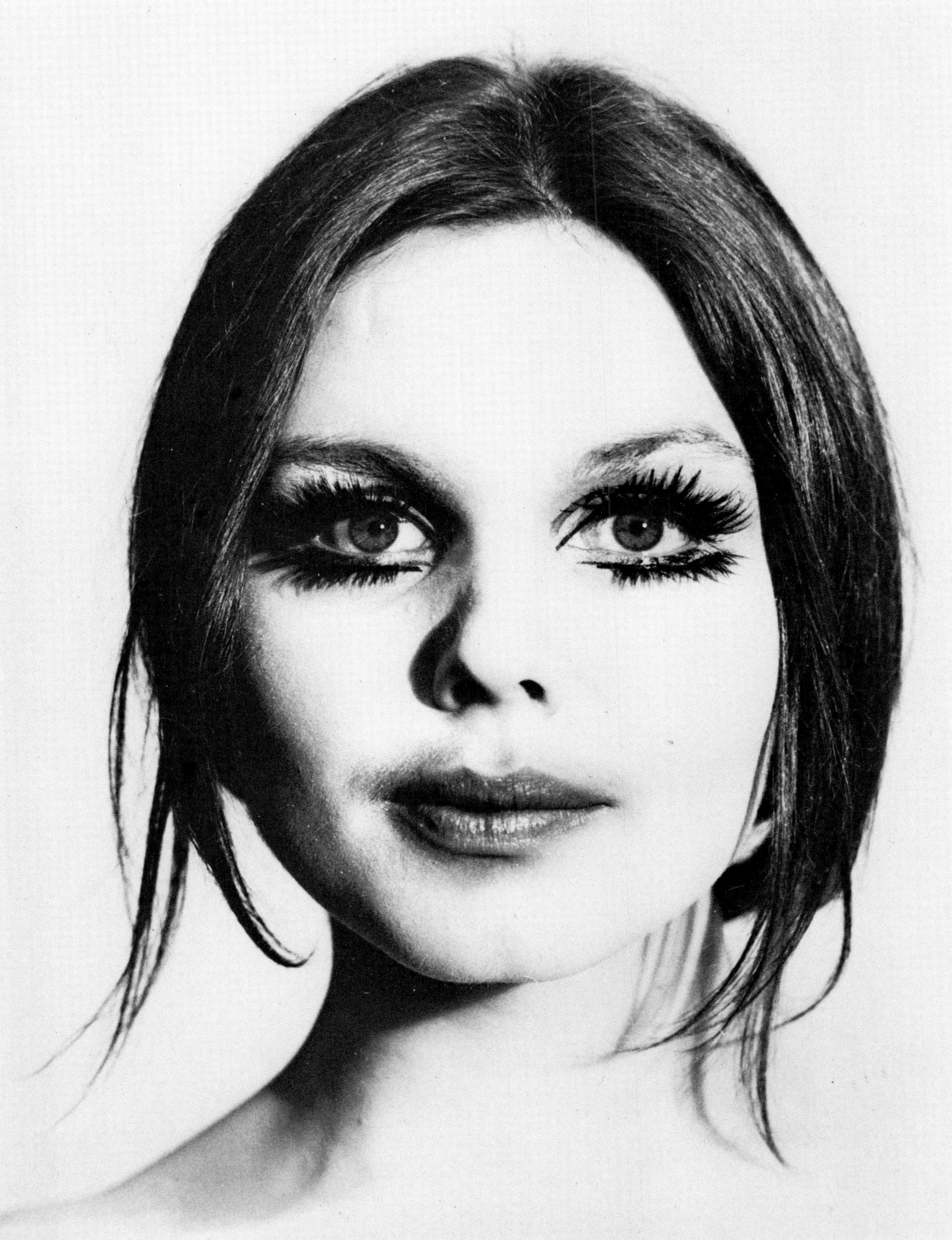

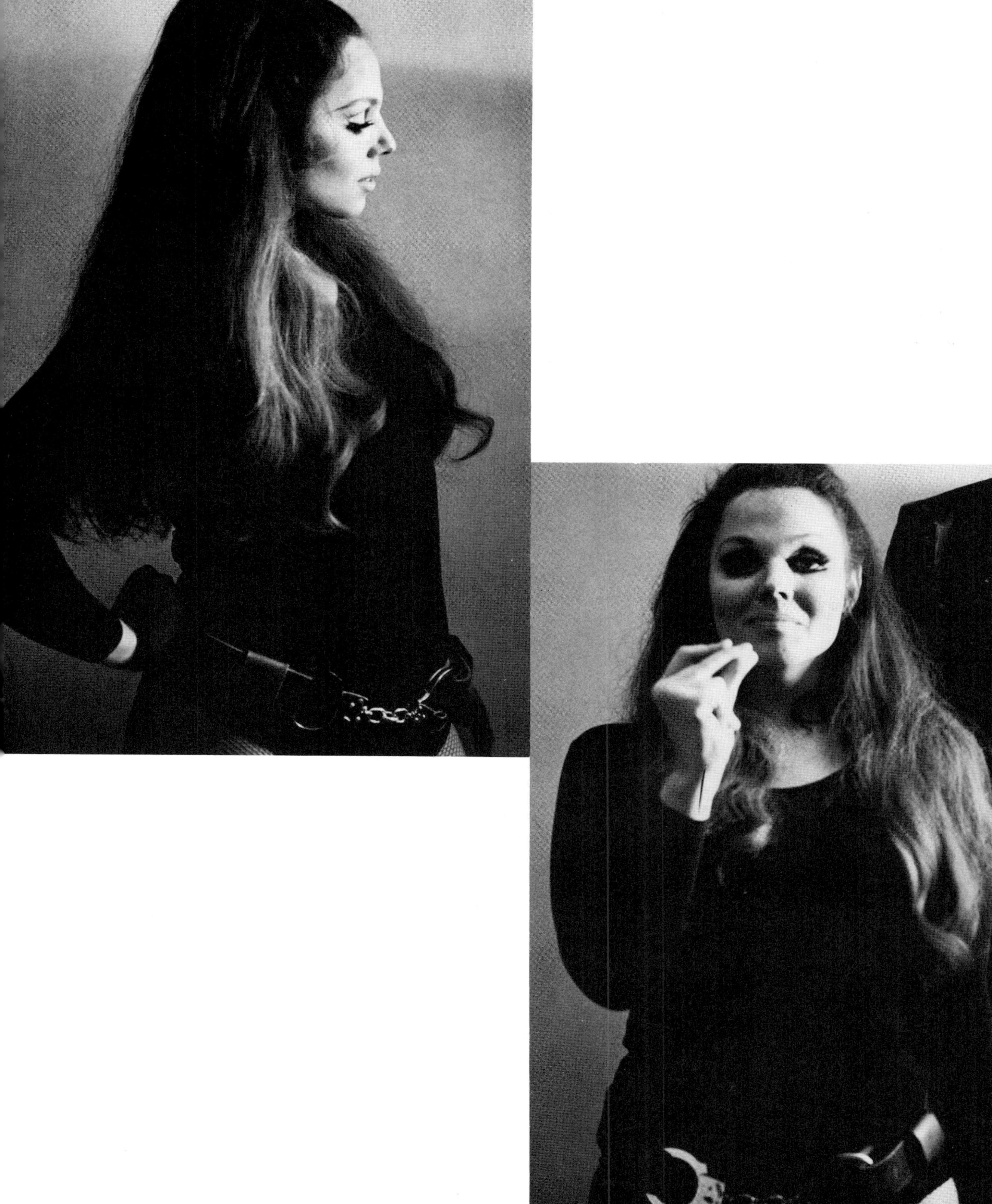

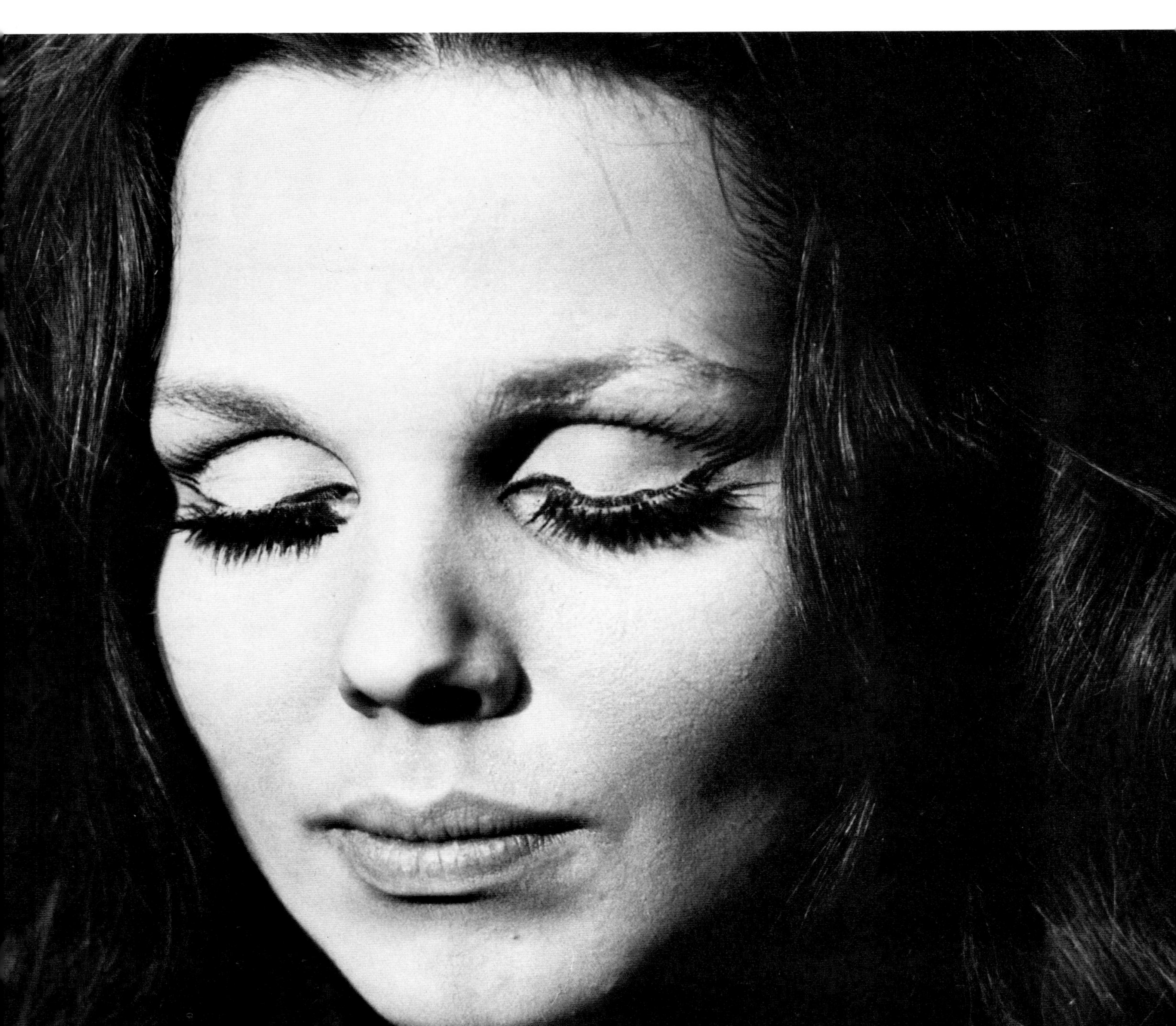

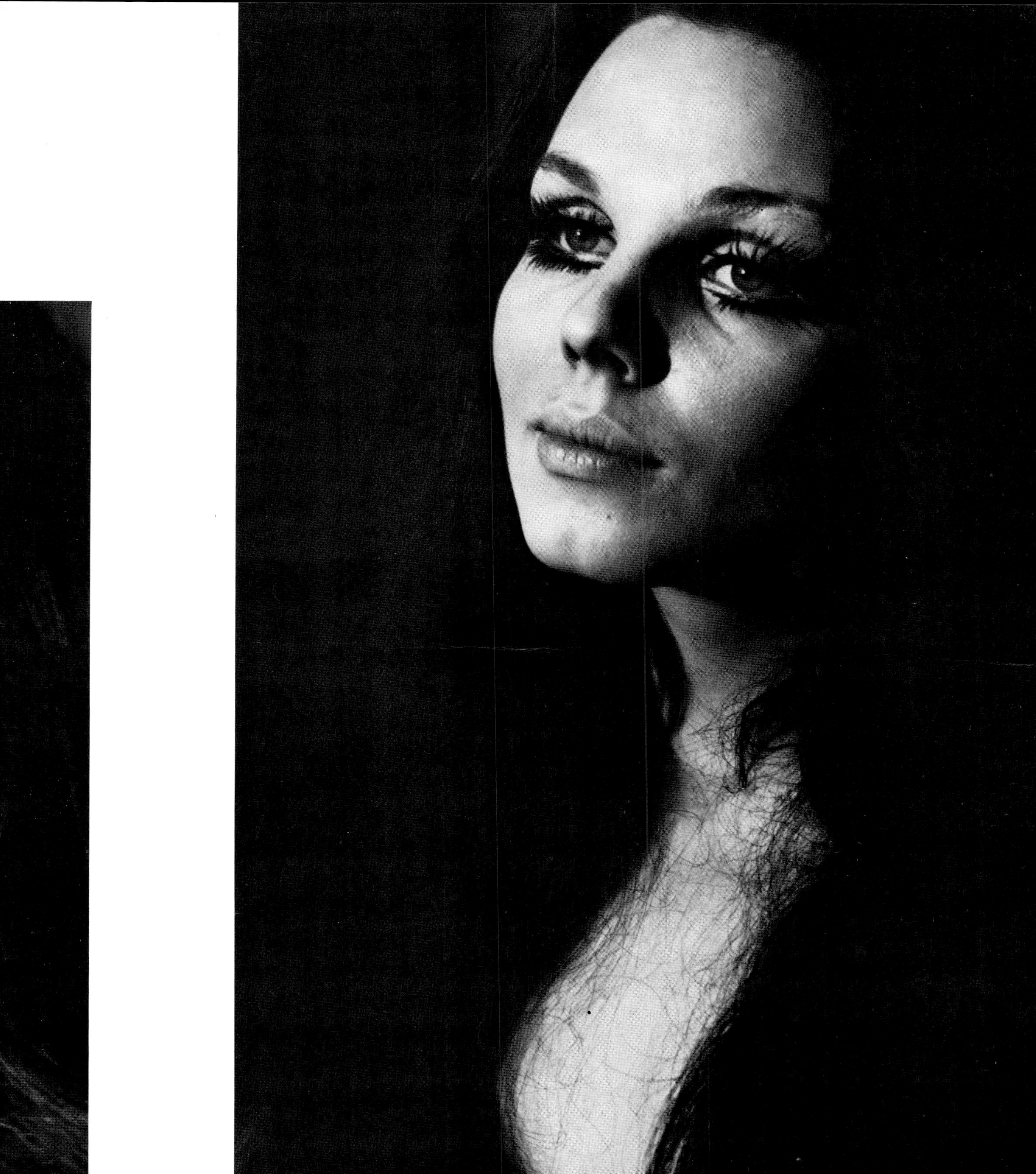

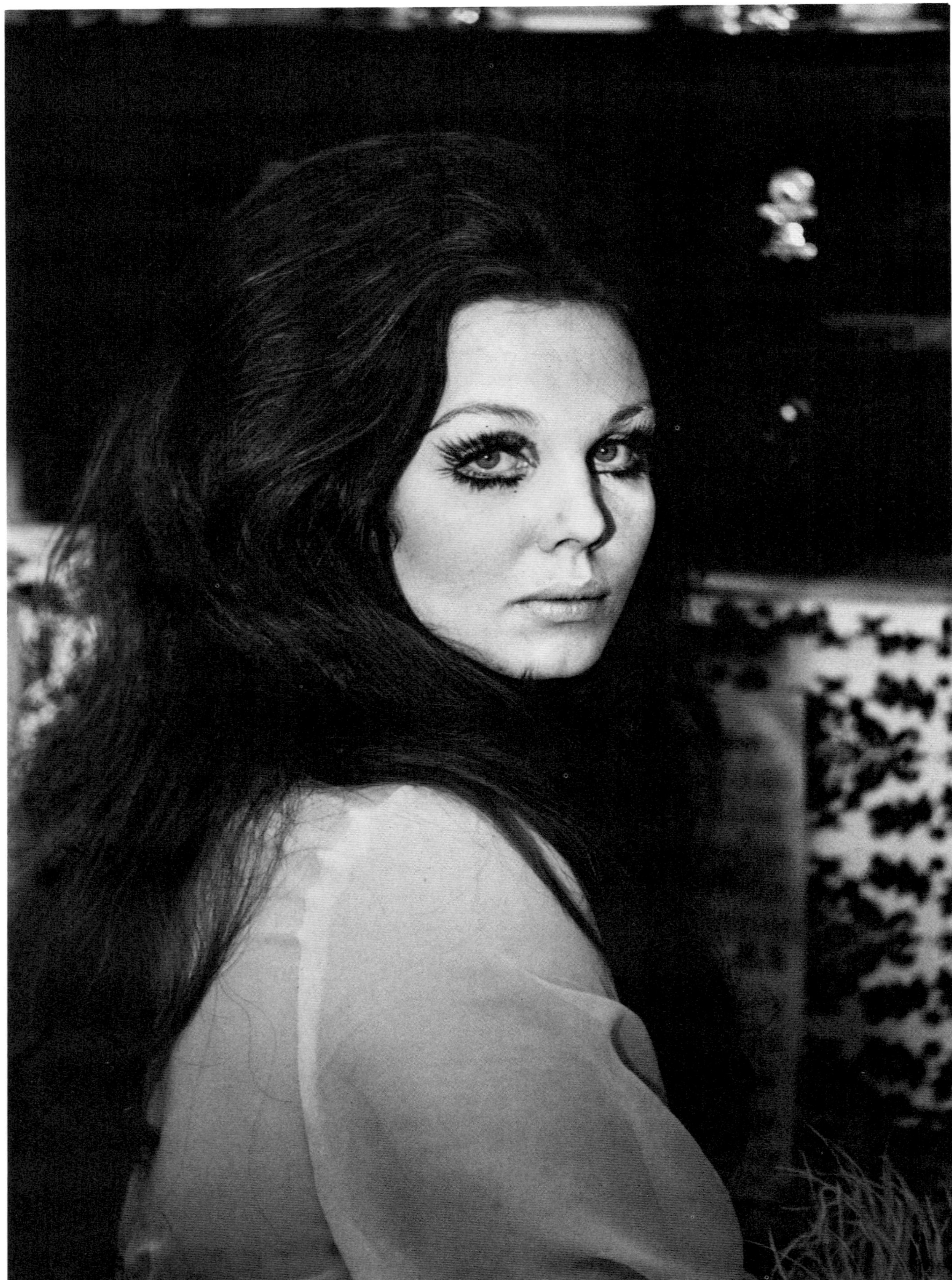

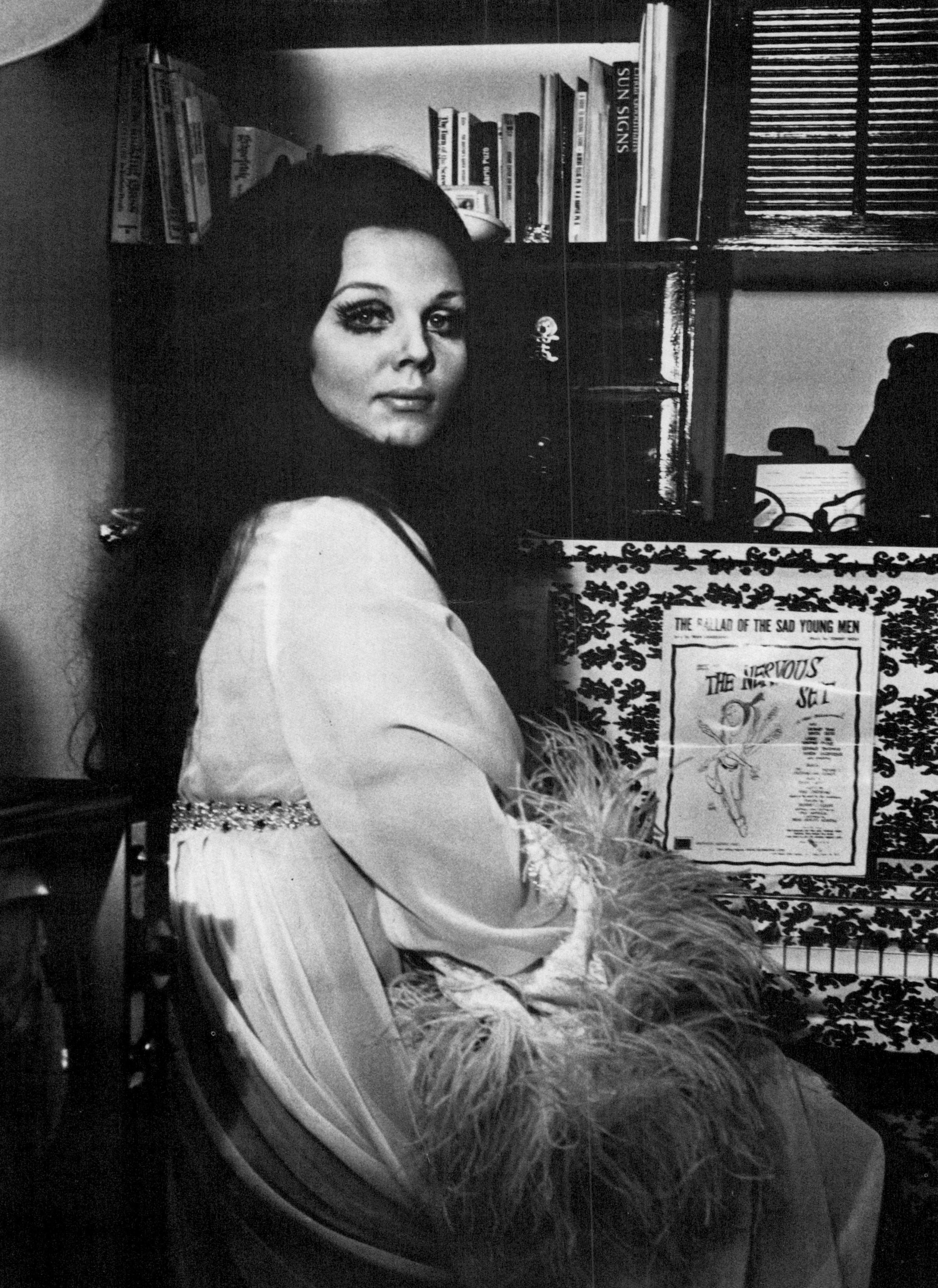

SUN SIGNS
THE BALLAD OF THE SAD YOUNG MEN
THE NERVOUS SET

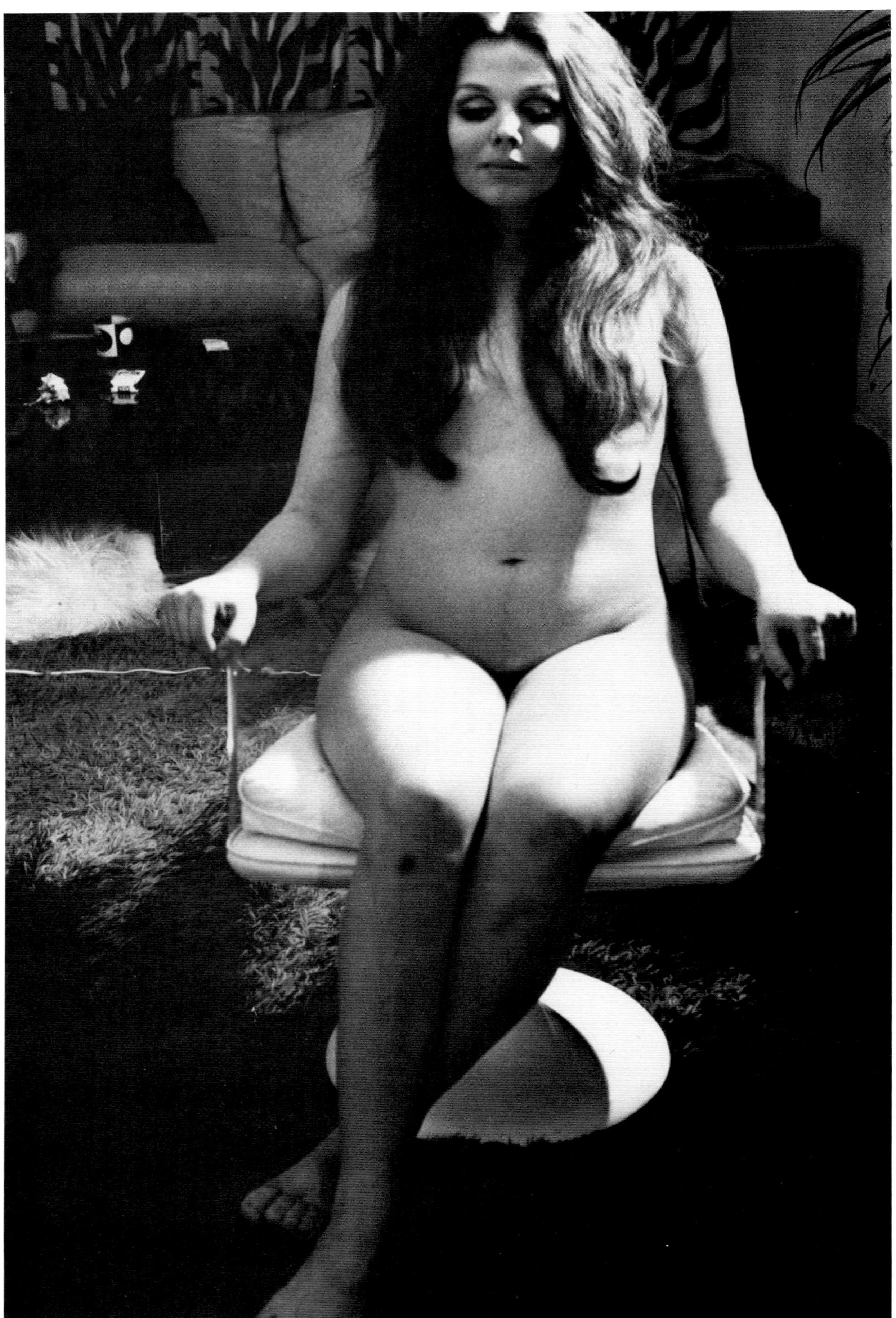

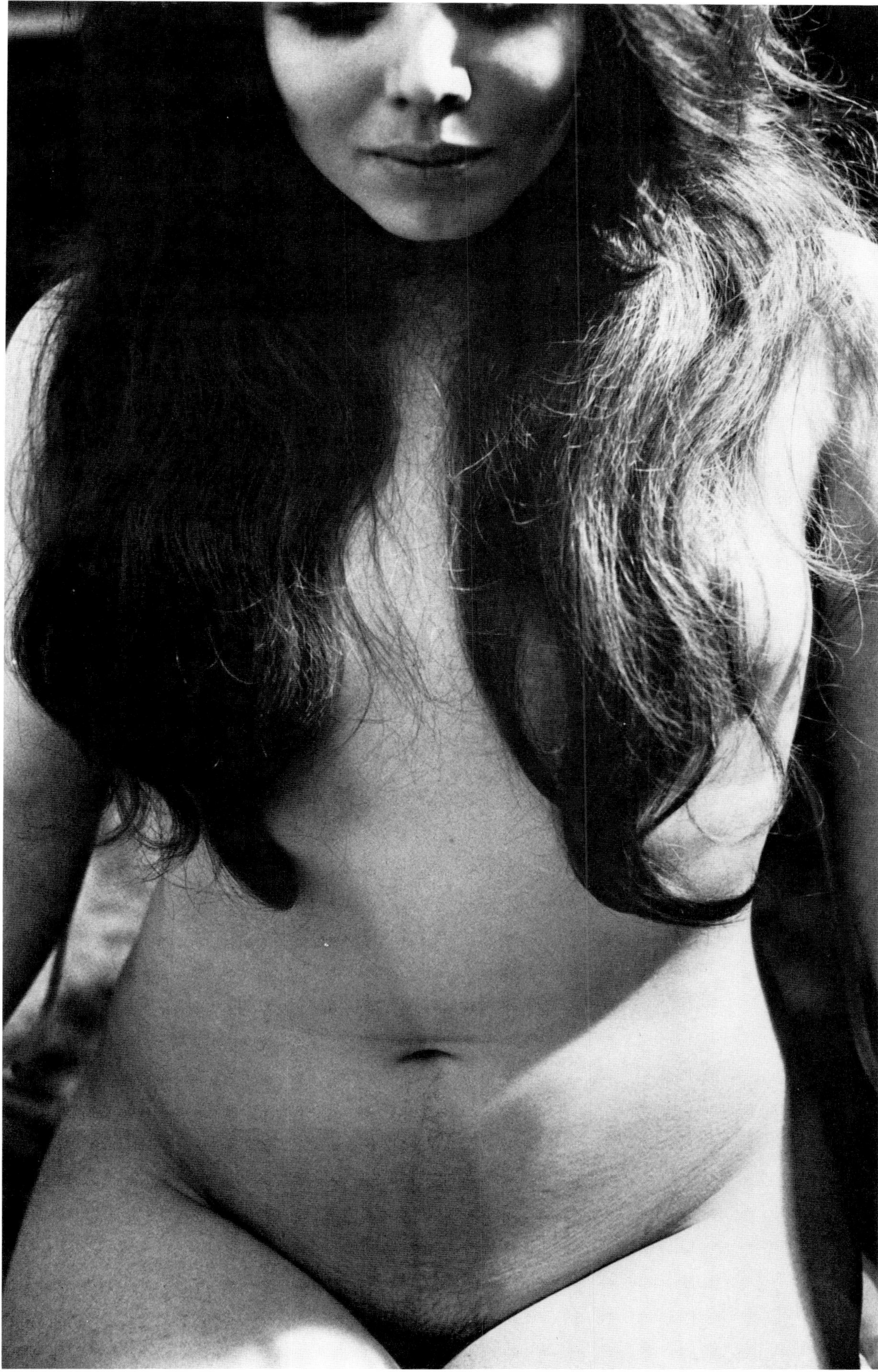

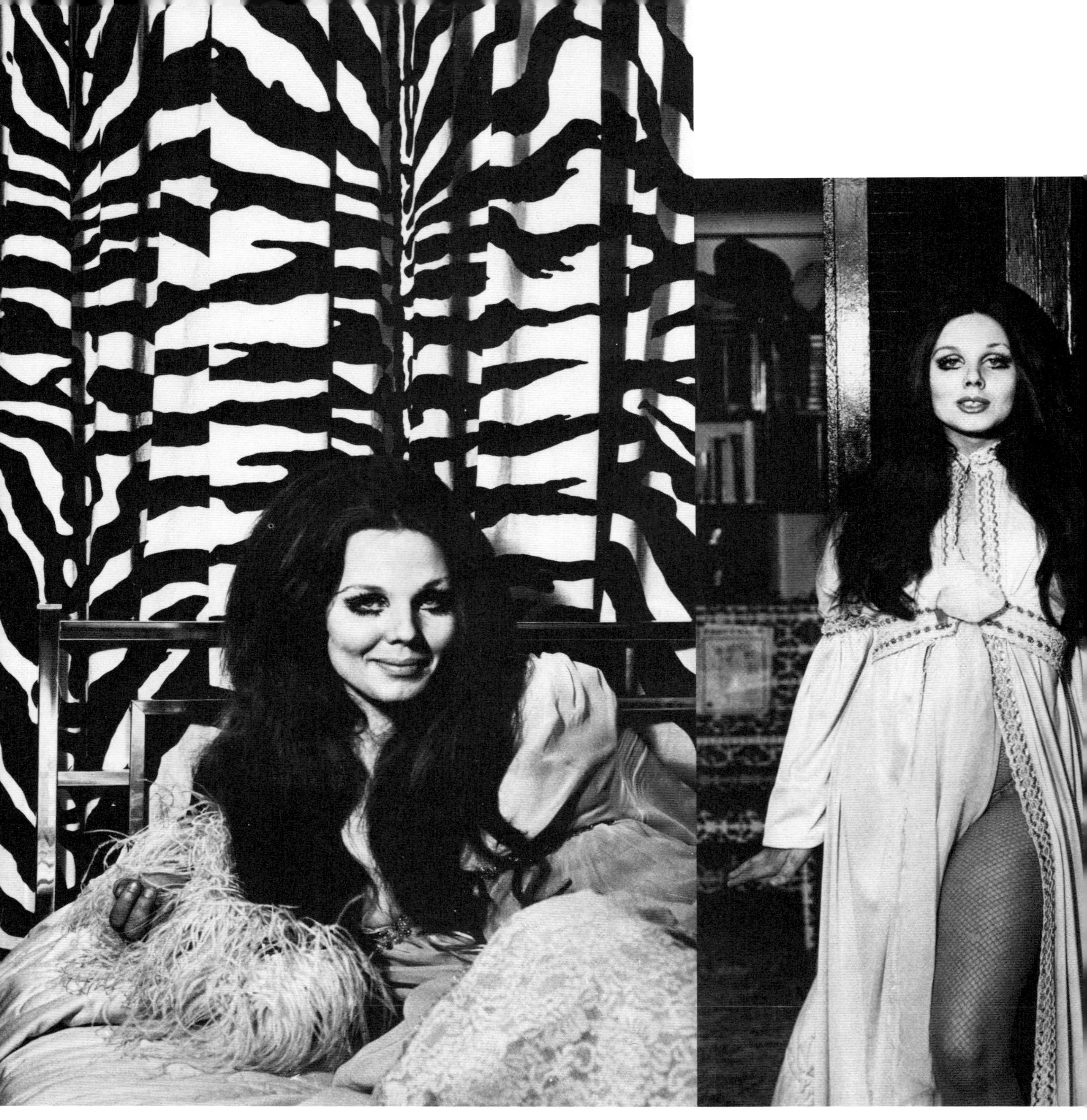

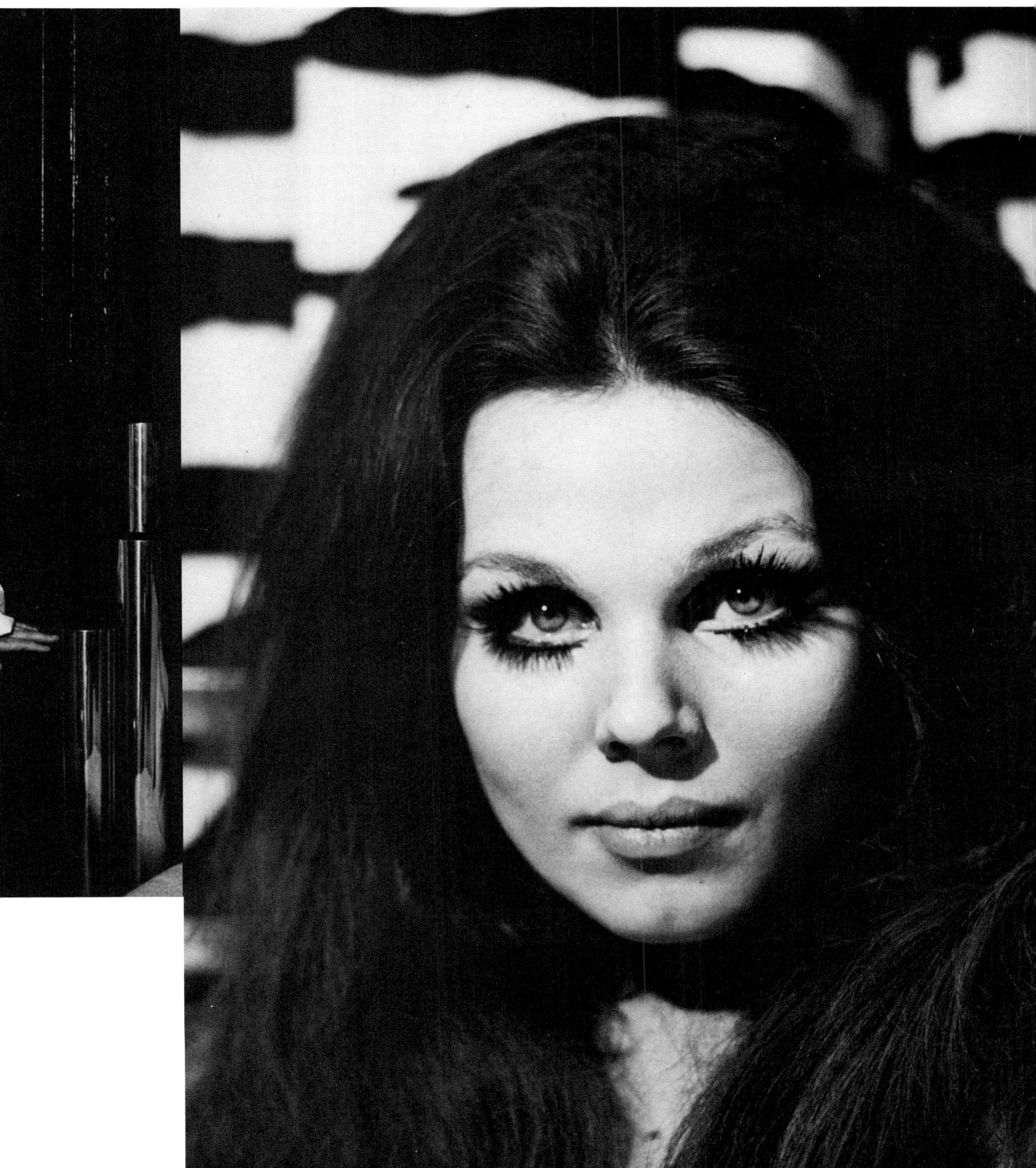

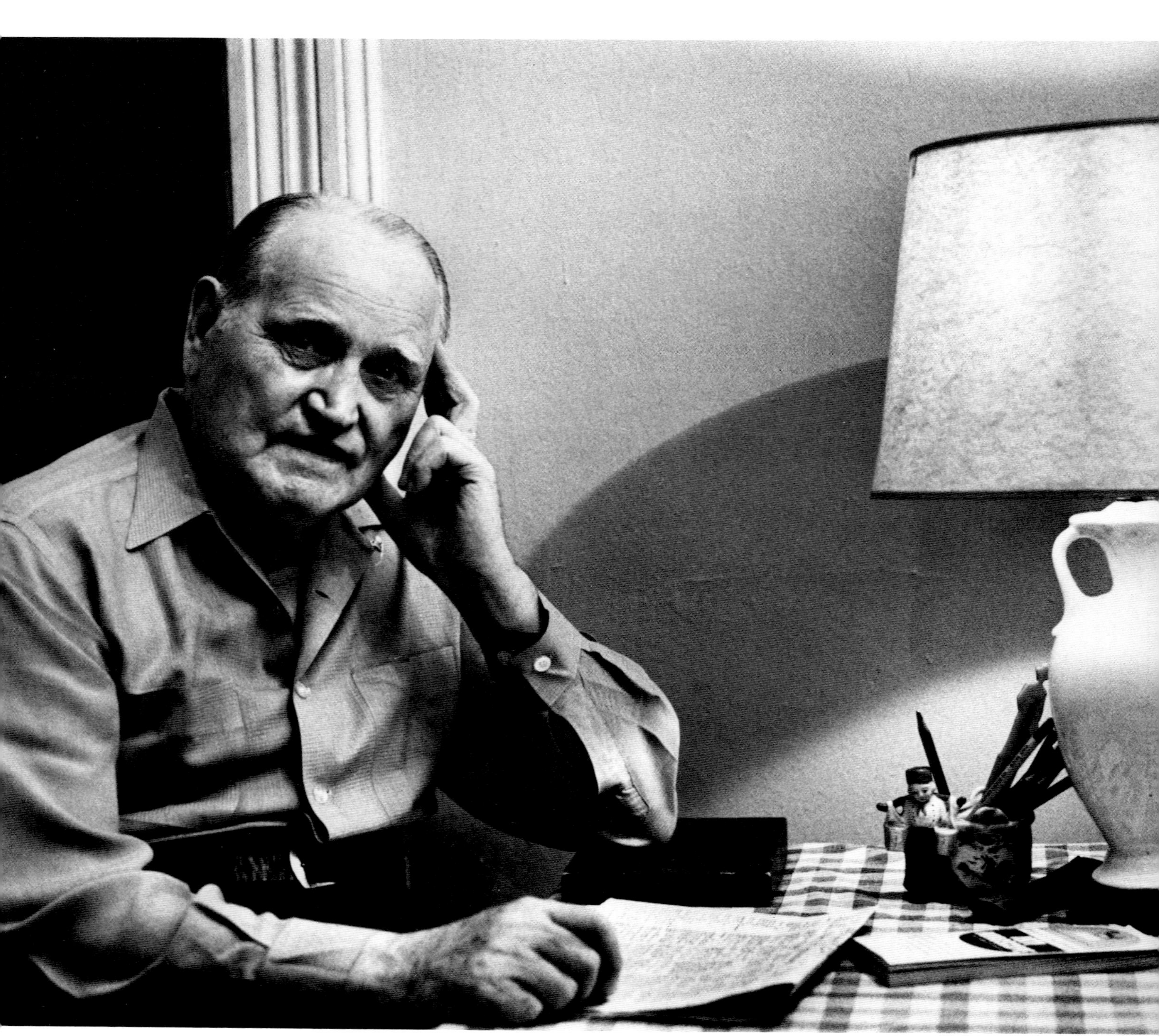

This is Jack

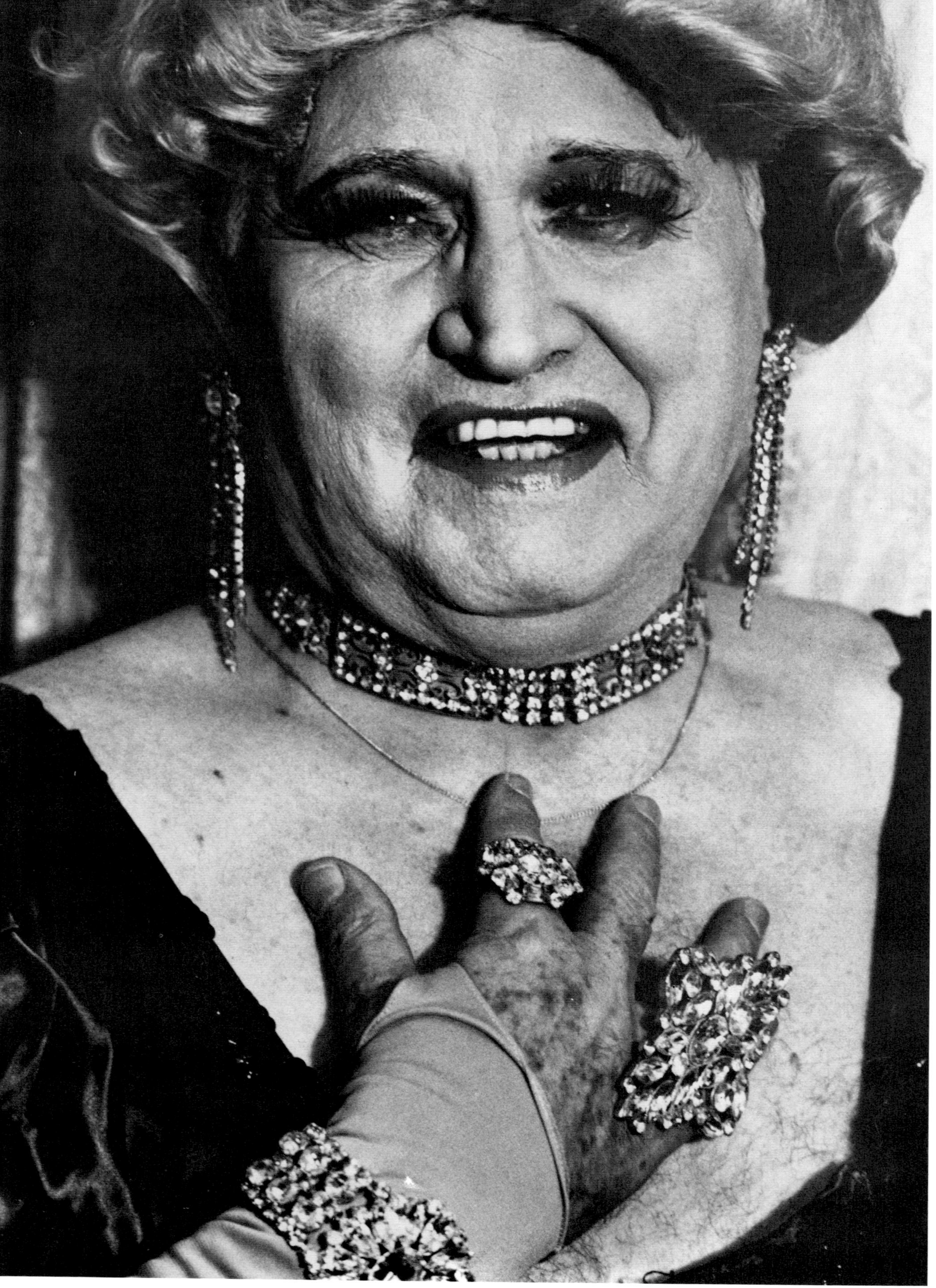

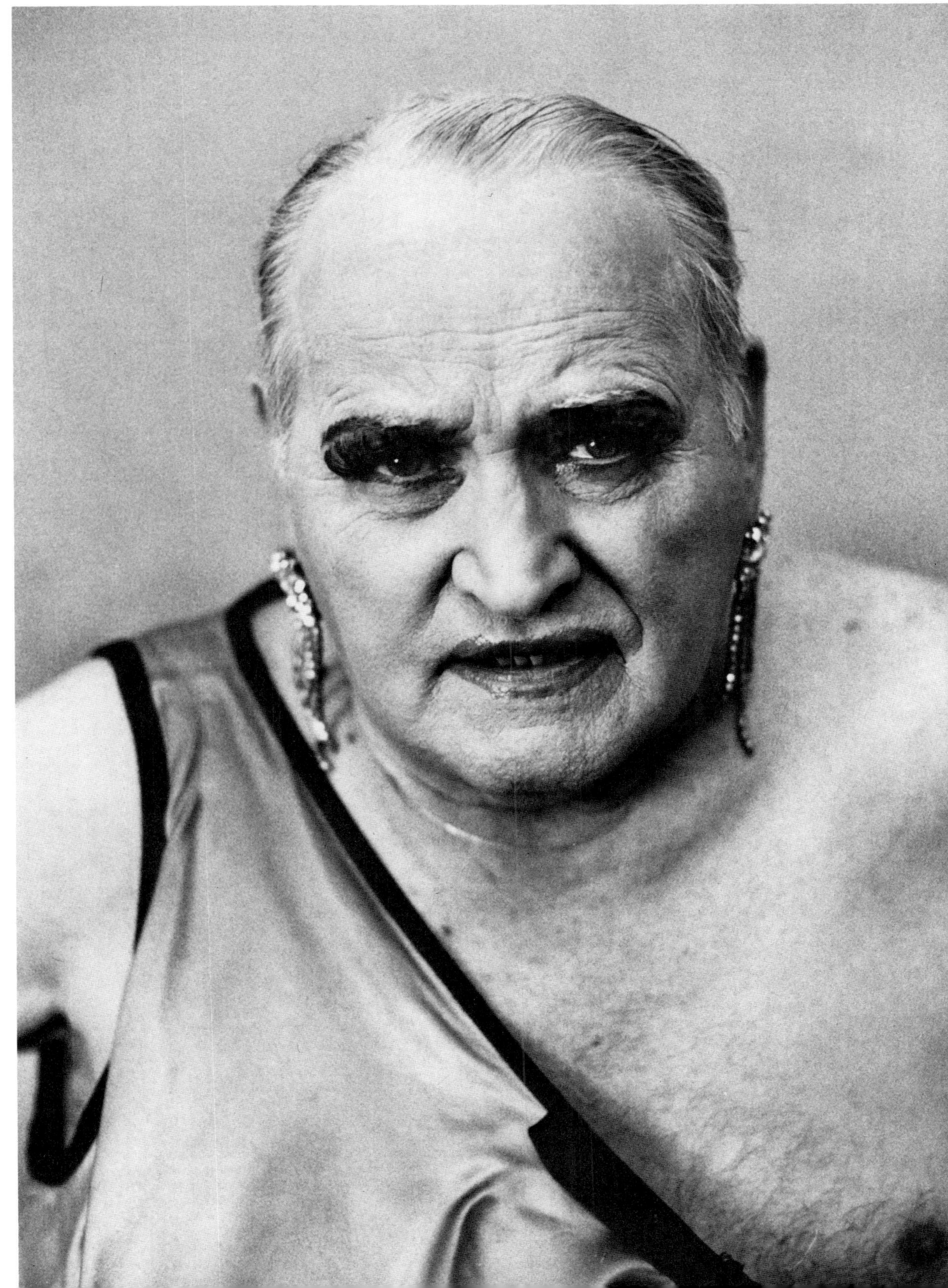

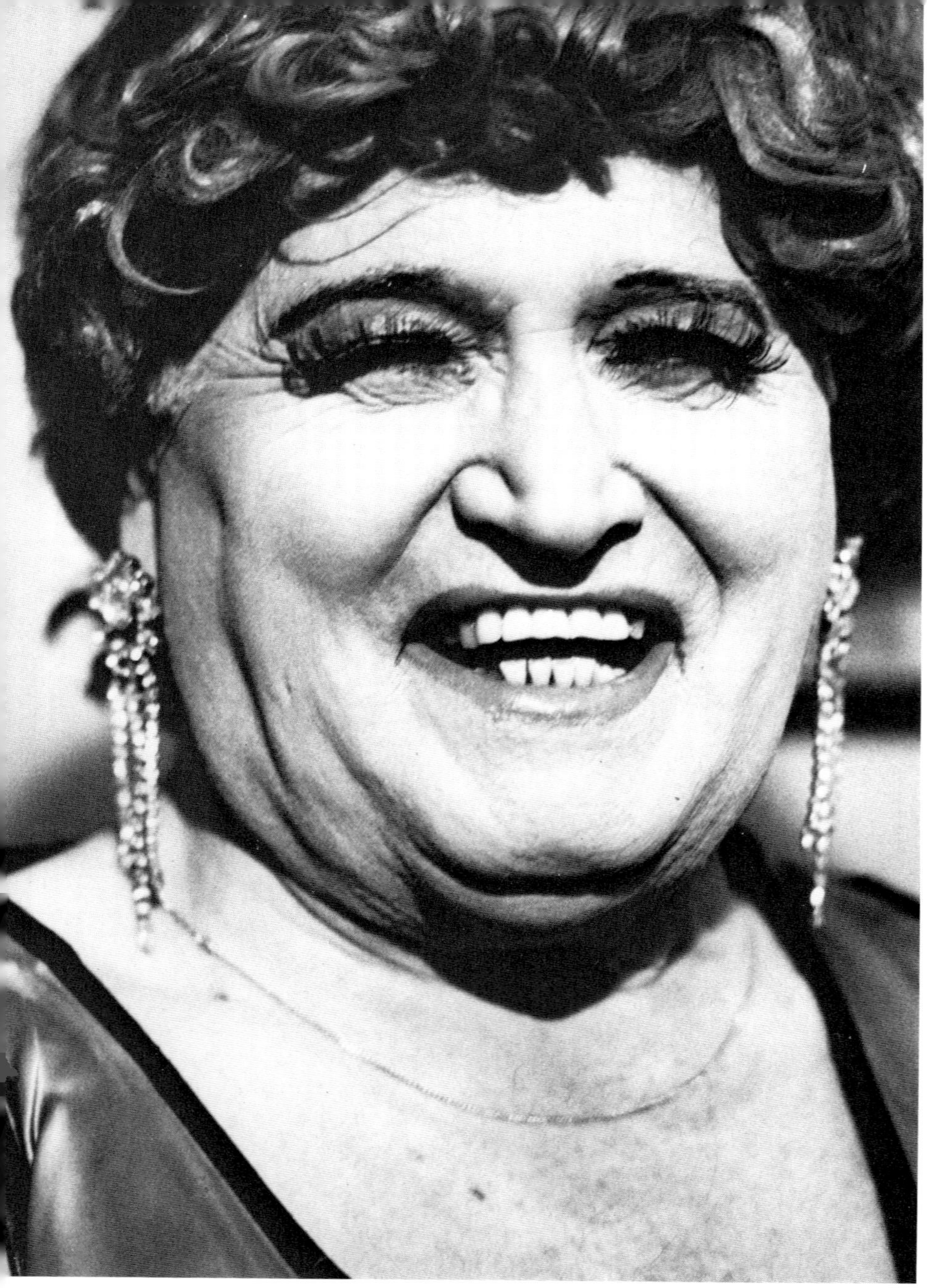

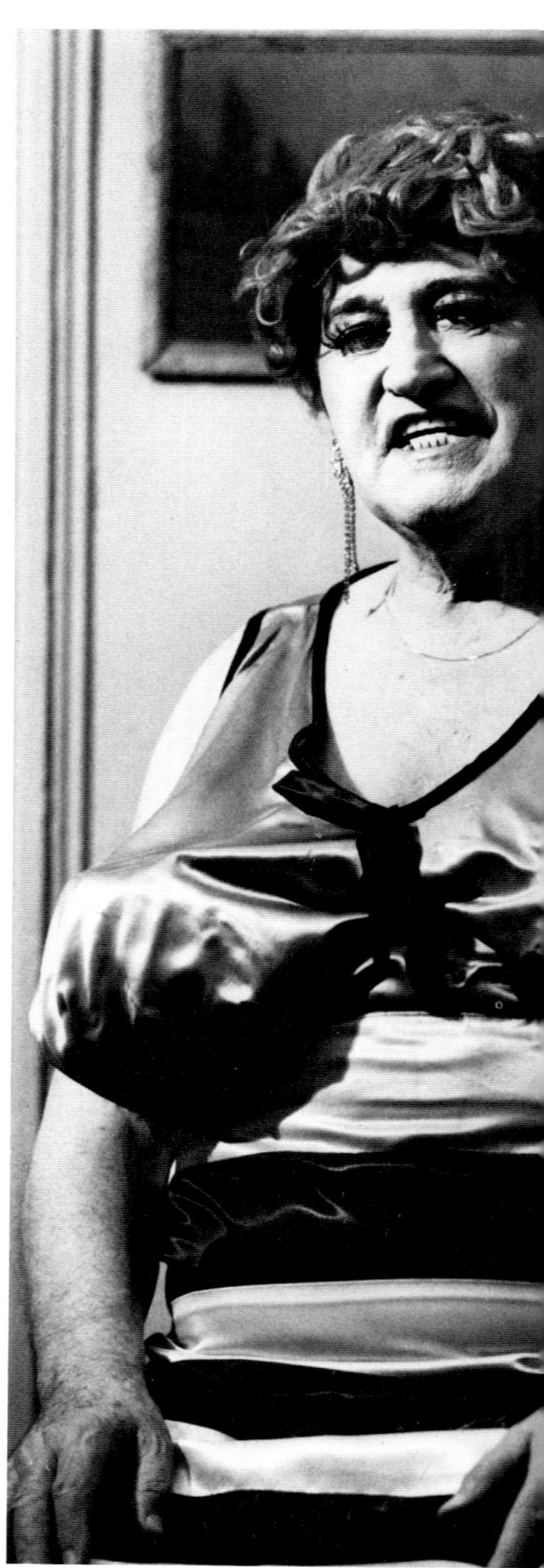

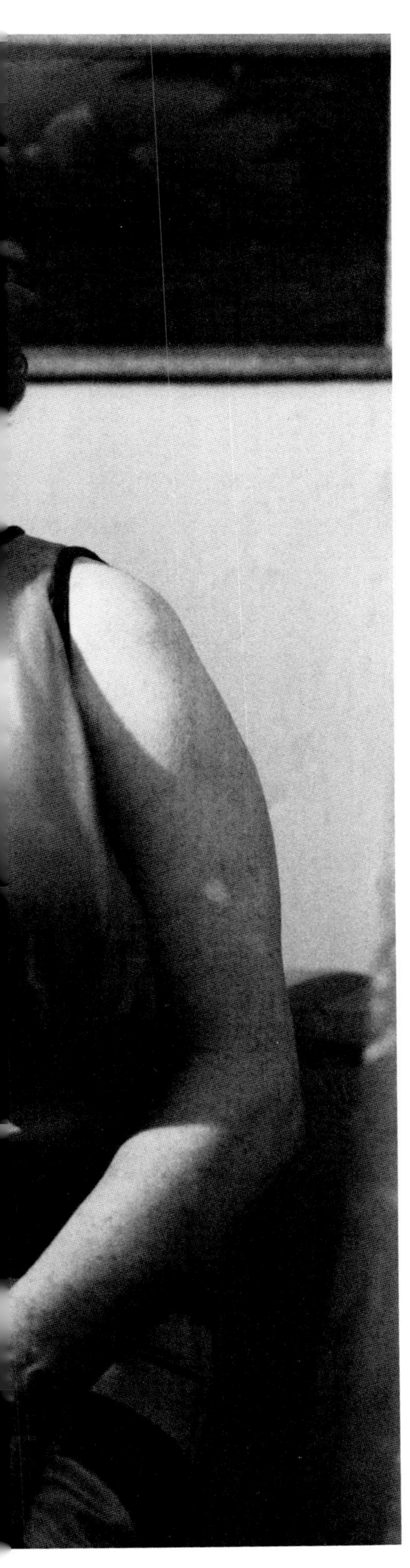

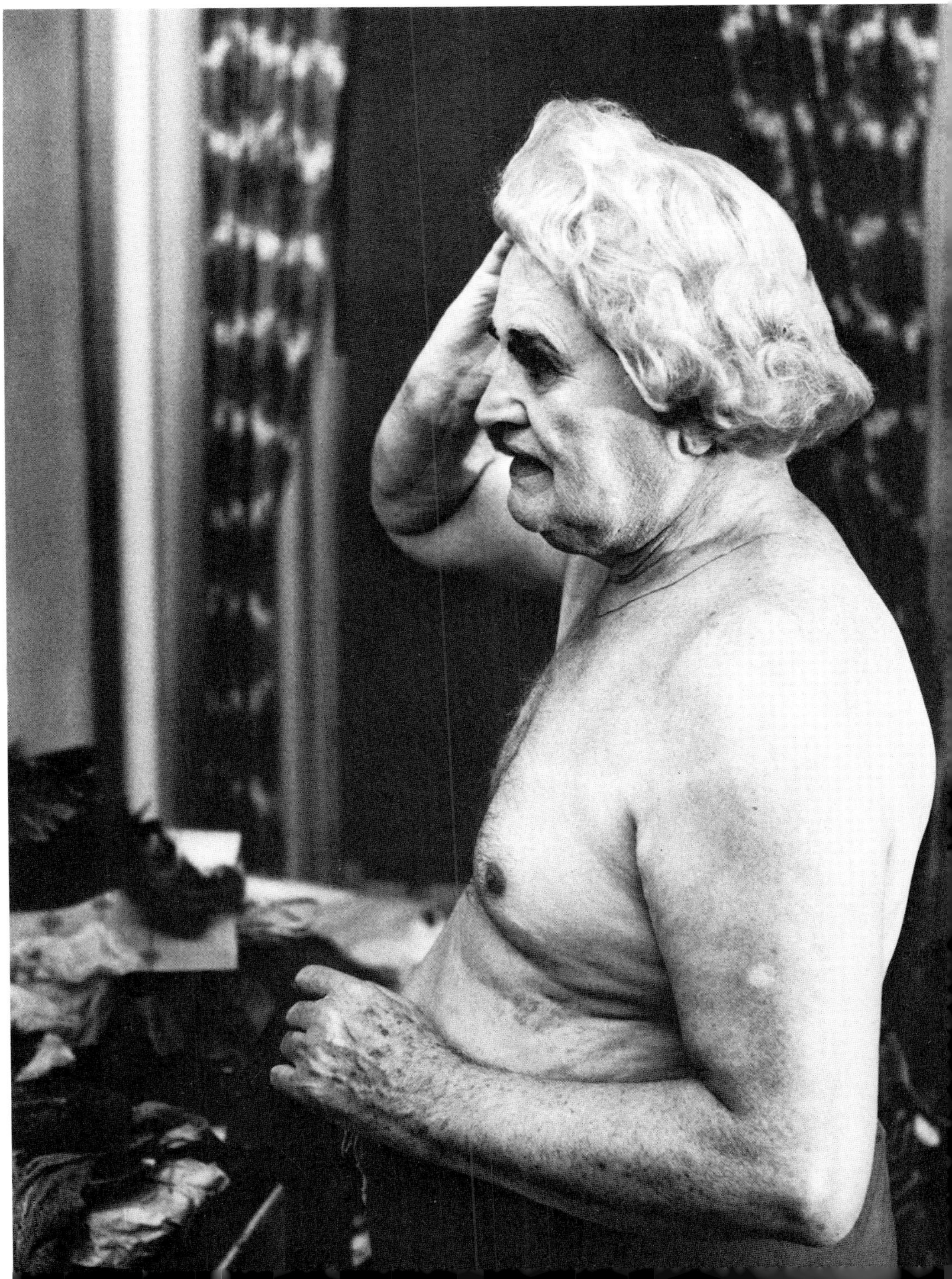

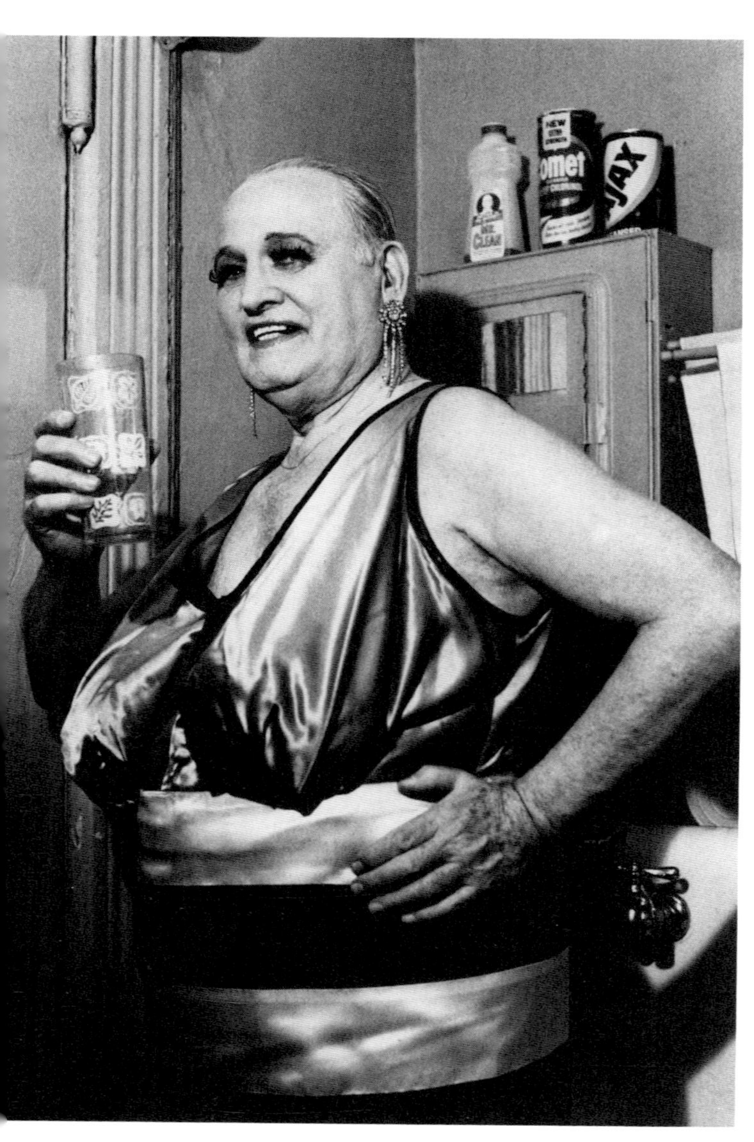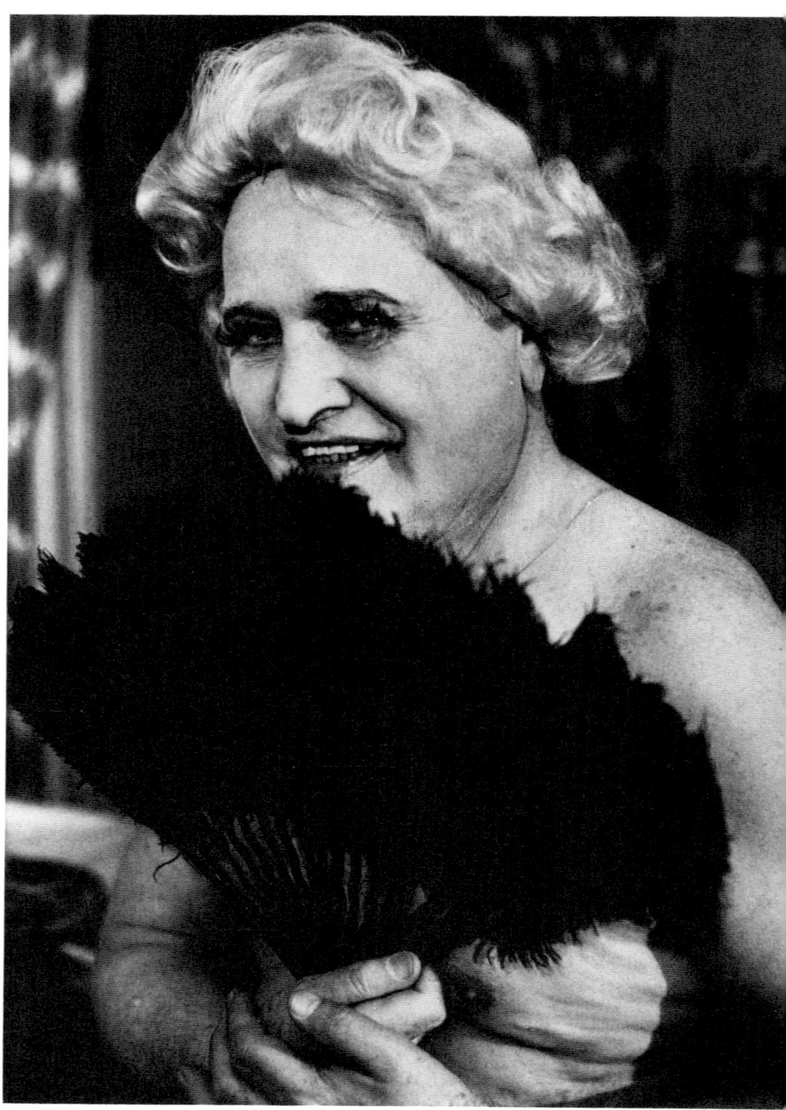

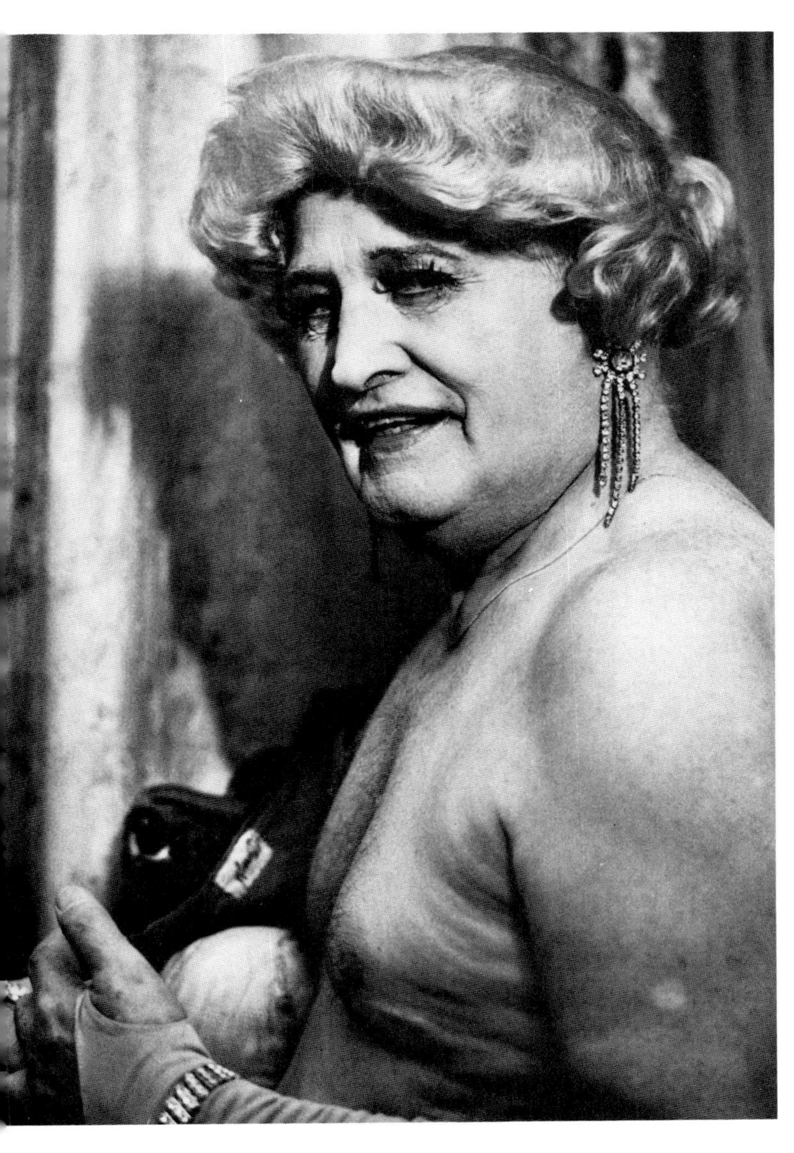
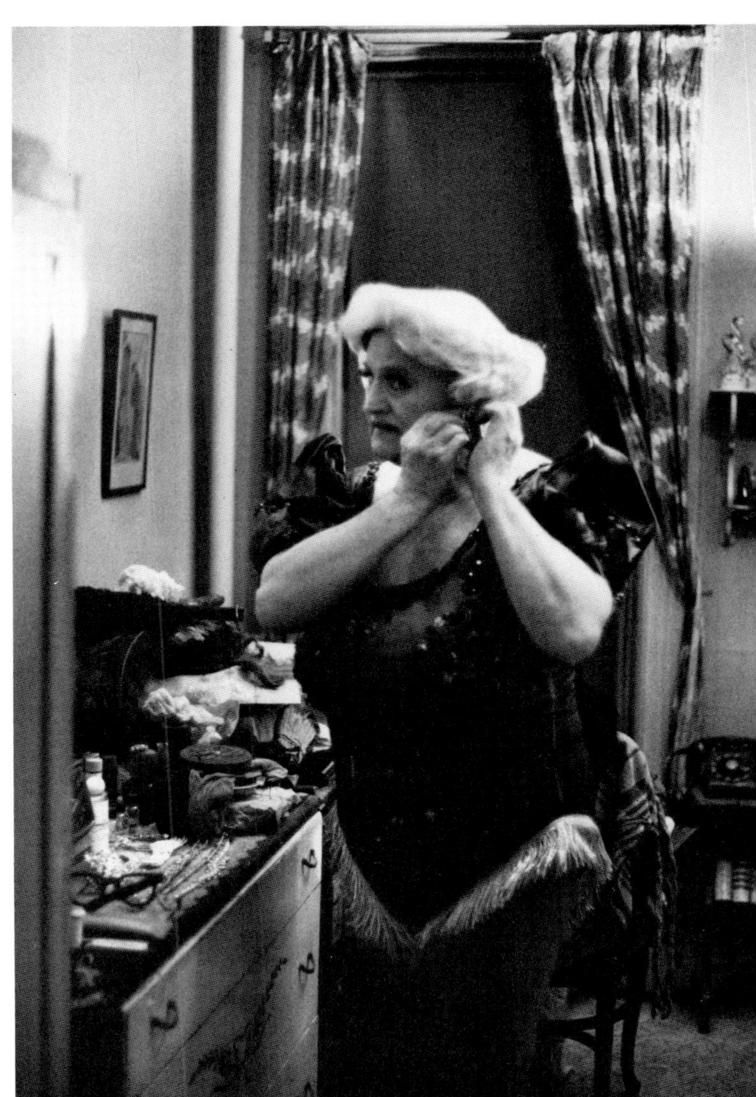

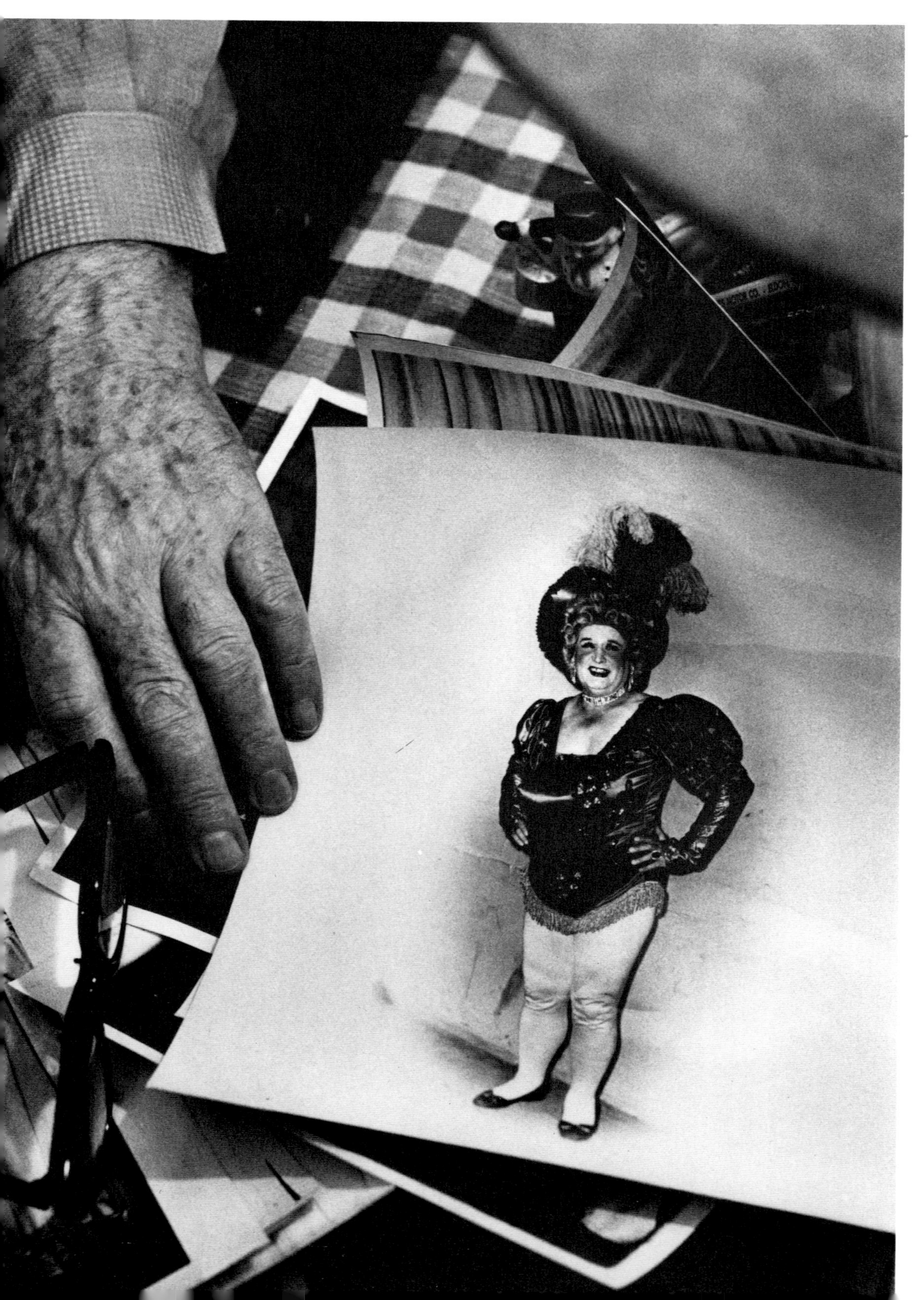

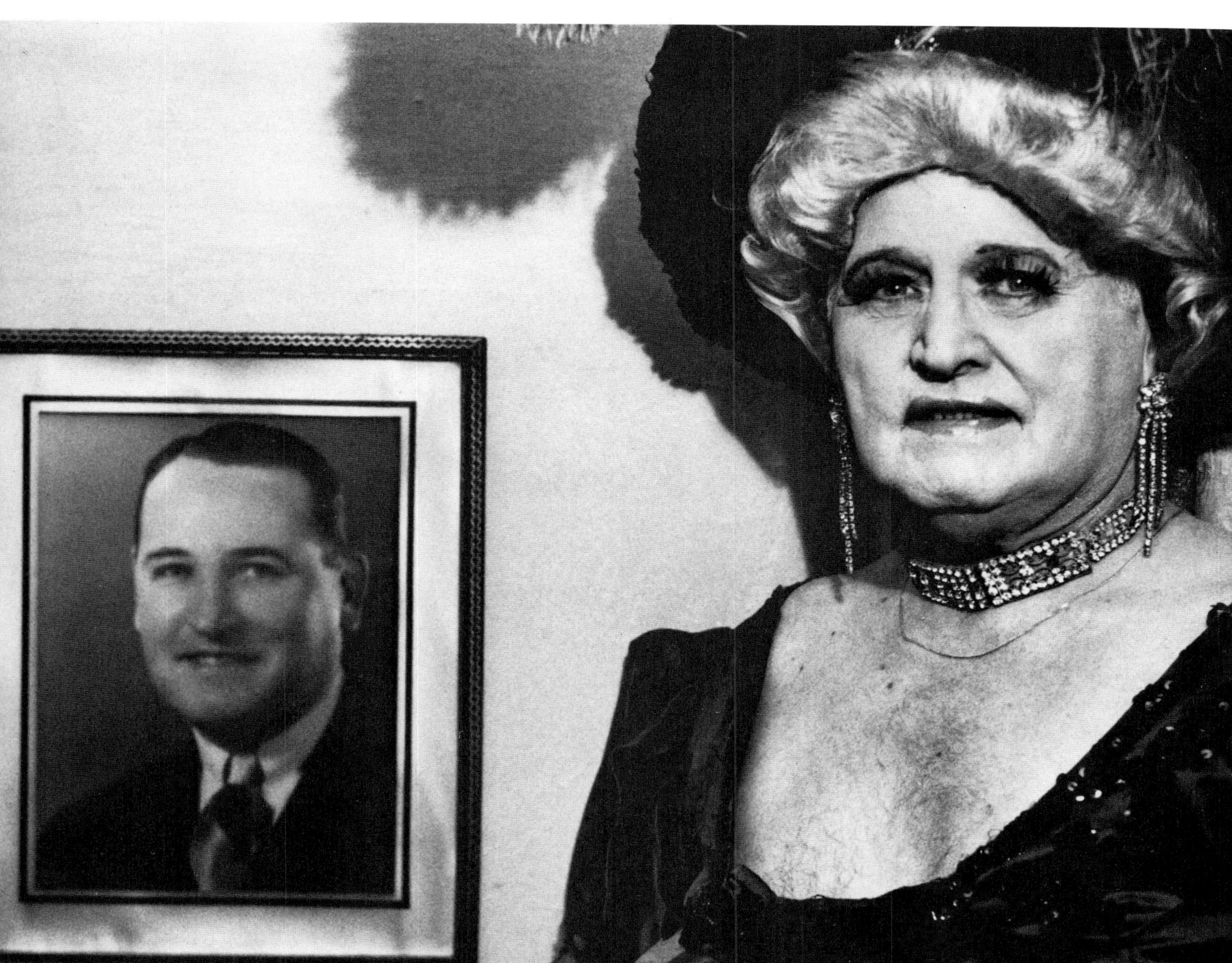

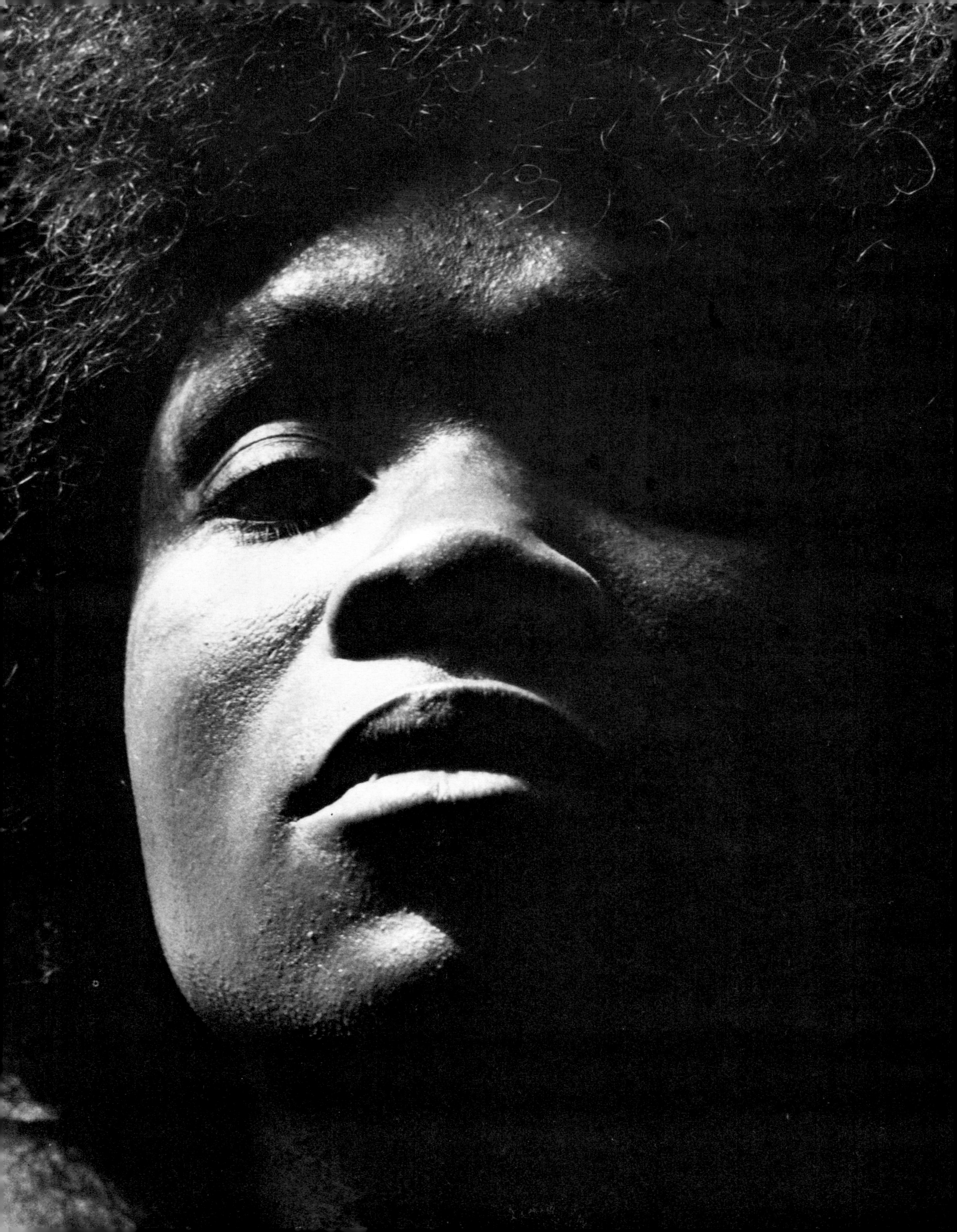

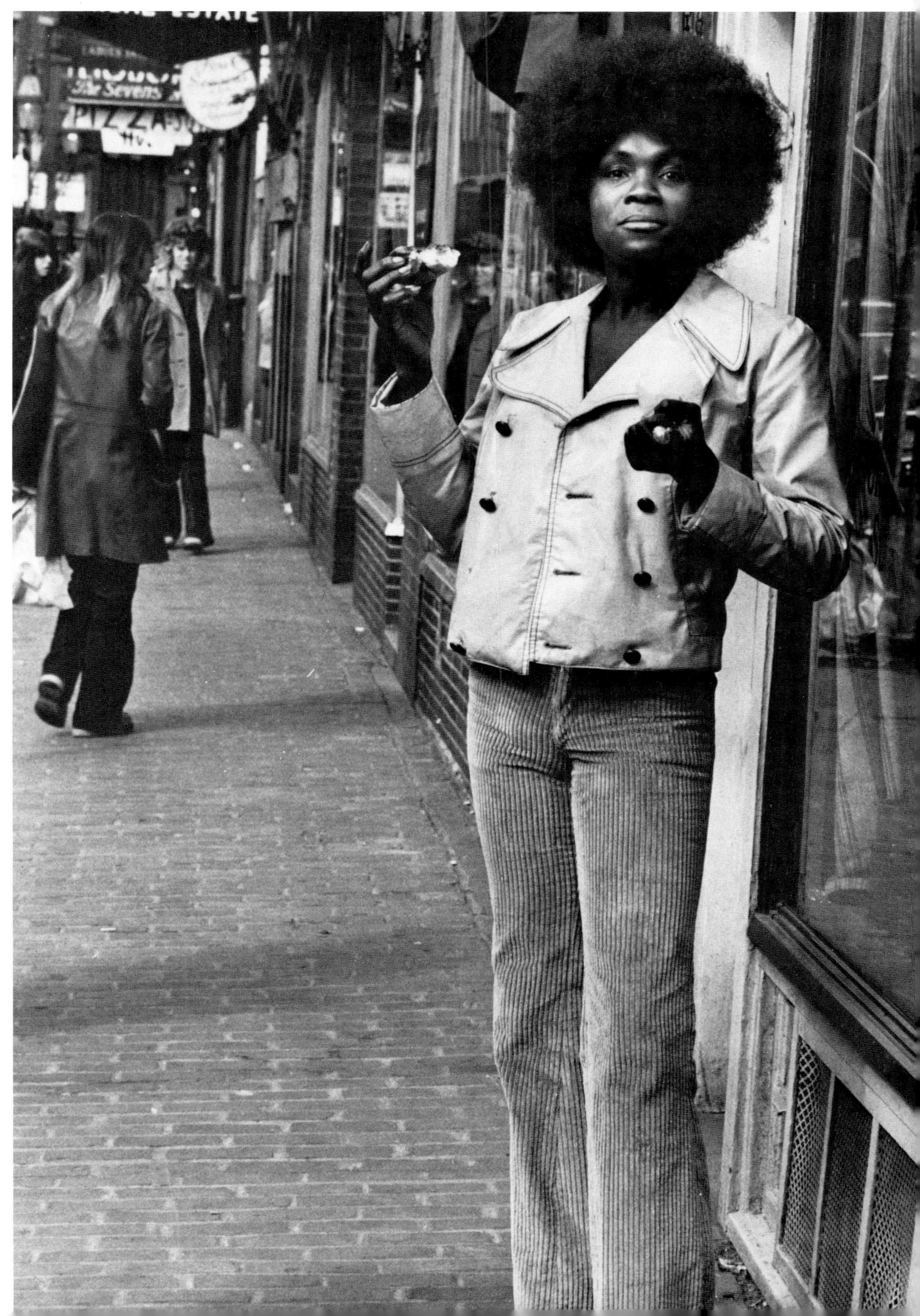

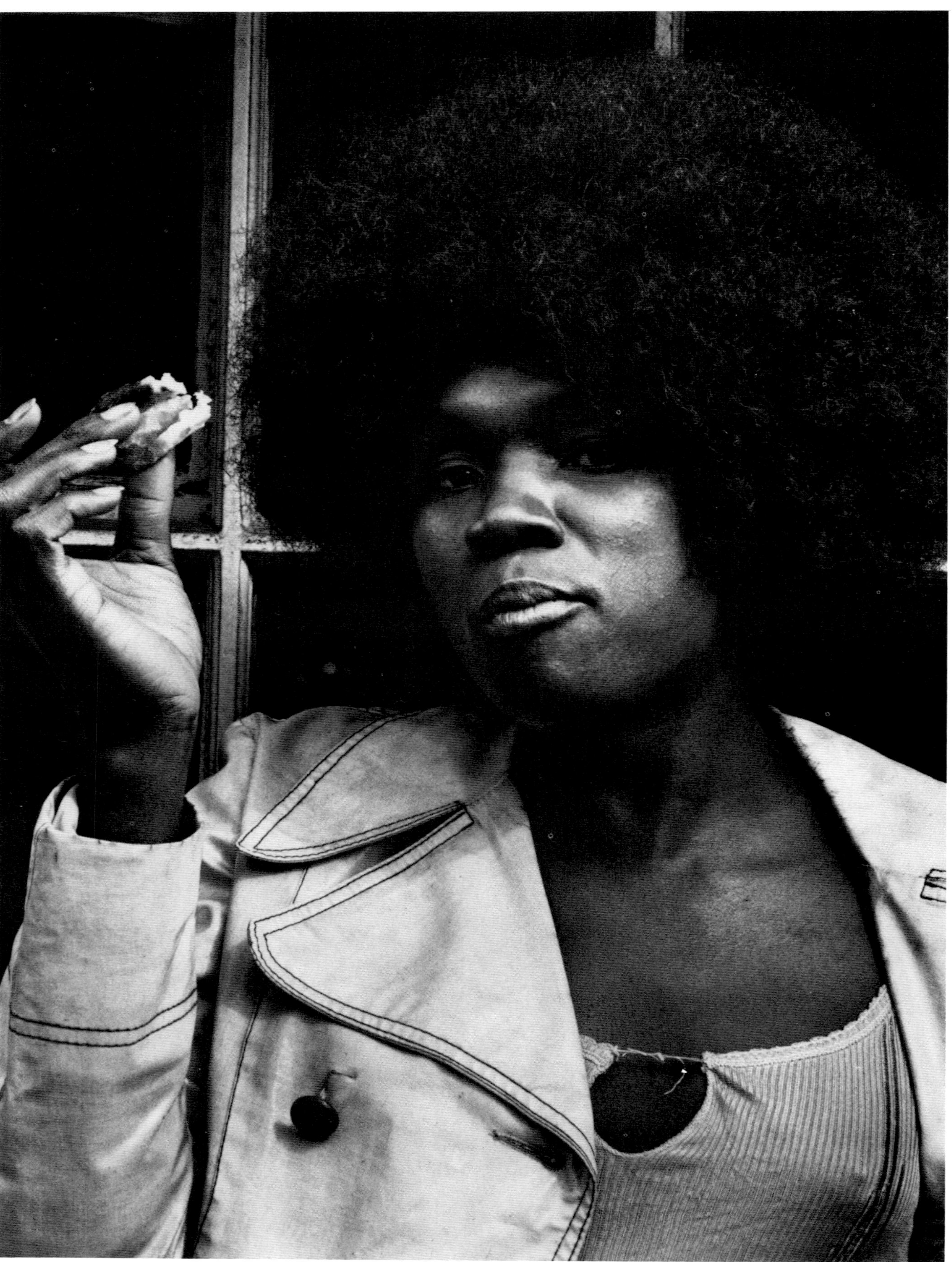

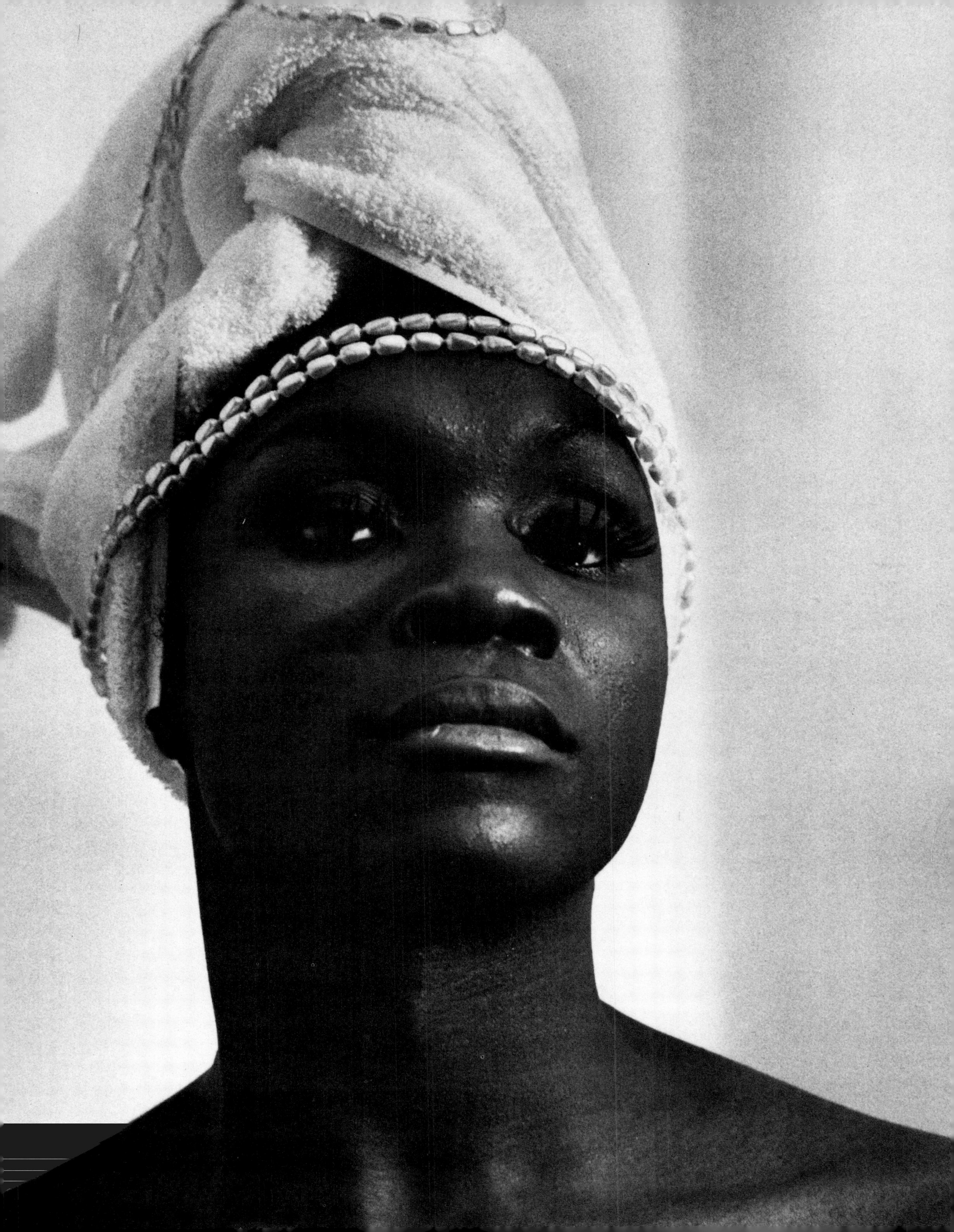

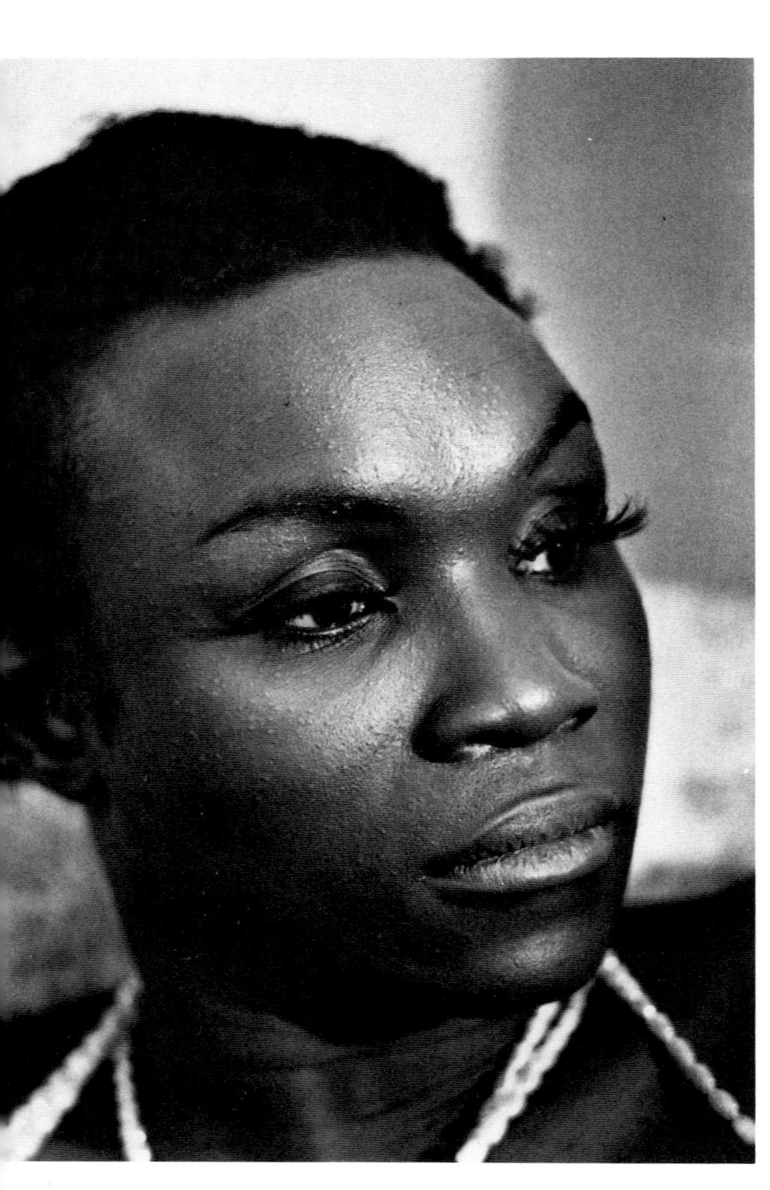

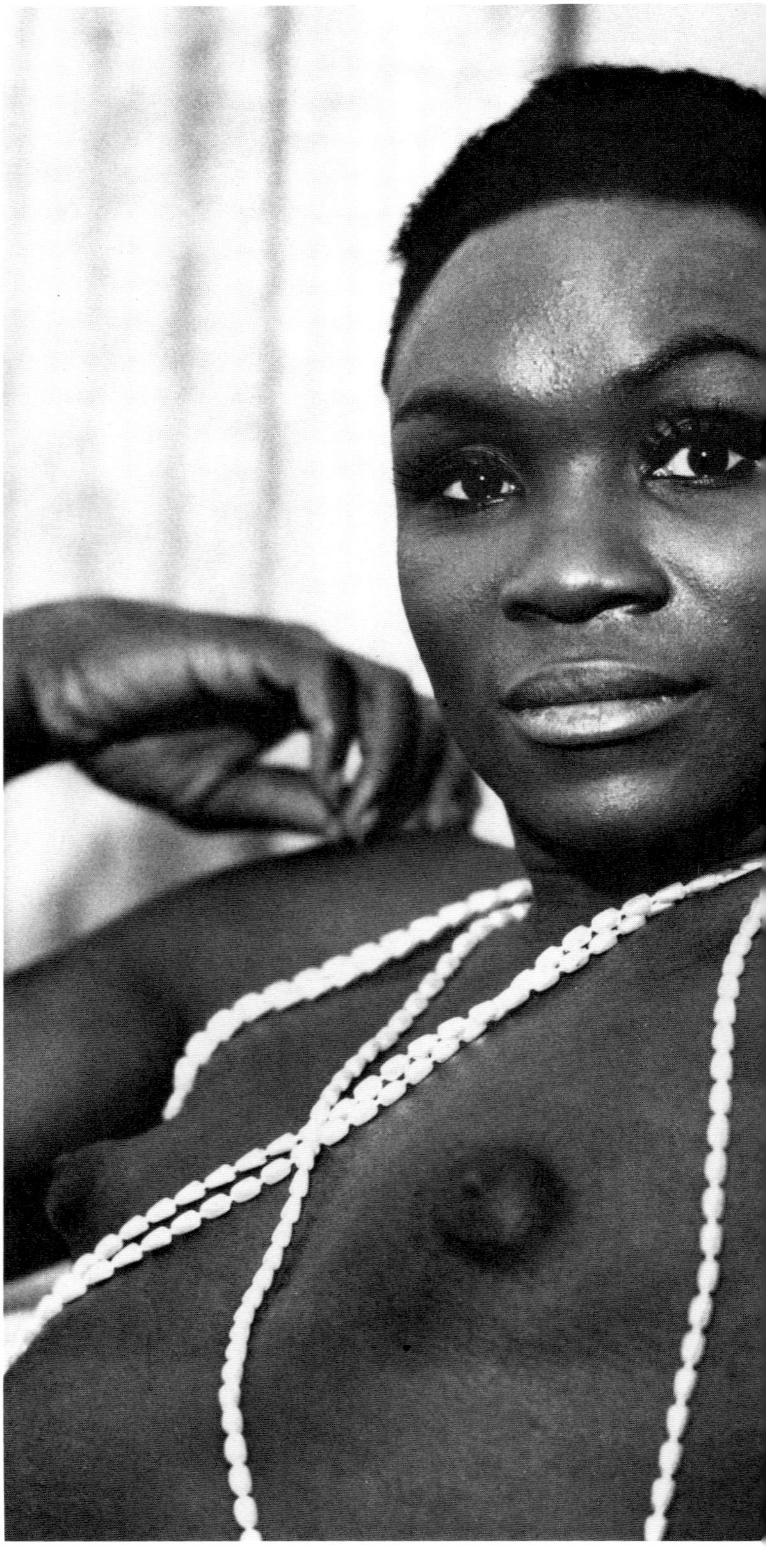

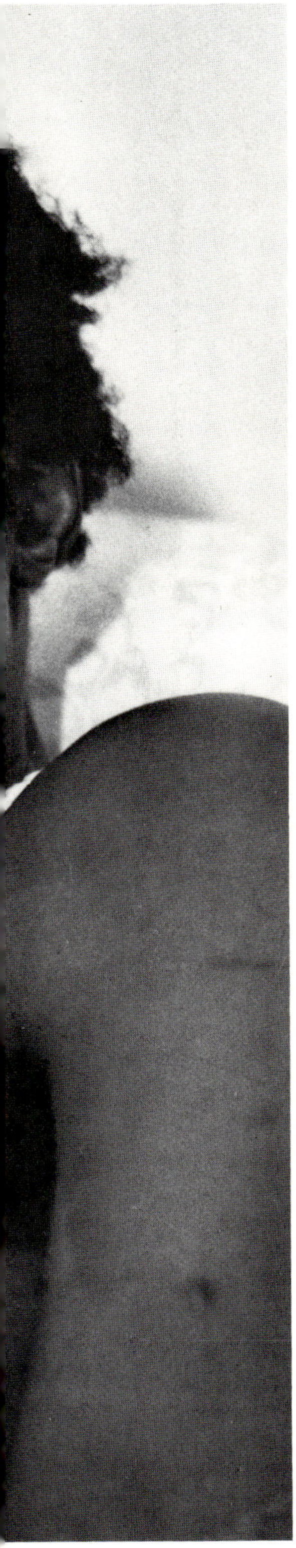

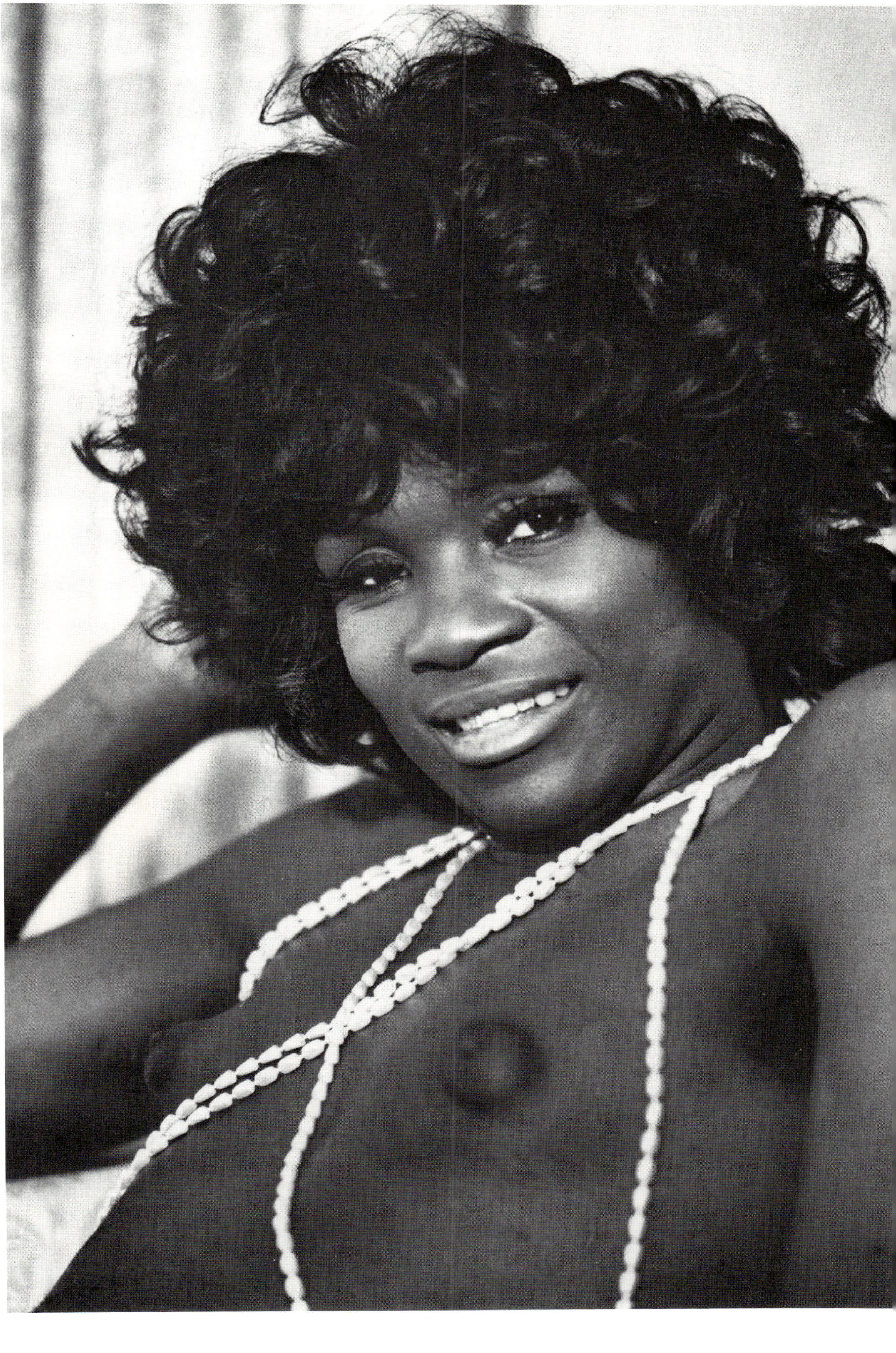

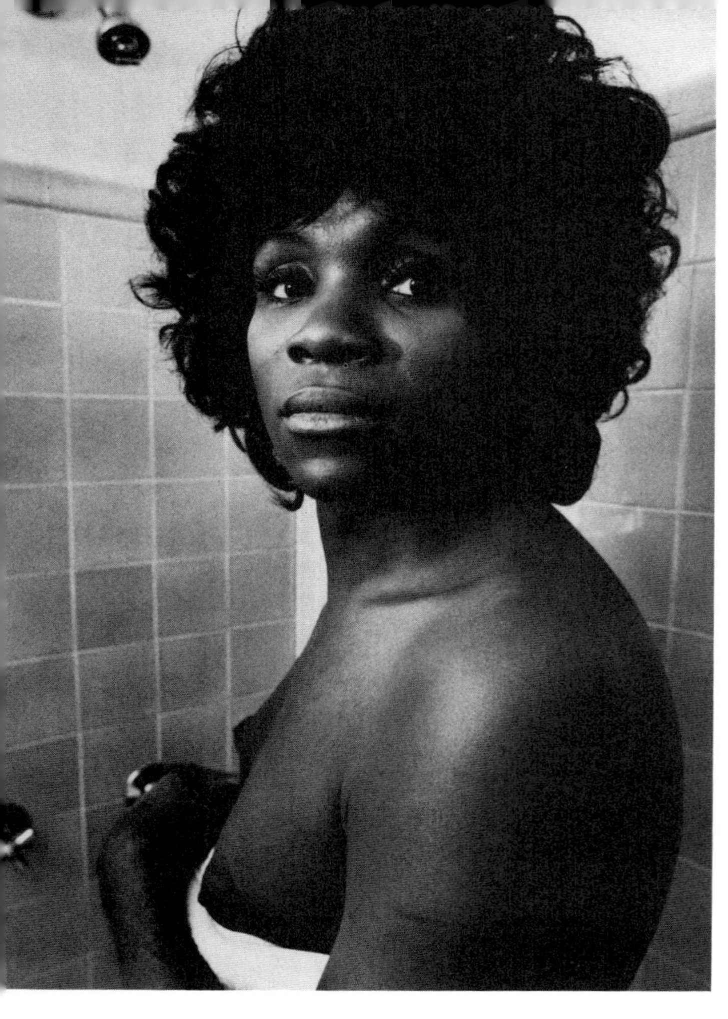
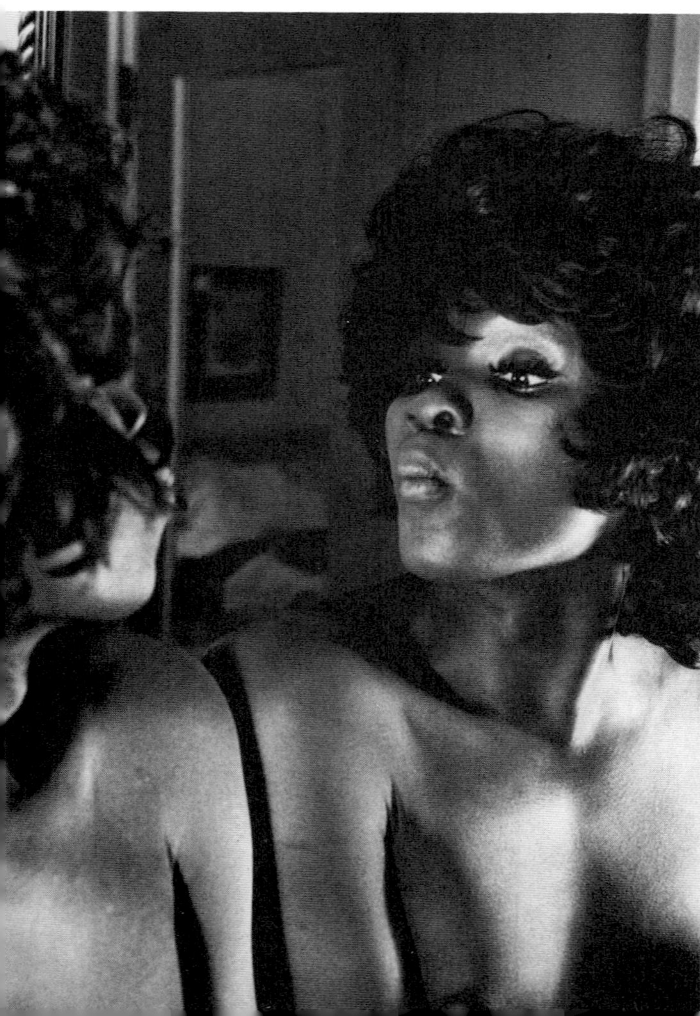

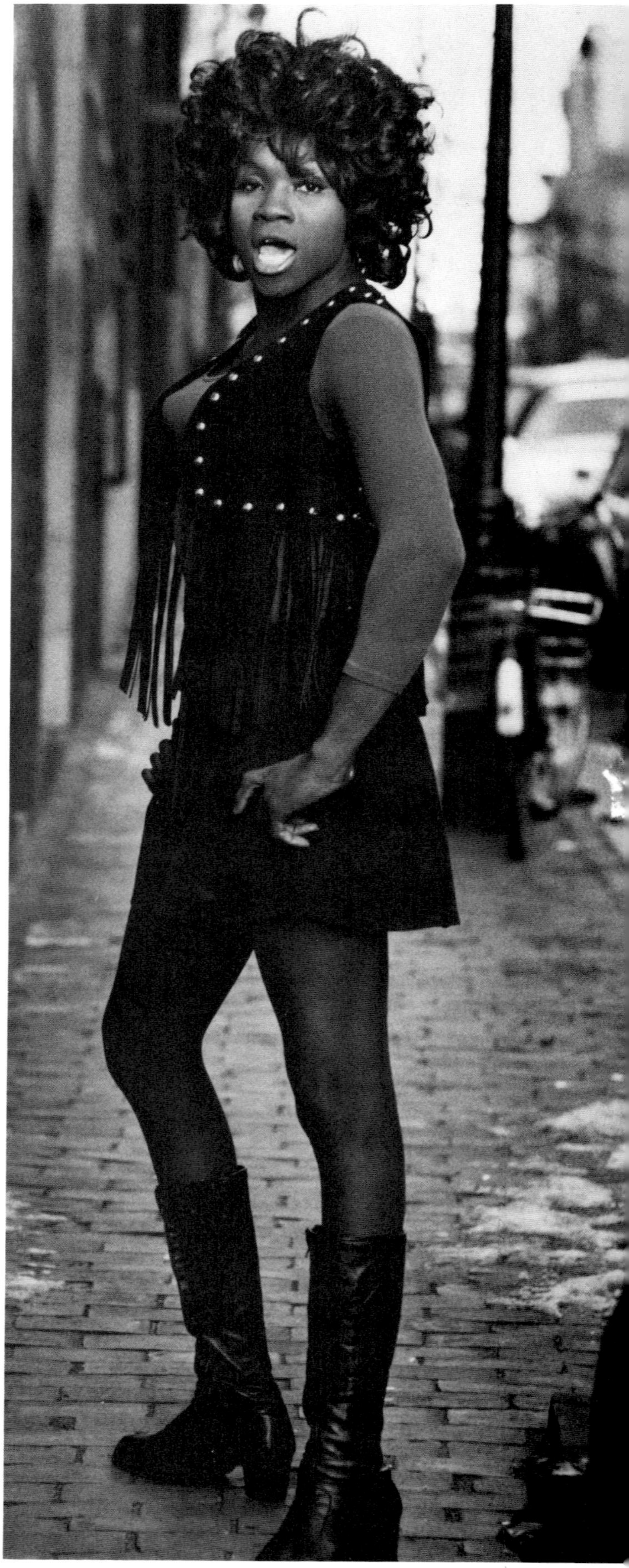

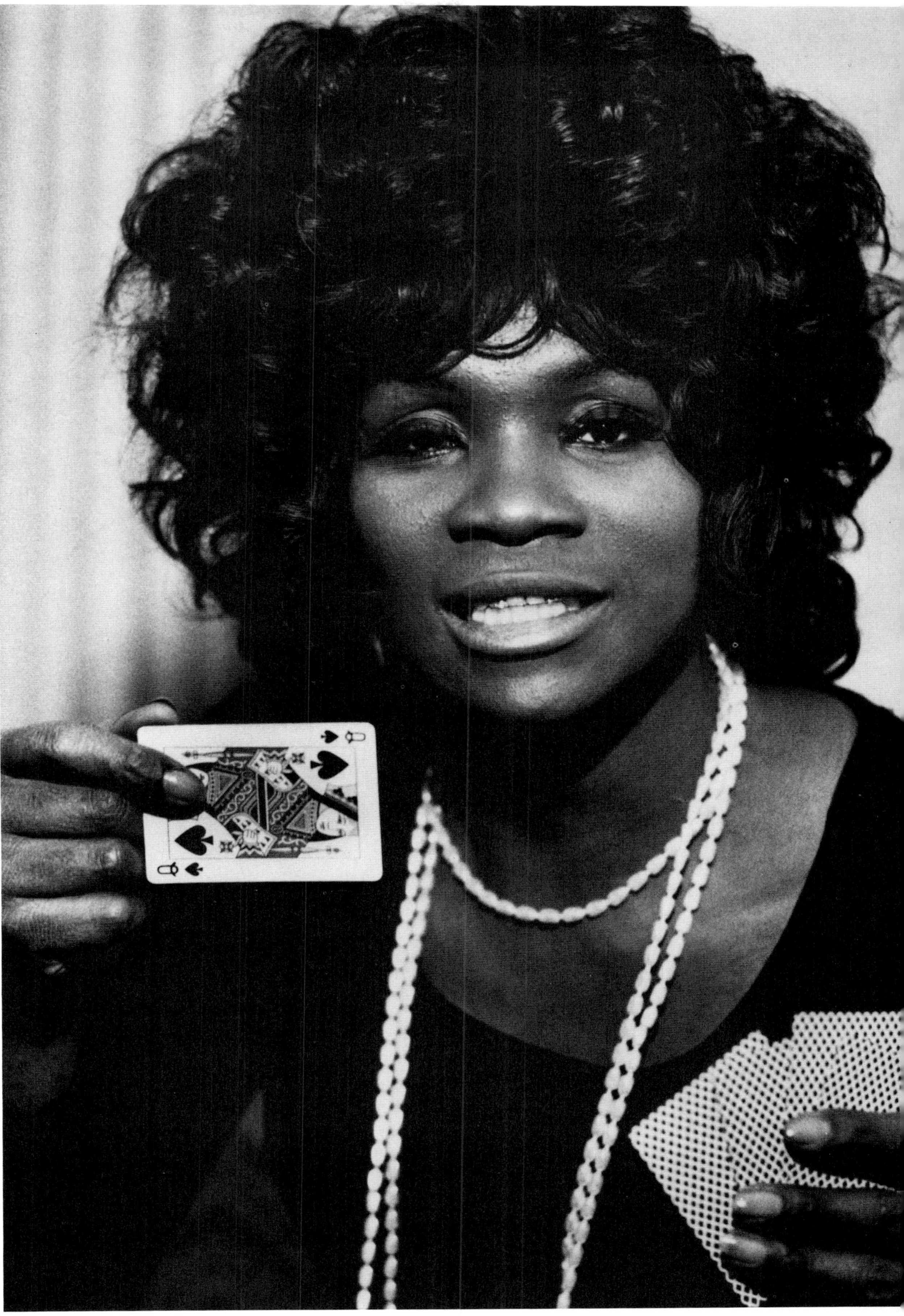

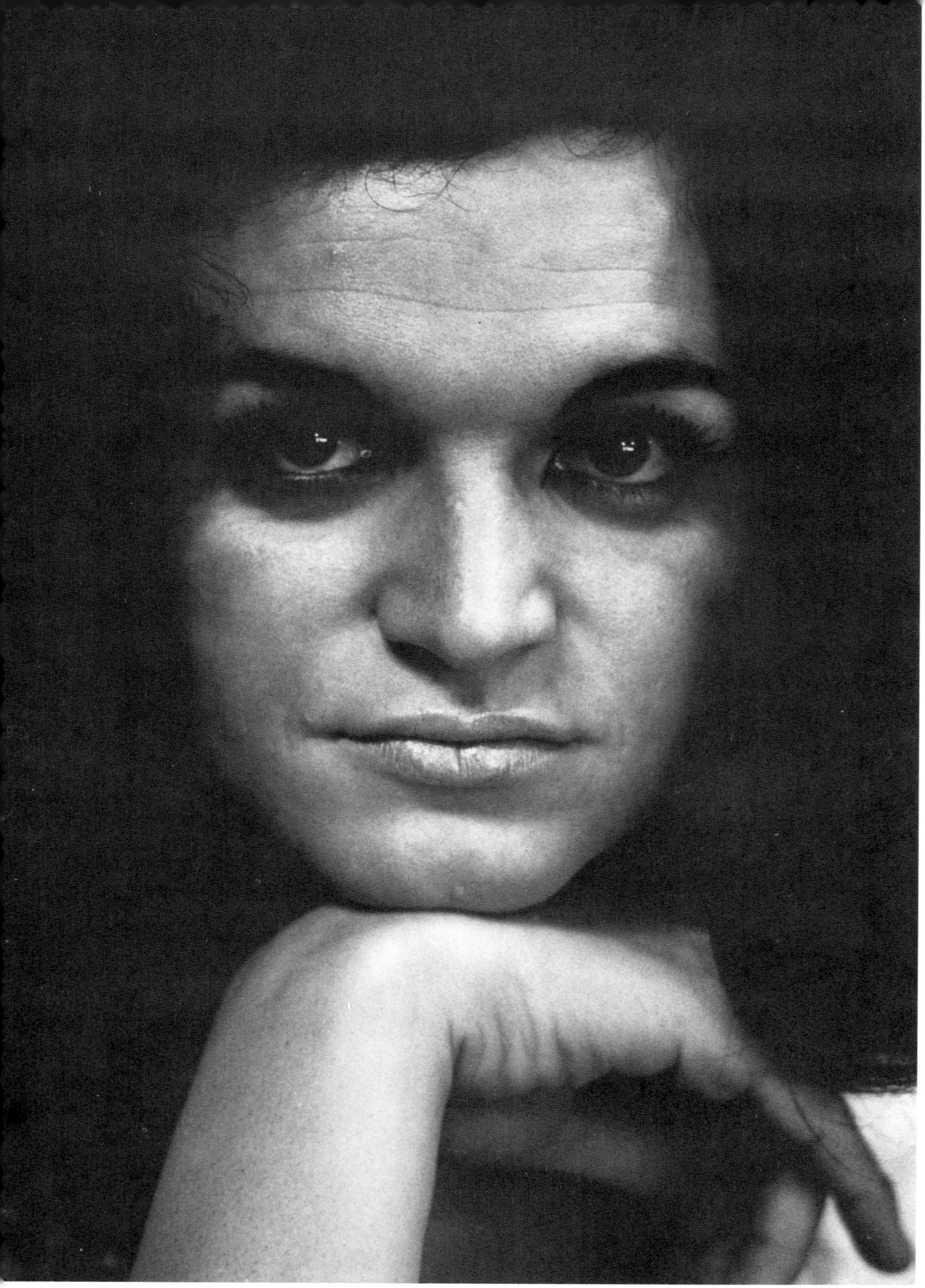

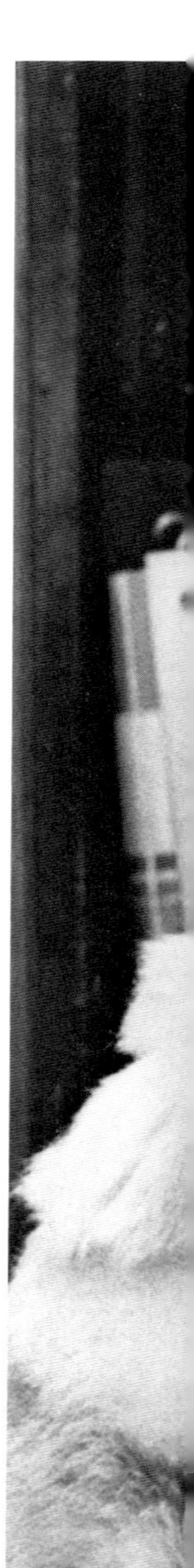

This is Toni

ELLERY QUEEN'S
Mystery Magazine
ALL-NEW ISSUE
14 NEW
stories
LAWRENCE TREAT
ANTHONY GILBERT
ROBERT L. FISH
BERKELY MATHER
WARD D. HOCH
11 mysteries that will make your
mouth water. All for $1
The Detective Book Club
beginning
a new kind
of serial
every
installment
a complete
story
but with
a cliffhanger!
The Will-o'-
the-Wisp
Mystery by
MR. X
MAD
MAD
TANKEE
PAGE

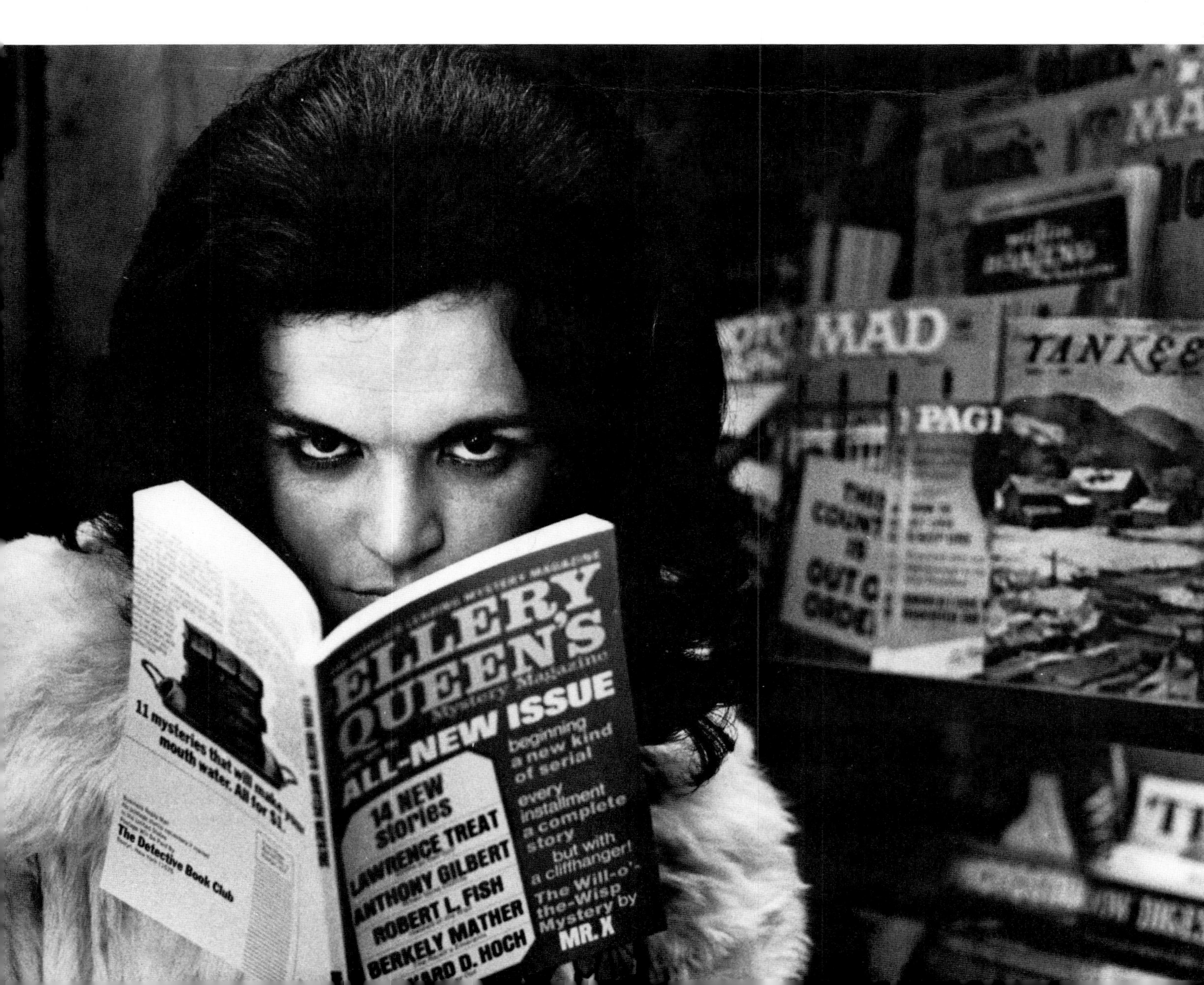

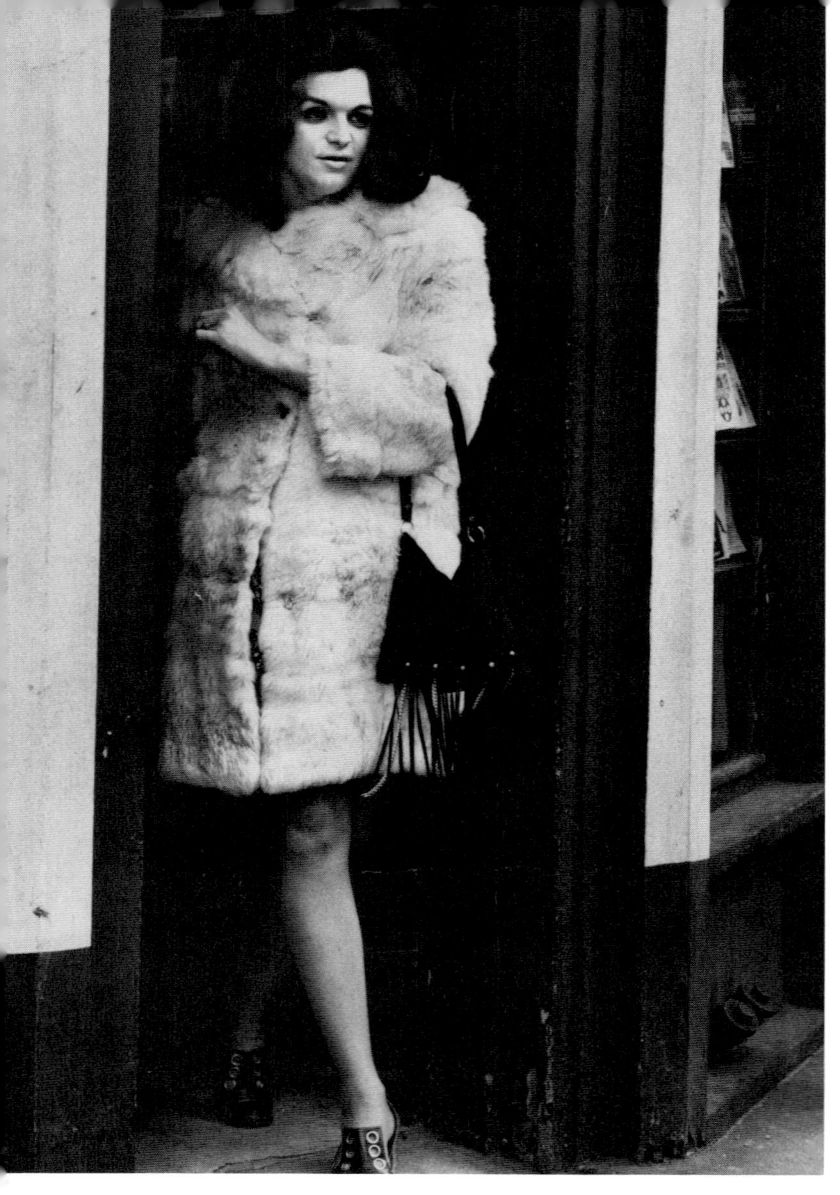
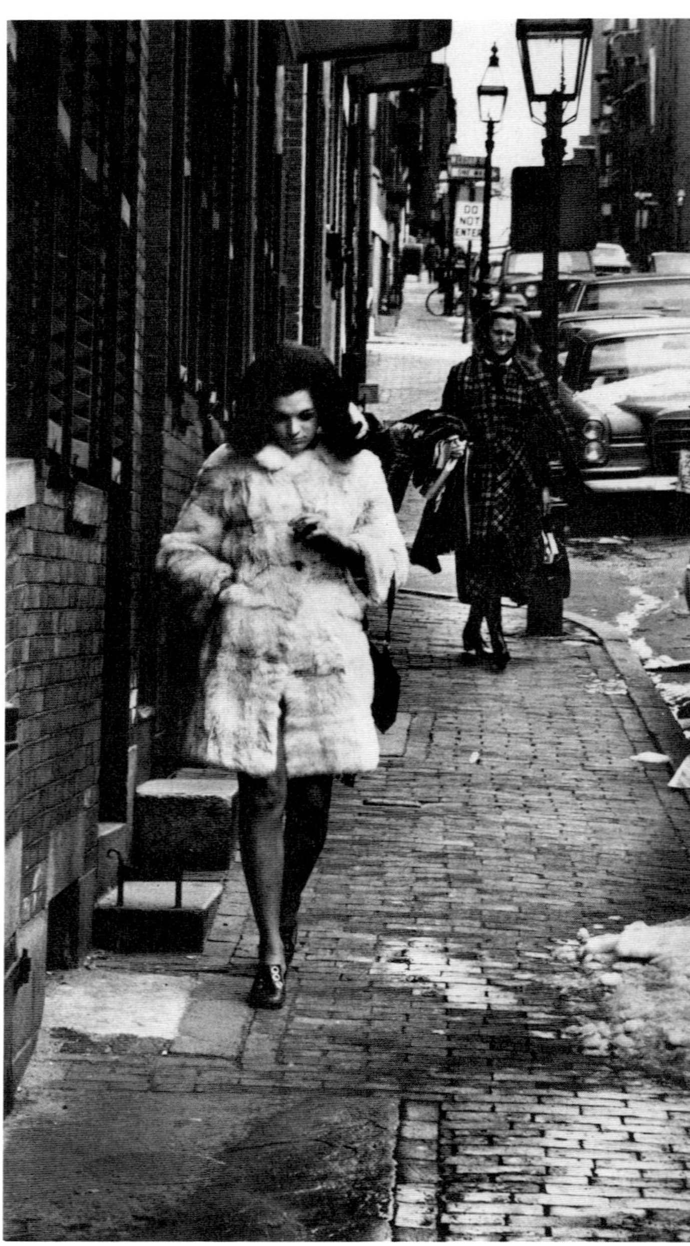

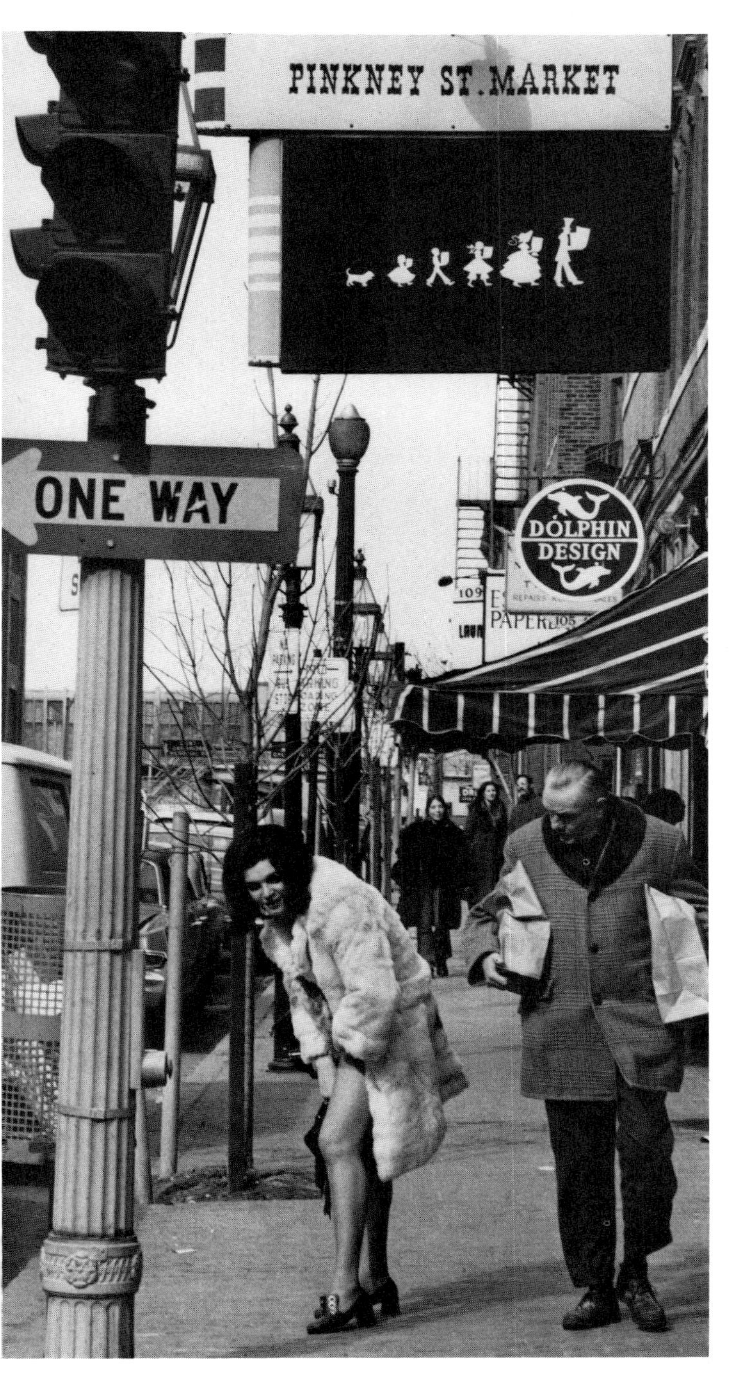

PINKNEY ST. MARKET
ONE WAY
DOLPHIN
DESIGN

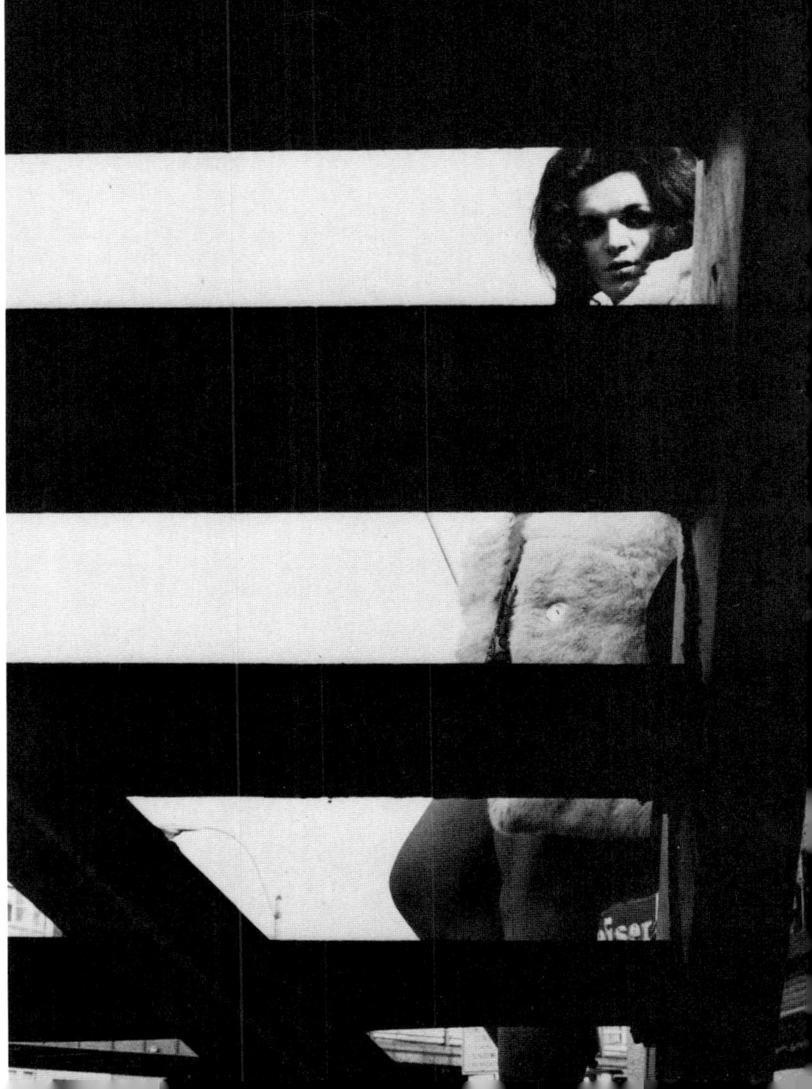

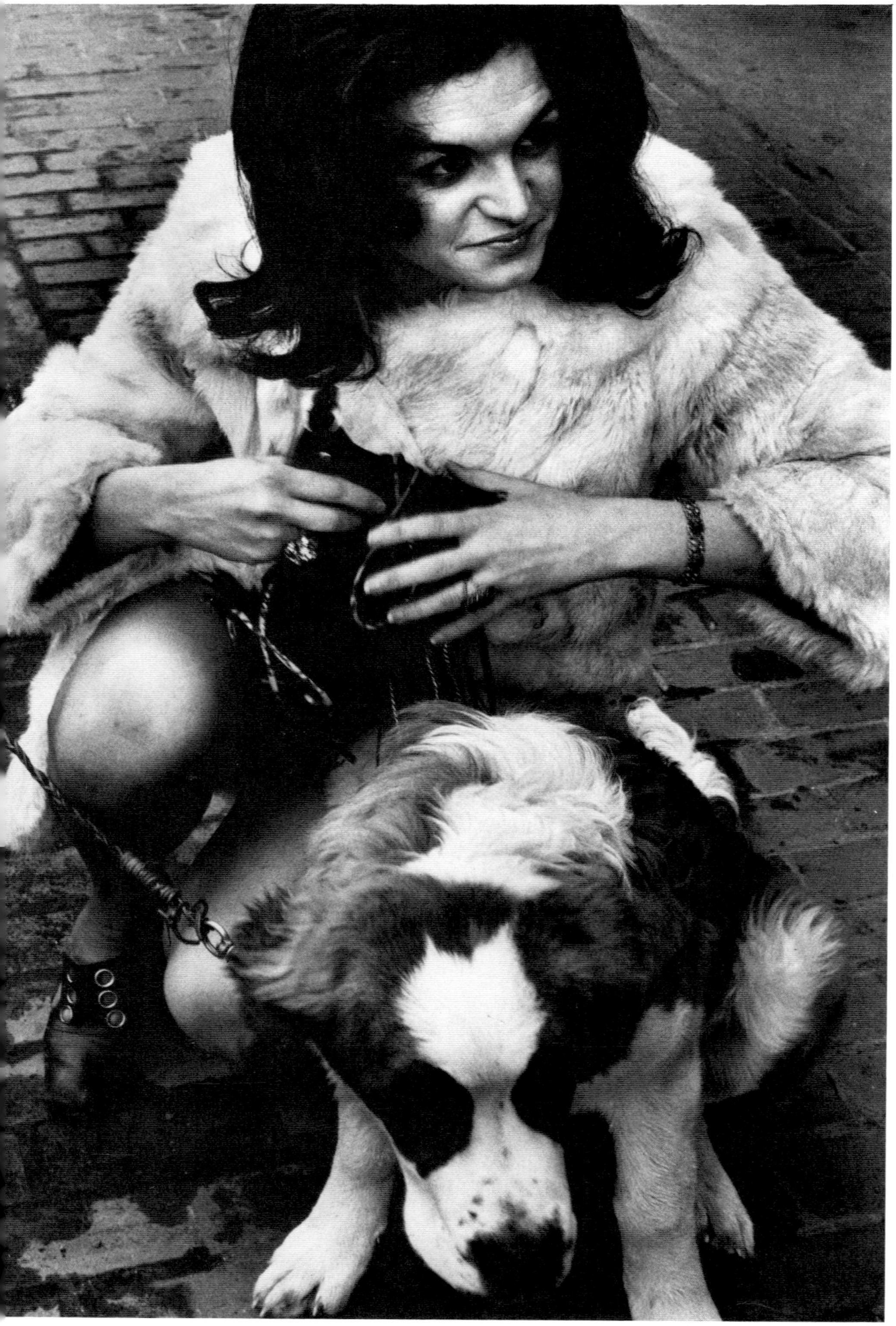

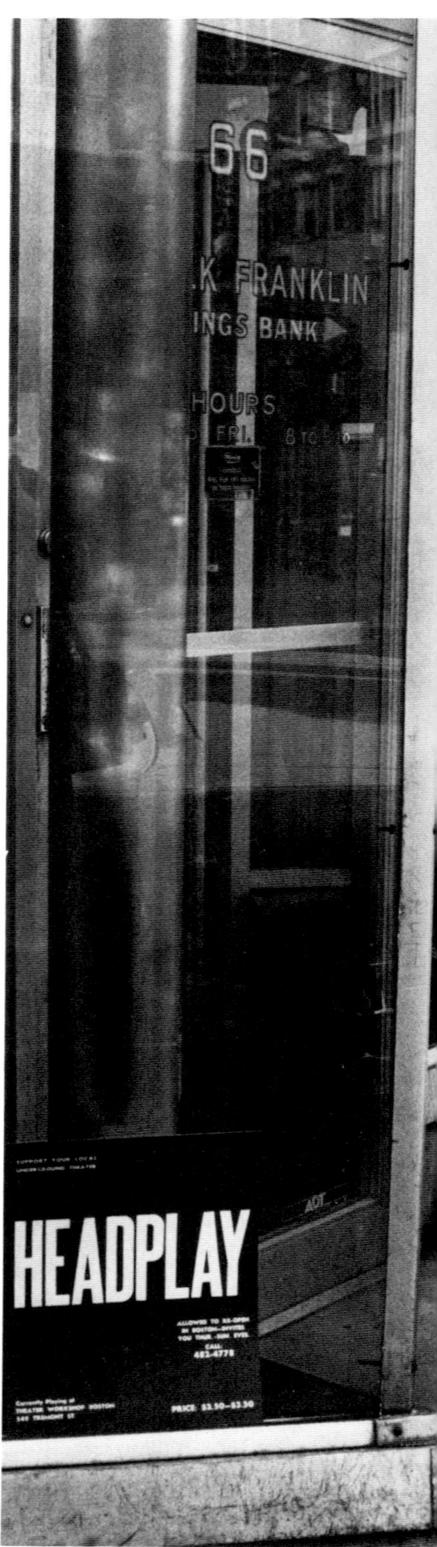
66
K FRANKLIN
INGS BANK
HOURS
FRI.
HEADPLAY

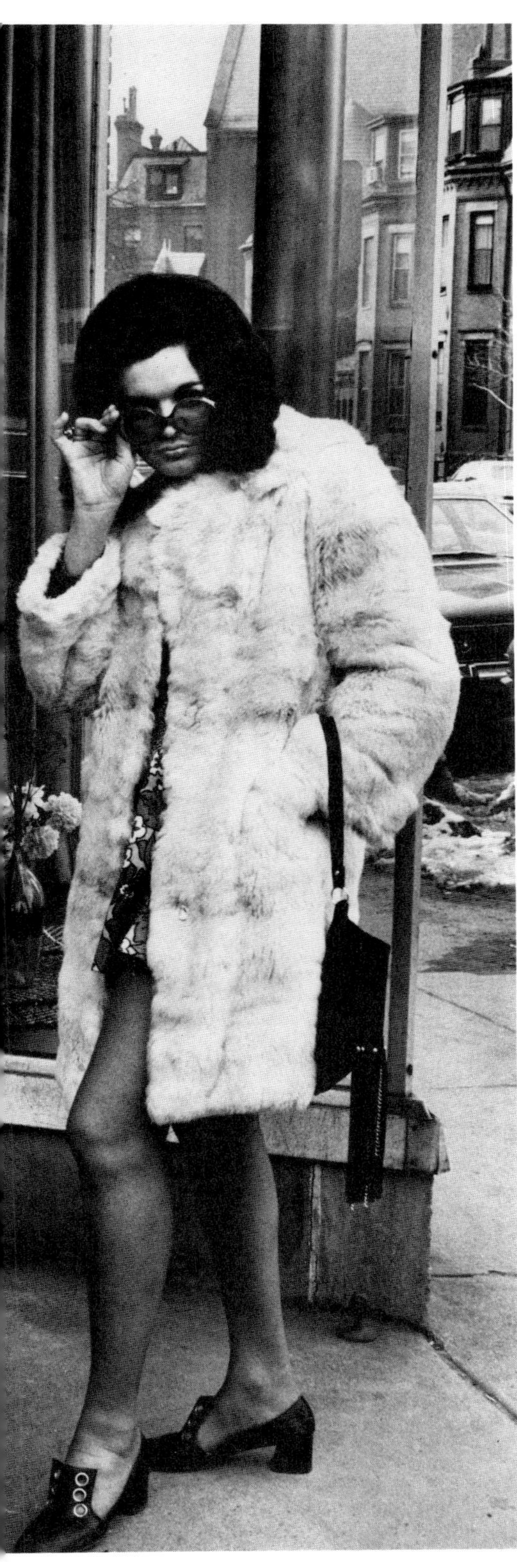

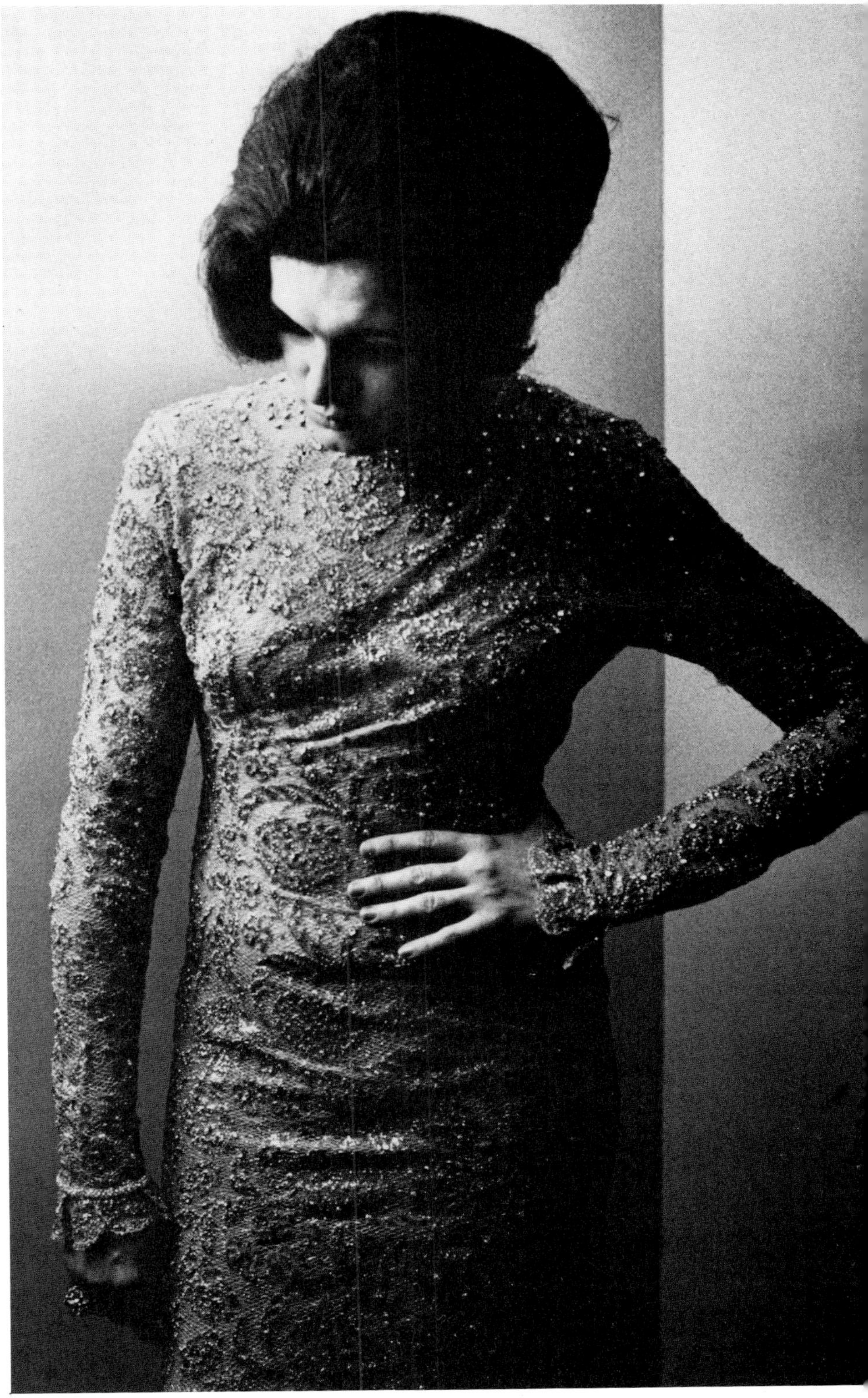

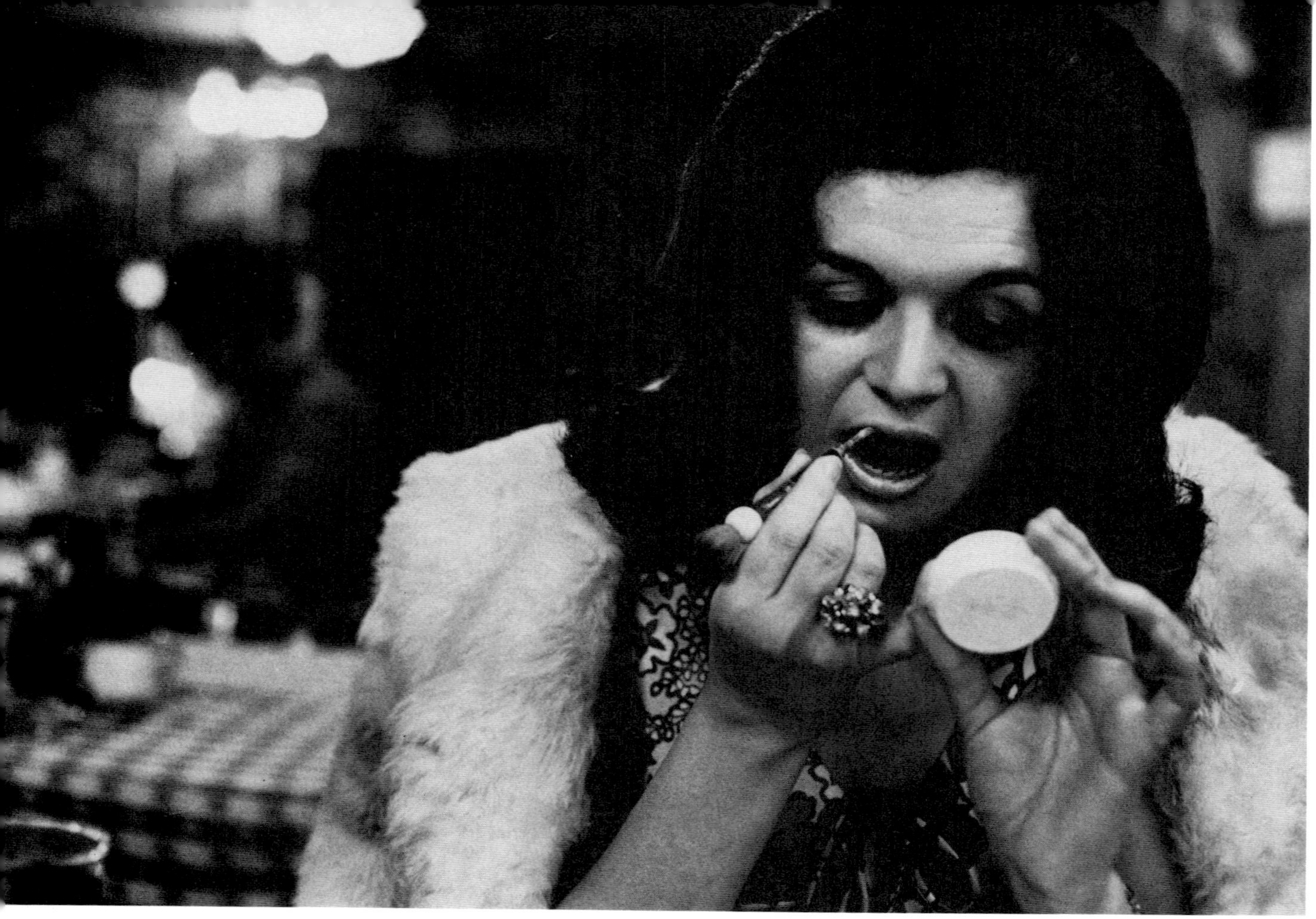

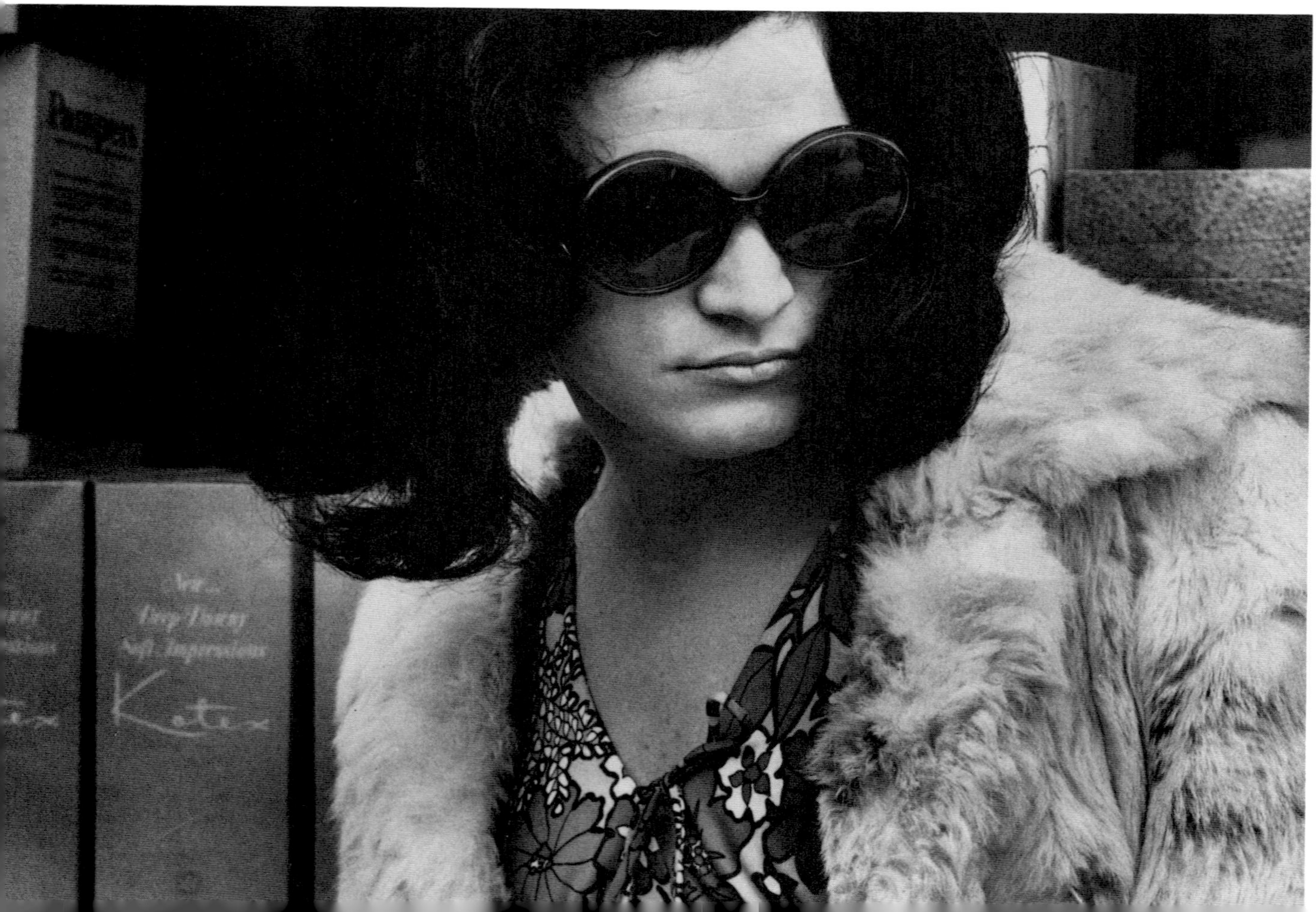

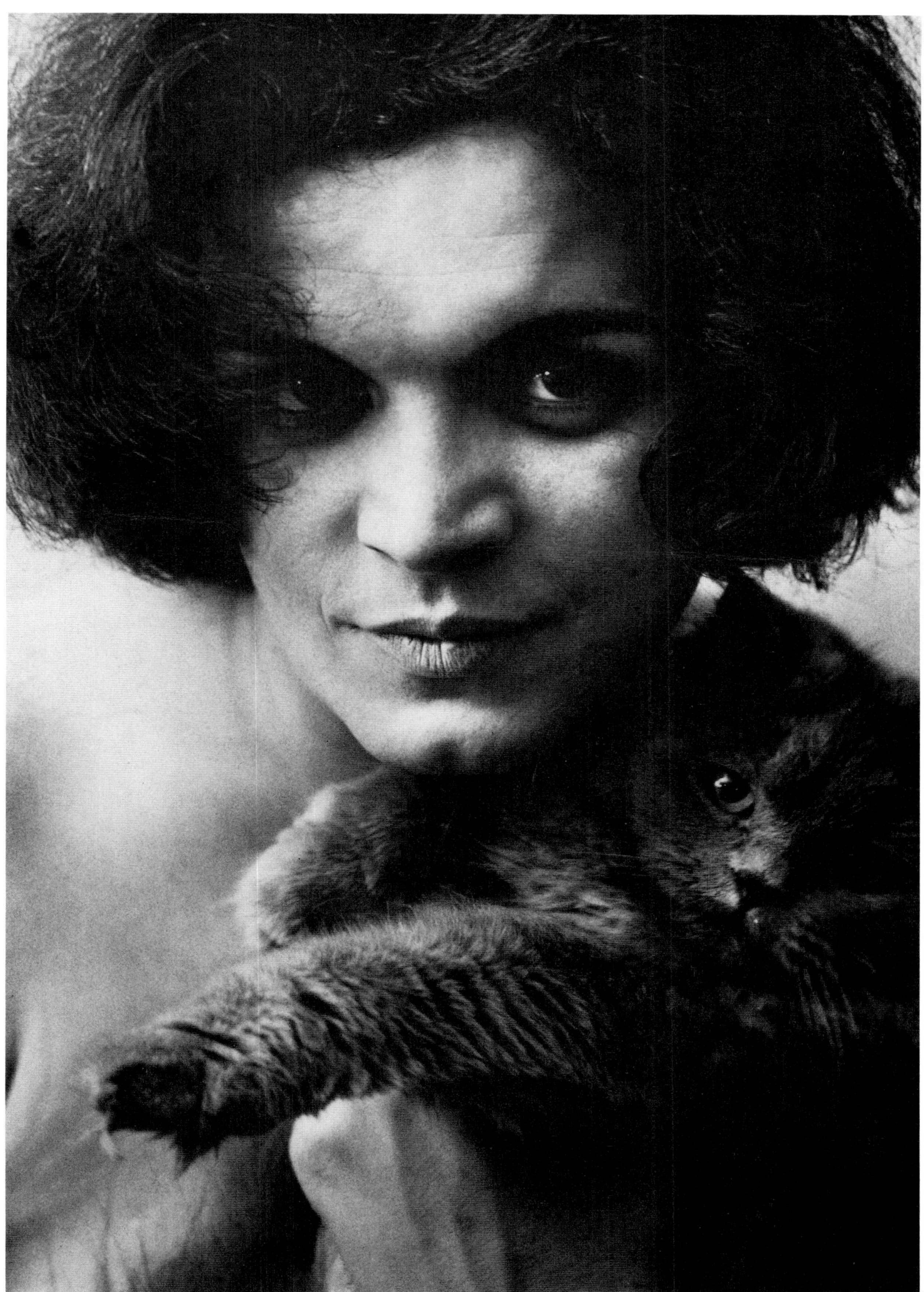

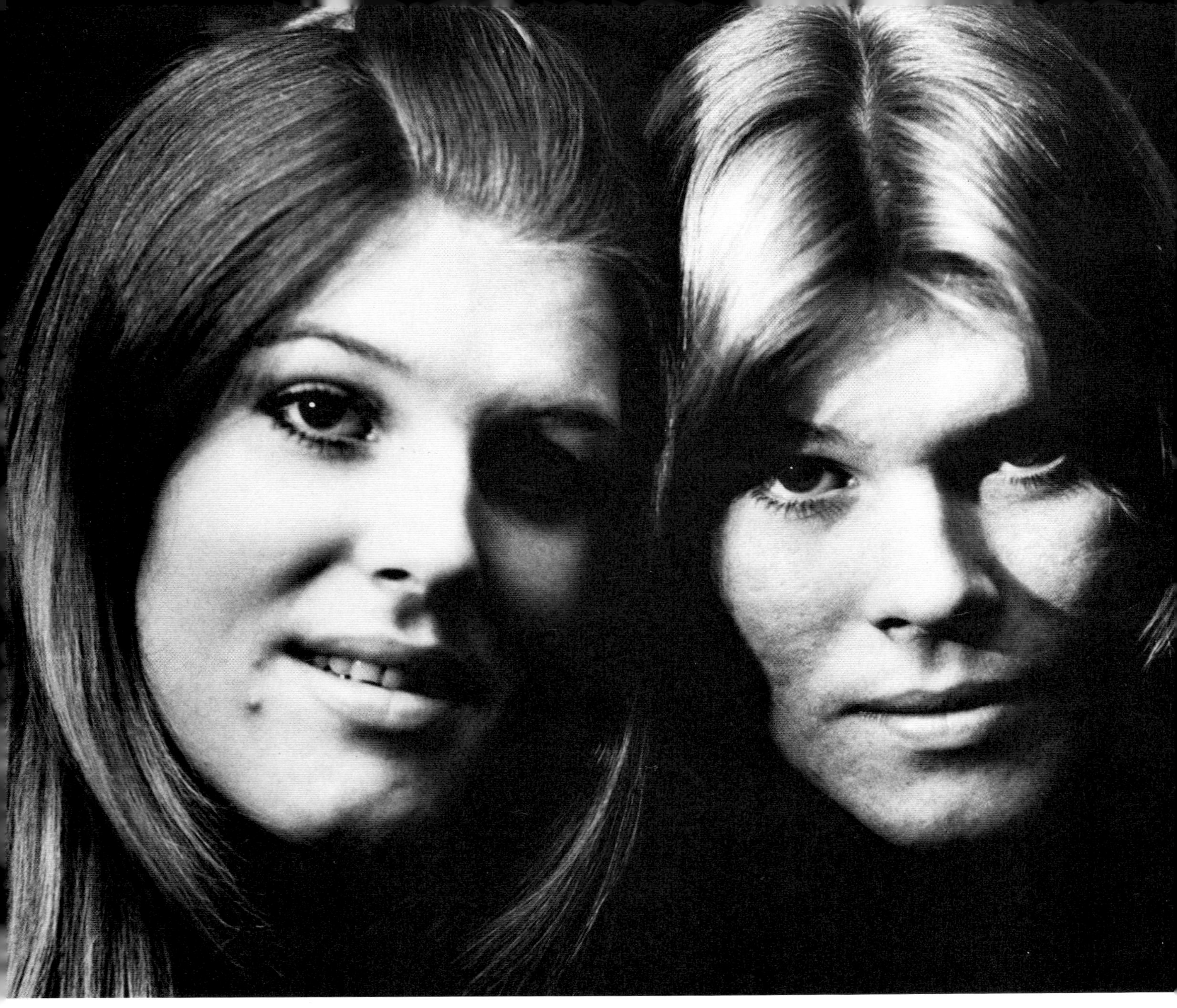

These are the twins—Kim and Bobbie

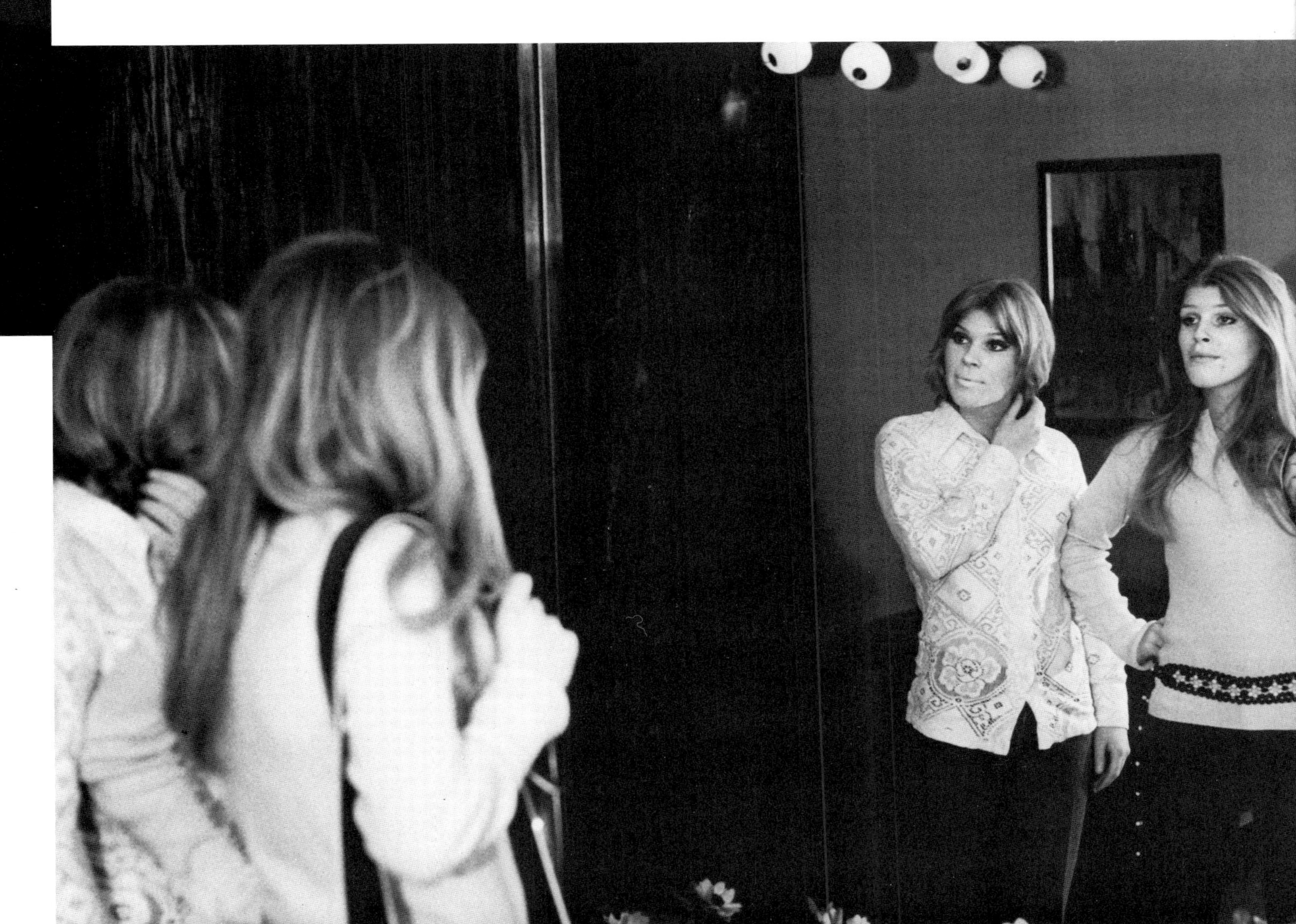

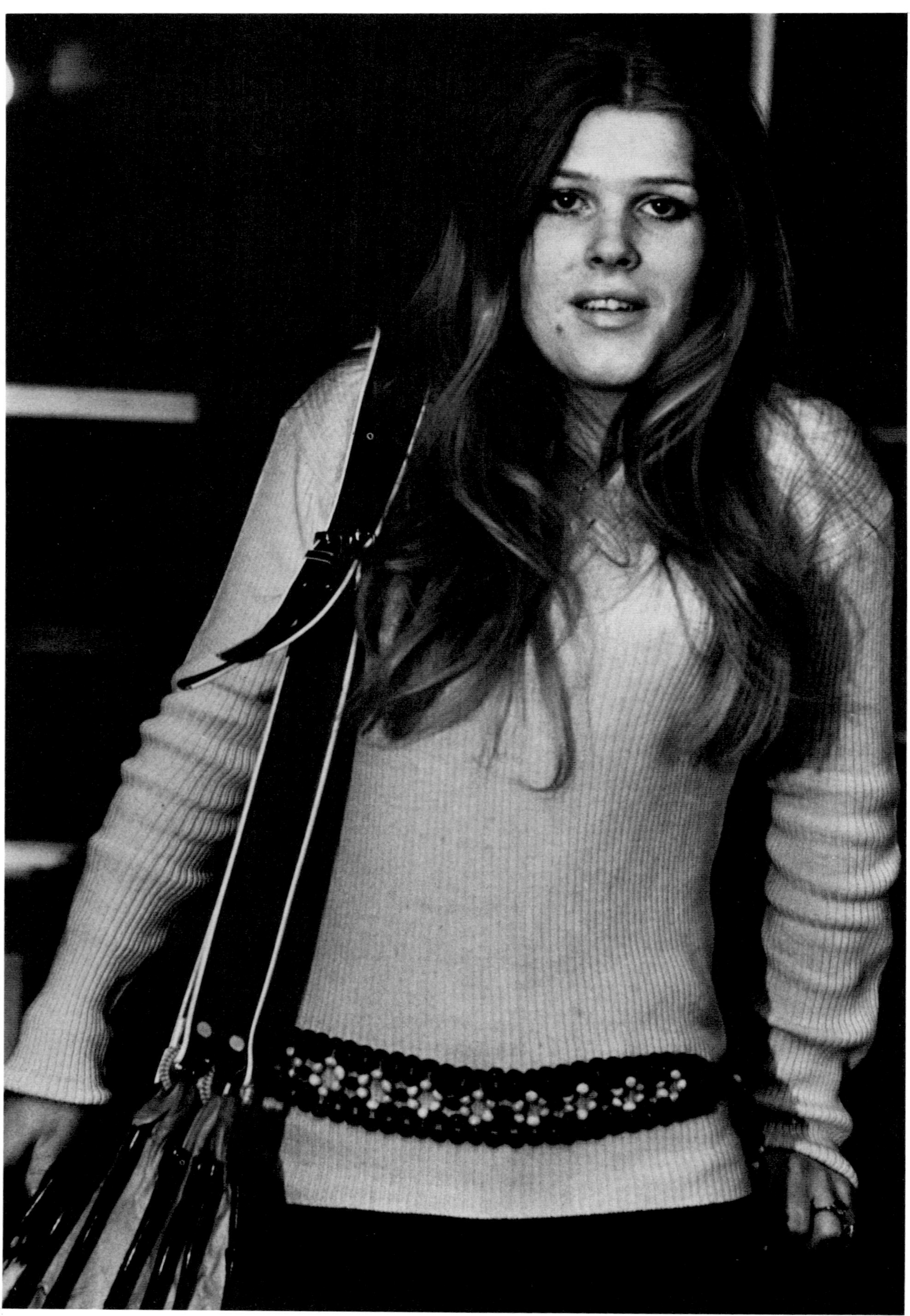

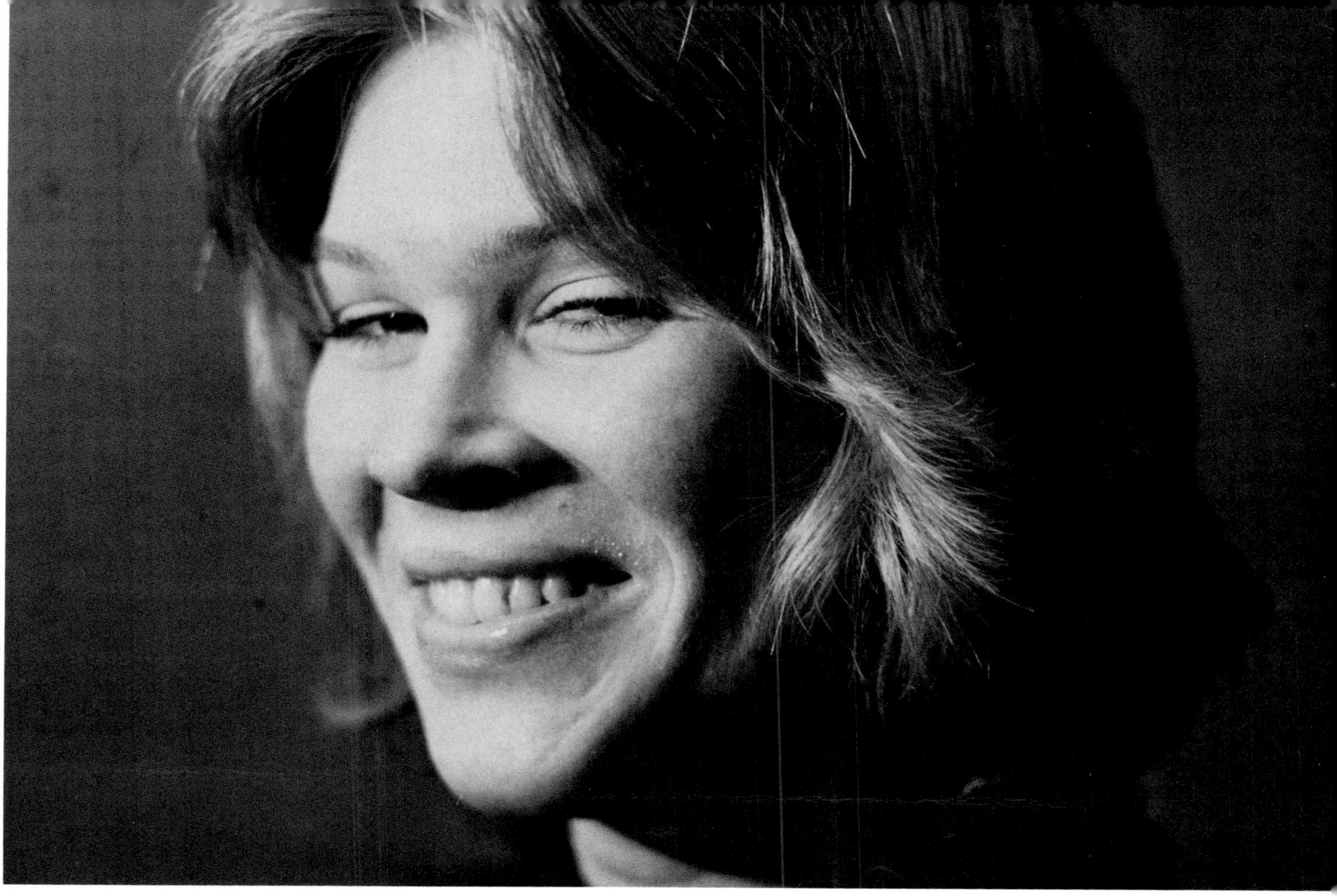

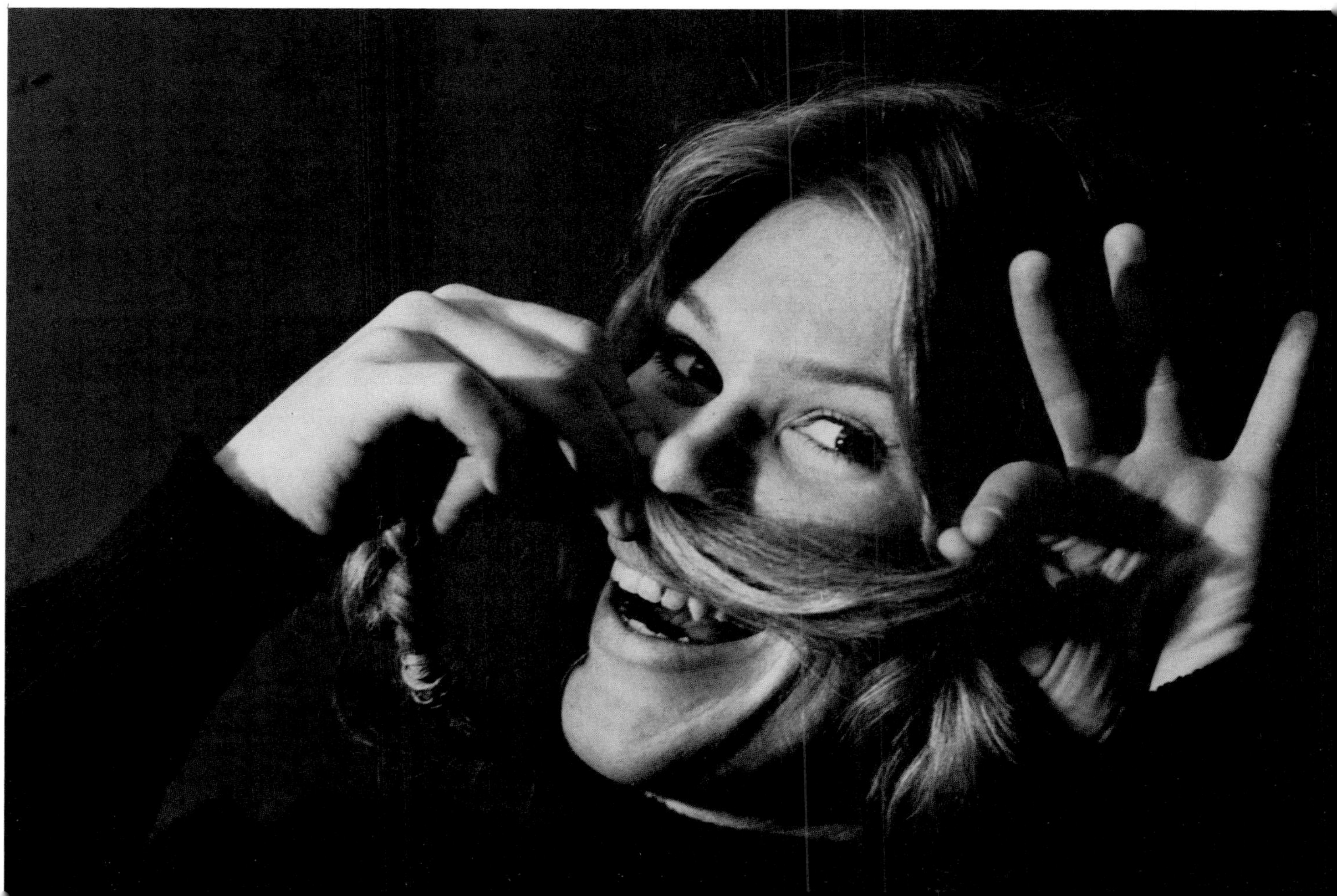

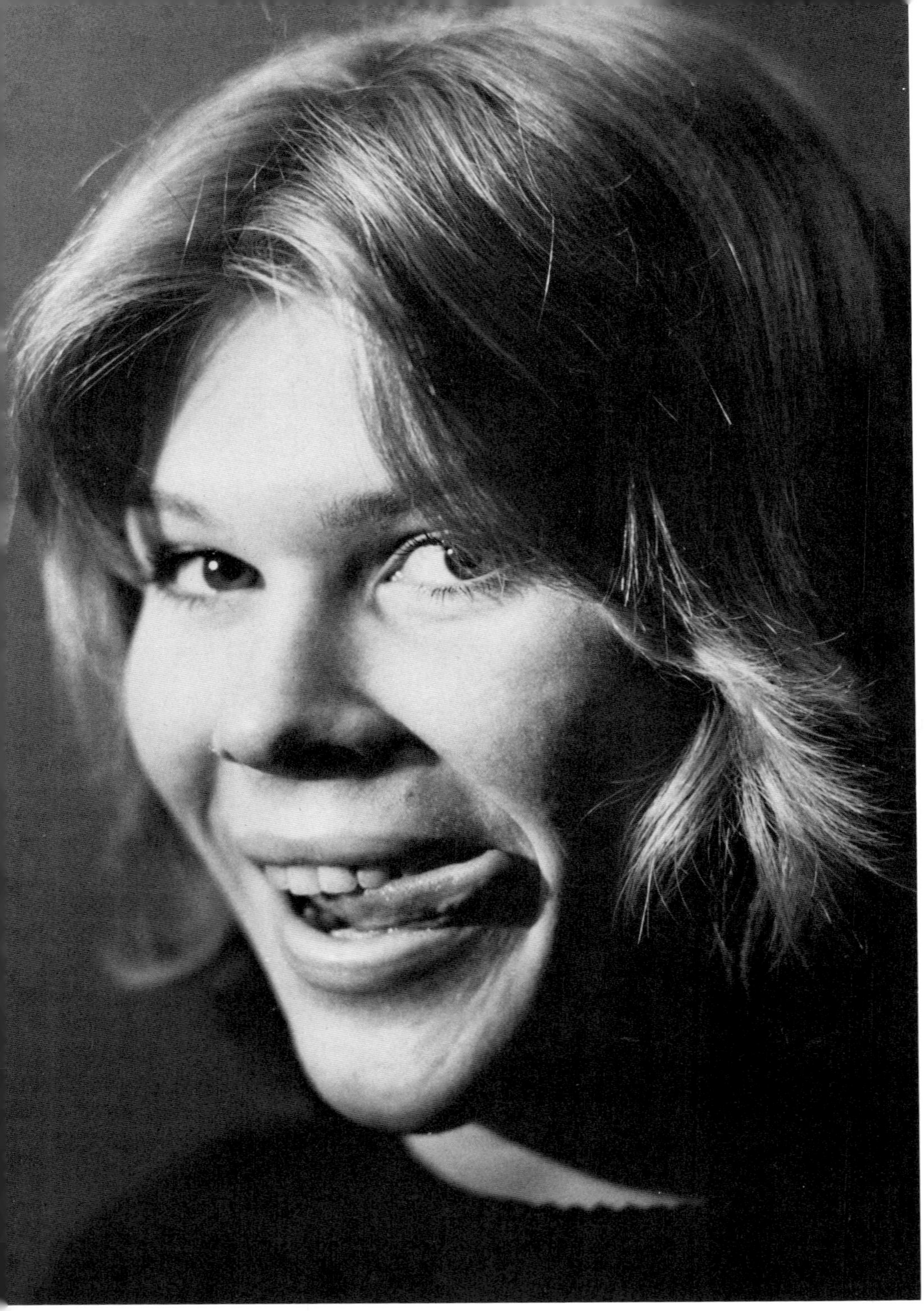

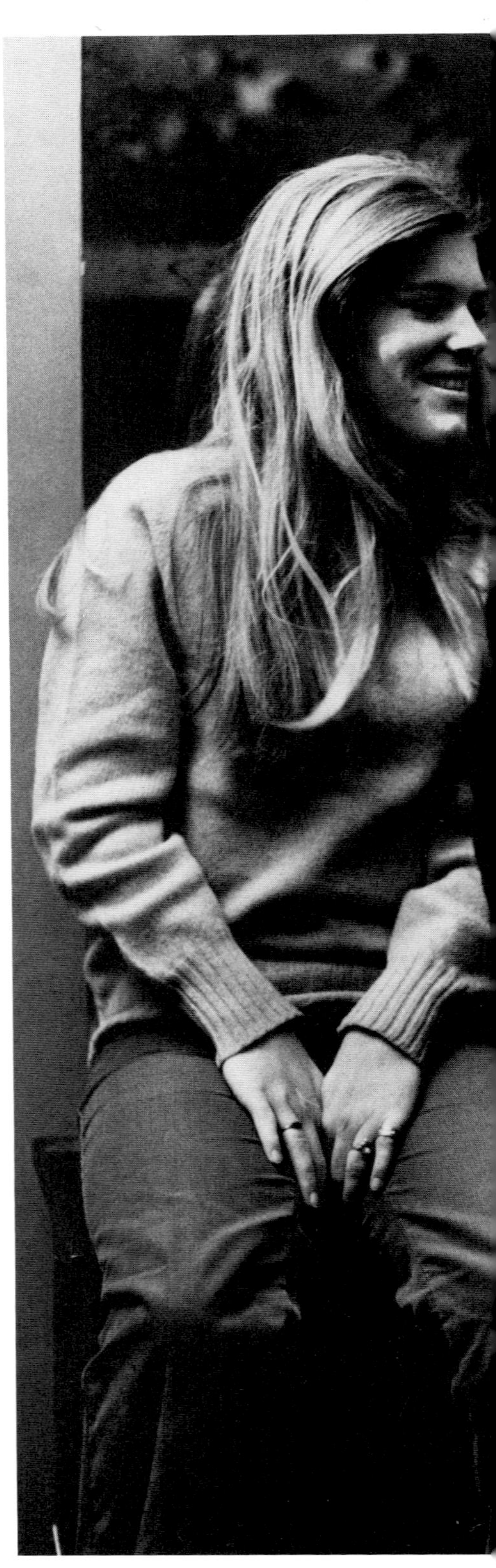

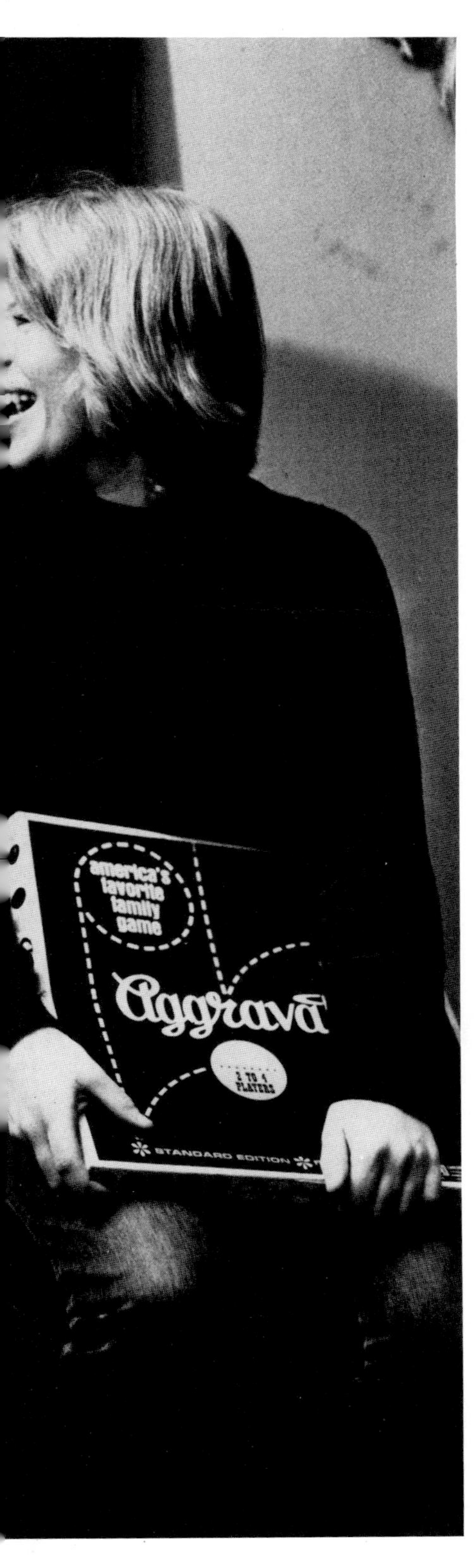
america's
favorite
family
game
Aggrava
2 TO 4
PLAYERS
STANDARD EDITION

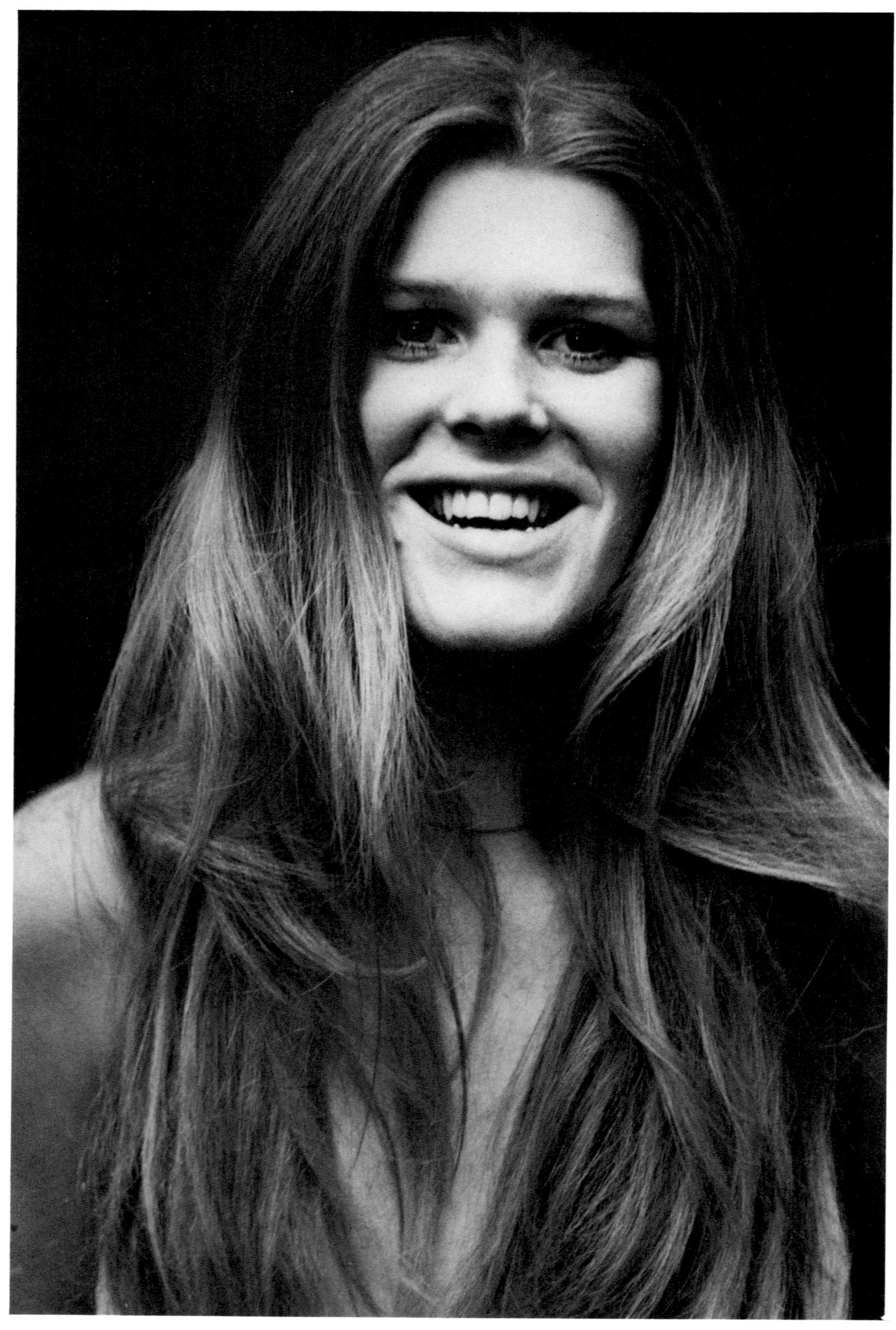

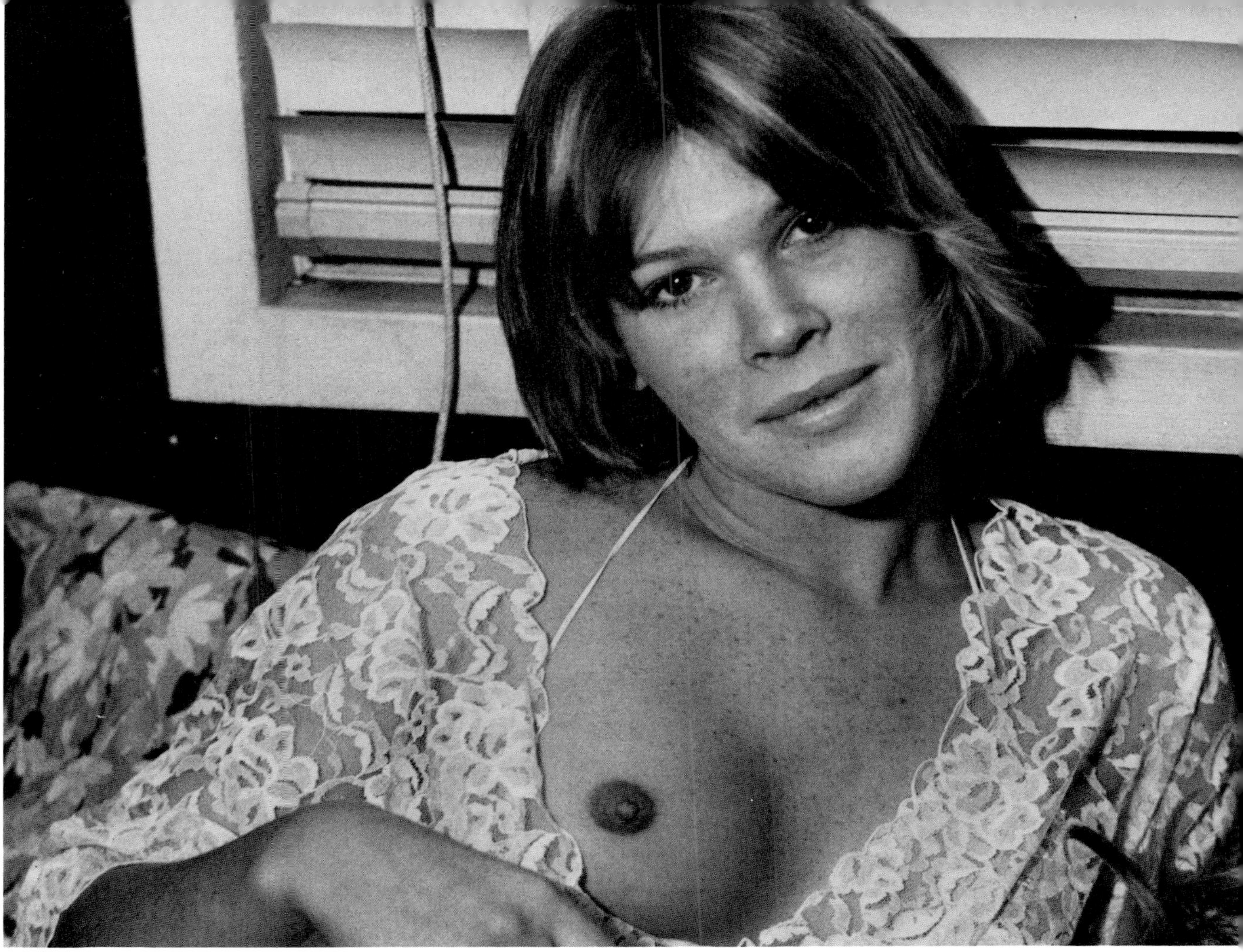

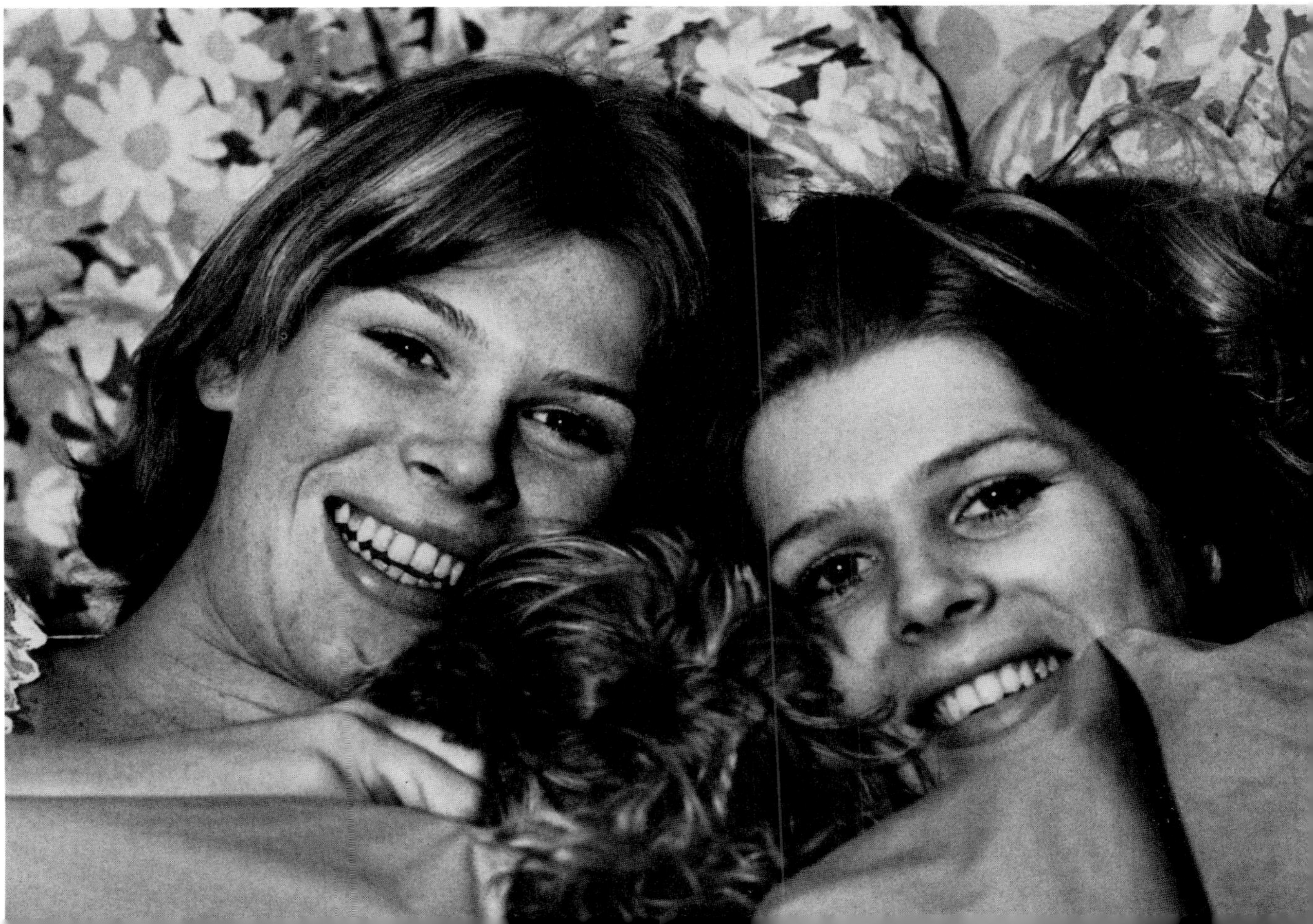

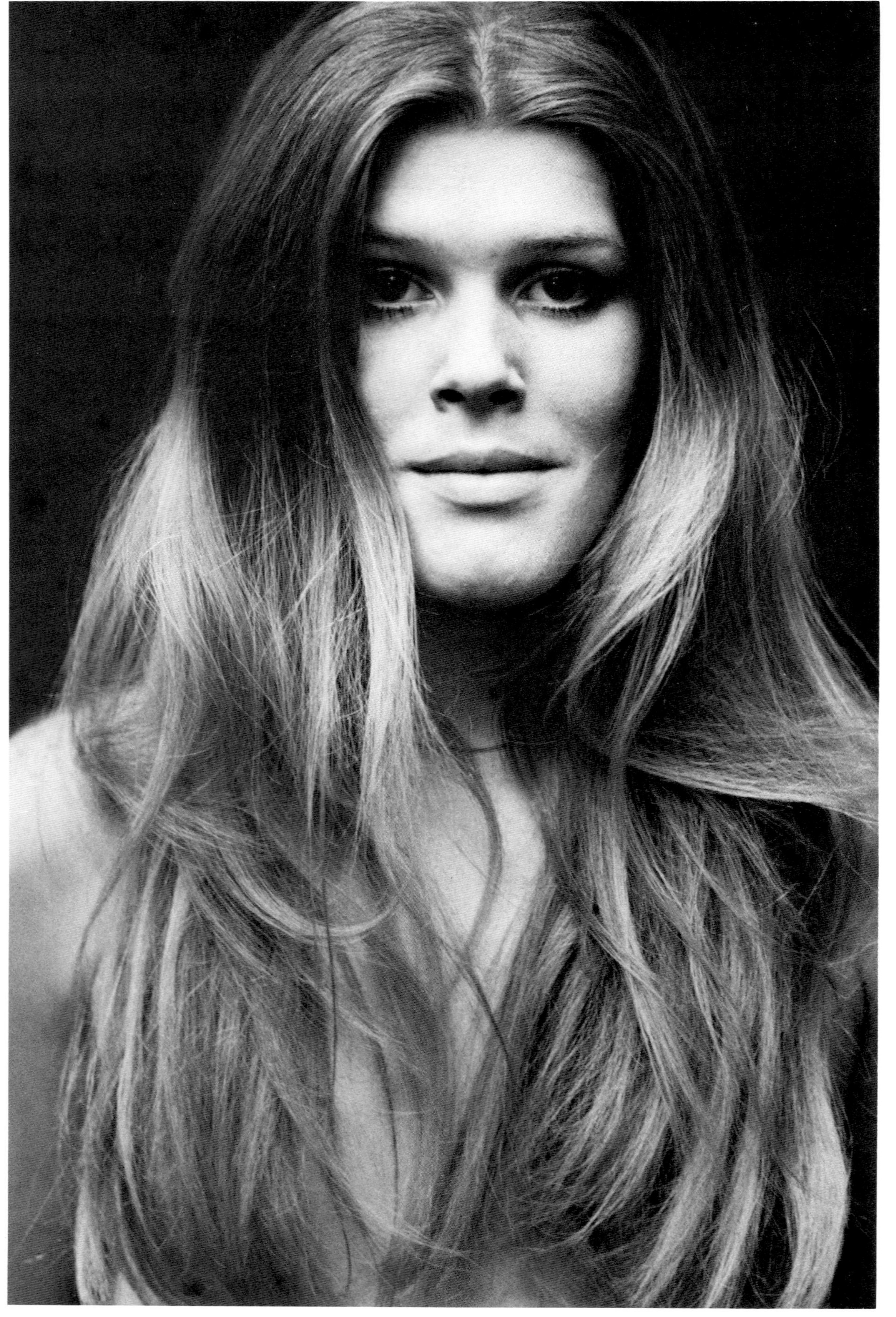

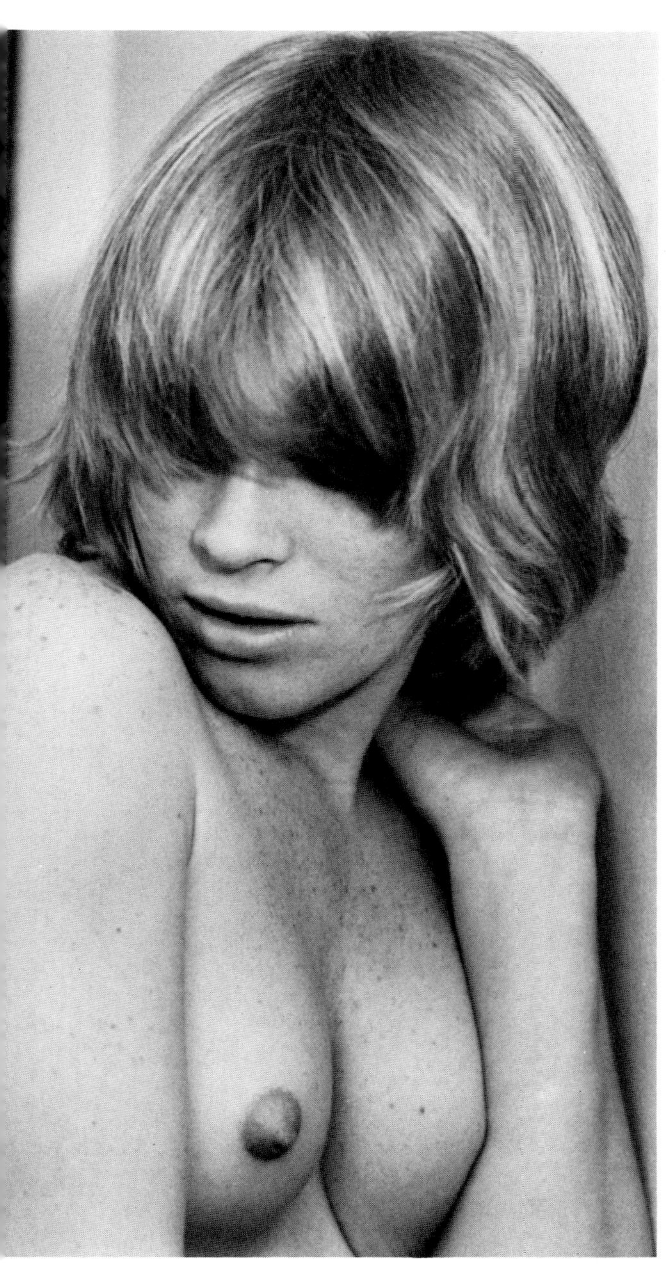

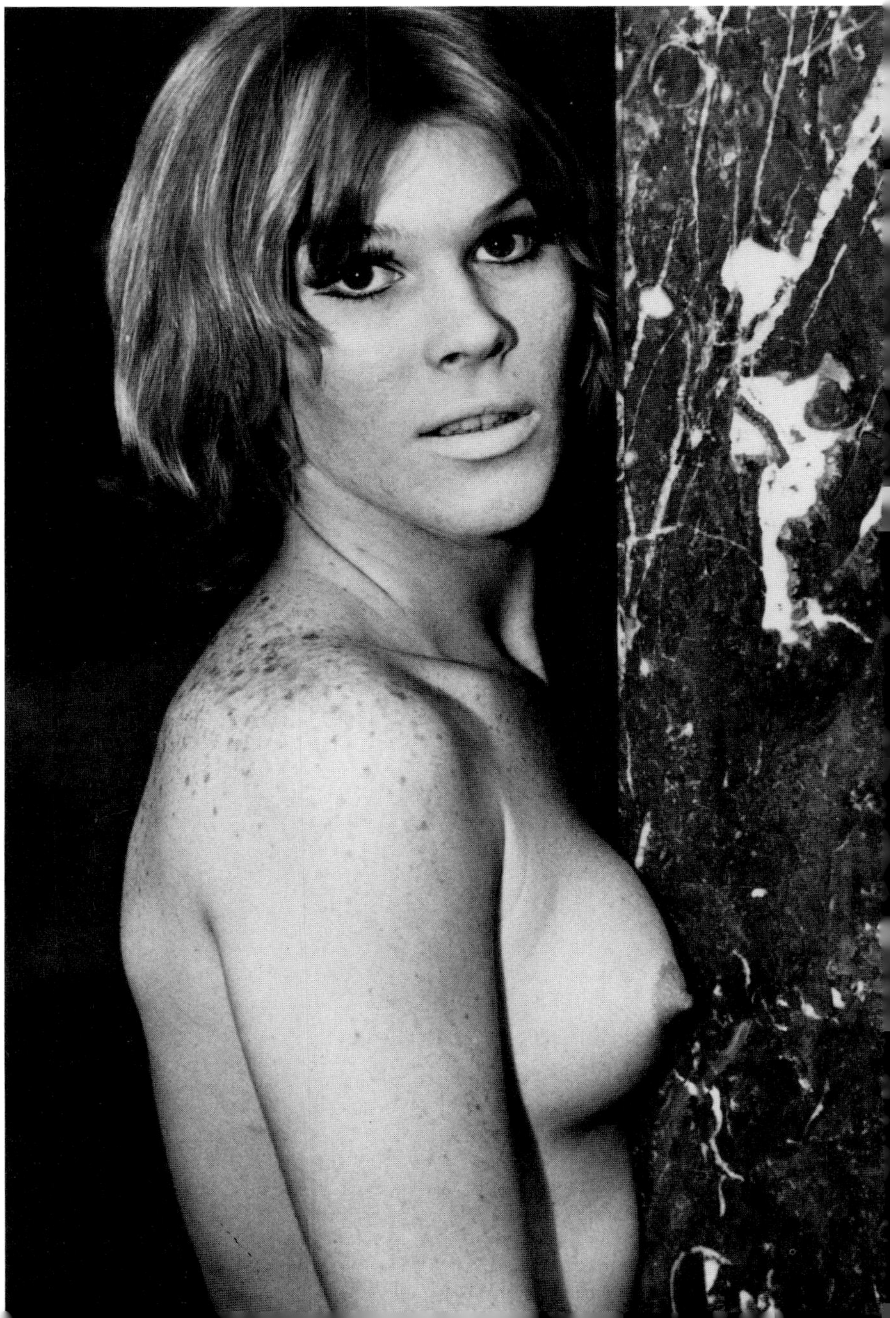

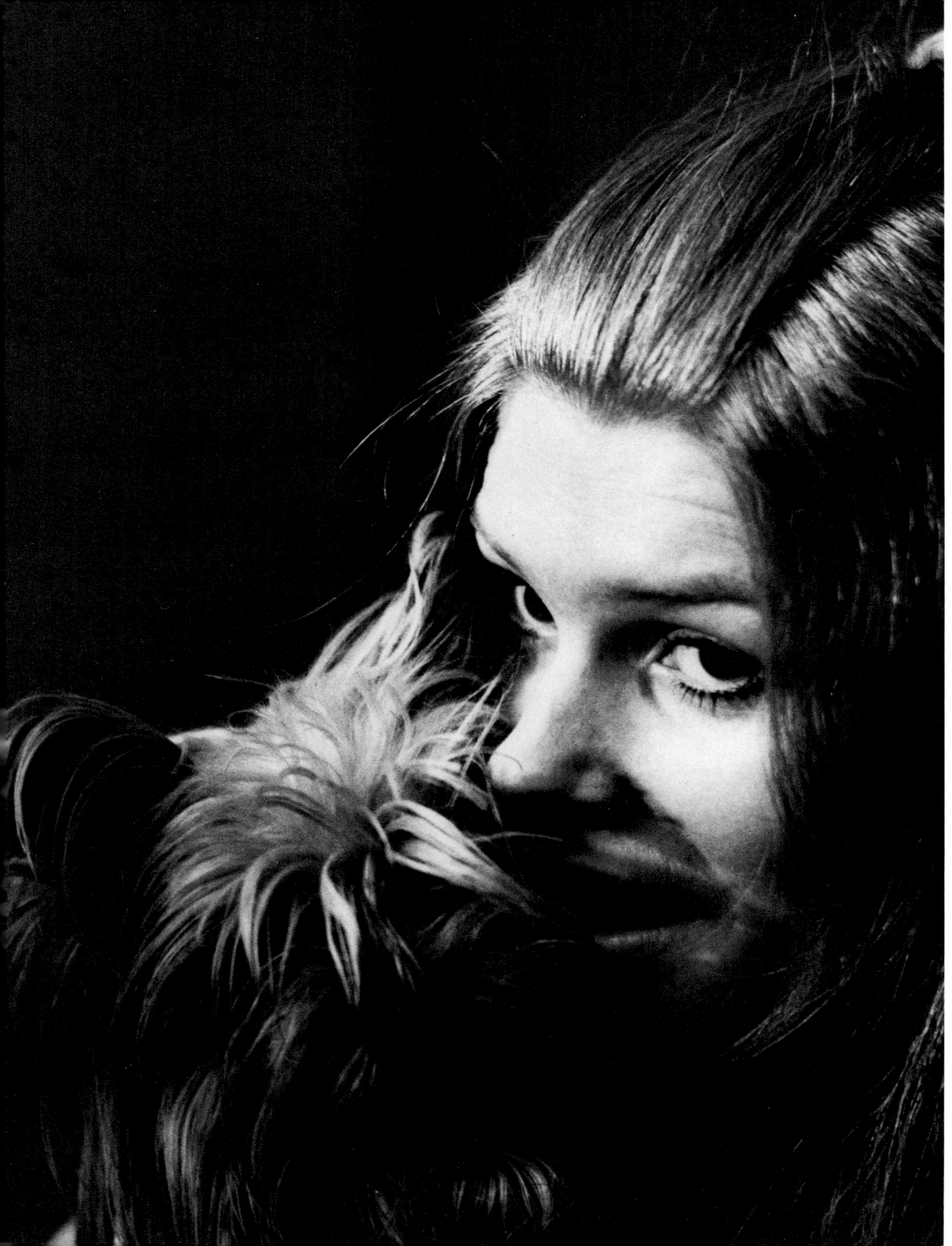

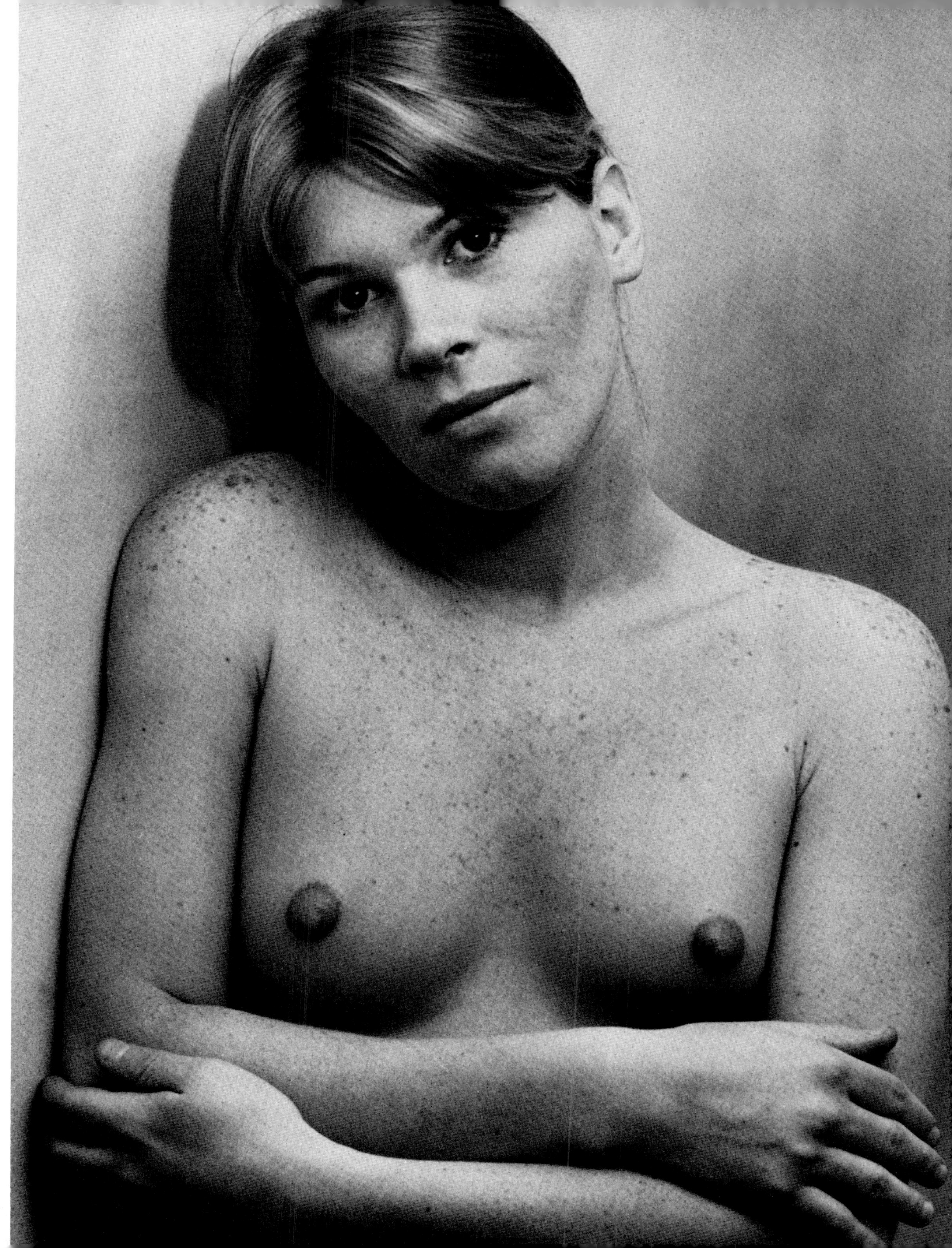

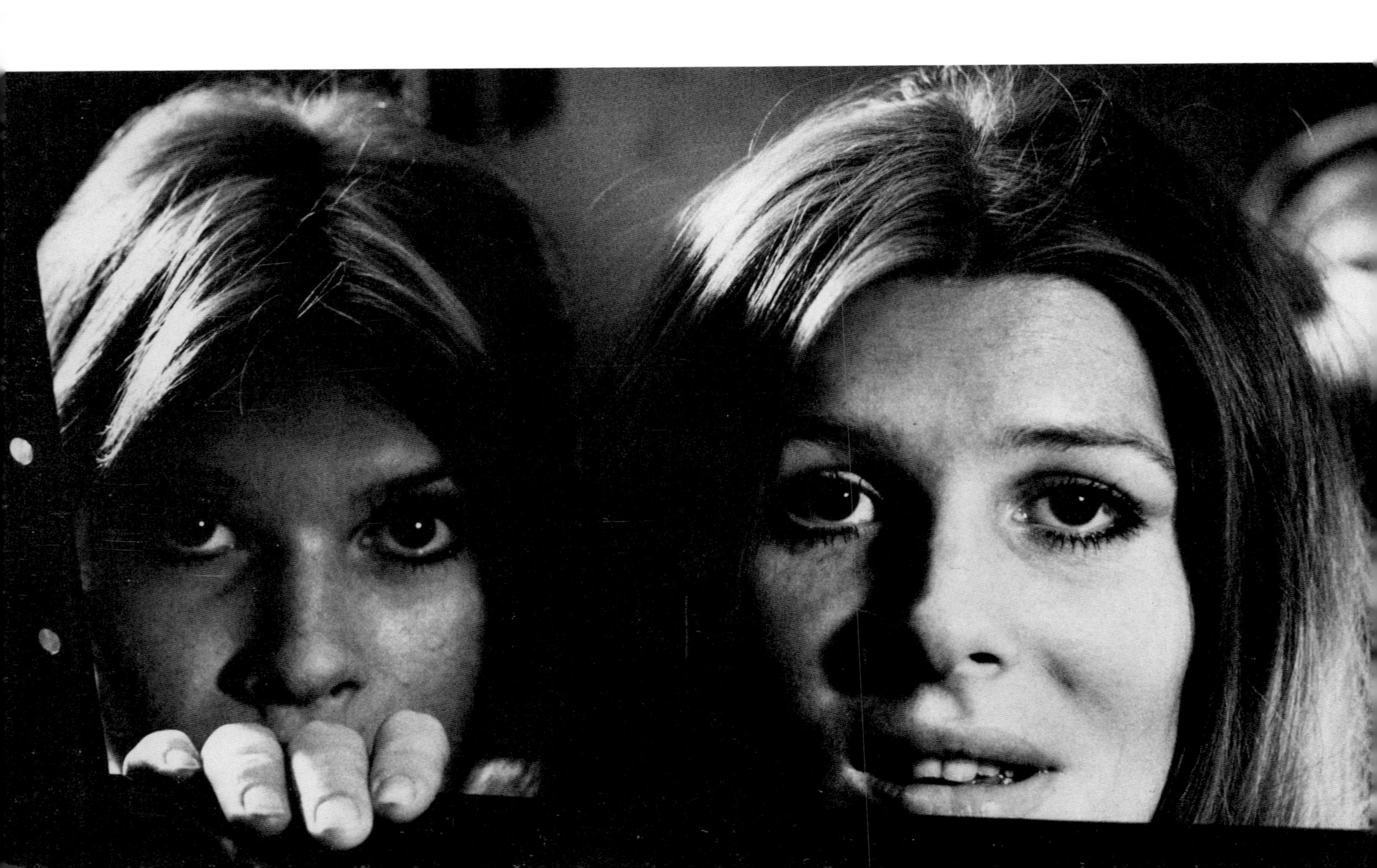